Bury My Bones
In America

DATE DUE

*Dedicated to the Chinese miners
who helped to develop America.*

Bury My Bones In America

The Saga of a Chinese Family in California 1852–1996
From San Francisco to the Sierra Gold Mines

By Lani Ah Tye Farkas

CARL MAUTZ PUBLISHING
NEVADA CITY 1998

Copyright 1998
All rights reserved in all countries
10 9 8 7 6 5 4 3 2

Edited by Rosemarie Mossinger
Designed by Richard D. Moore
Composed in Gill Sans and Joanna types
Printed in the United States of America

Library of Congress Catalog Card Number: 98-066456
Cataloging-in-Publication Data
    Farkas, Lani Ah Tye.
        Bury my bones in America: the saga of a Chinese family in
        California, 1852–1996: from San Francisco to the Sierra gold
        mines/Lani Ah Tye Farkas.—1st ed.
        p.cm.
        Includes bibliographical references and index.
        ISBN: 1-887694-11-0 paper
               1-887694-12-9 cloth

    1. Ah Tye family. 2. Farkas, Lani Ah Tye—Family. 3. Chinese American
families—California, Northern. 4. California, Northern—Ethnic
relations. I Title.

F867.F37 1998   979.4'004951073
                          QBI98-748

Frontispiece: Temple remnants of the old Lone Mountain cemetery,
now a part of Lincoln Park, San Francisco, California.
Photograph by Richard D. Moore.

Carl Mautz Publishing
228 Commercial Street, No. 522
Nevada City, California 95959
Telephone 530 478-1610   Fax 530 478-0466

CONTENTS

INTRODUCTION

A Chinese presence has been recorded in these United States for over two centuries. The earliest instance occurred only two years after the end of the Revolutionary War. In 1783, three Chinese seamen arrived on the East Coast as part of the crew of the *Pallas*, a ship that sailed from Canton, China. In subsequent decades a few more dozen Chinese followed their footsteps and landed on the East and West Coasts. However, a permanent Chinese community in America did not spring into existence until the mid-nineteenth century.

The California Gold Rush of 1849 attracted thousand upon thousands of gold seekers, fortune hunters and adventurers from all parts of the globe, including large numbers of Chinese. The latter were largely villagers from the Pearl River Delta, Guangdong Province on the southeast China coast. Chinese soon became a familiar part of the California scene. They congregated in the gold mining areas, and in San Francisco they established the beginnings of Chinatown. As the state's economy developed, they settled in towns and cities throughout northern, central and southern California. From the Golden State they migrated to all corners of the West and eventually to all parts of this nation.

Since their arrival, Chinese have been part of the mosaic making up America's multi-cultural, multi-ethnic society. They were key participants in California, contributing to the transformation of the state from a frontier wilderness into a region with flourishing agriculture and industries. Writings lauding California pioneers, however, often covered only sketchily, if at all, the important role of the Chinese. Moreover, the few references usually left the reader with the impression that the Chinese were merely a faceless and nameless mass of humanity that somehow were involved in gold mining, railroad construction and a multitude of other activities. One of the reasons usually given for this neglect is that very little biographical material has been available.

The present work on the Ah Tye family promises to make up for some of this deficiency. More than two decades ago, two junior members of this family, Lani Ah Tye Farkas and Doreen Ah Tye, took on the daunting and challenging task of combing through voluminous documents and conducting dozens of oral interviews. From these scraps of information, Lani has fashioned a coherent and detailed history of three generations of Ah Tyes. *Bury my Bones in America* is one of the few Chinese American family histories to have been published.

Yee Ah Tye, the progenitor of the family, was an immigrant to California during the early Gold Rush period. He was a California pioneer in every sense of the word. During his long, multi-faceted career as merchant, gold mine operator and Chinese community leader, he was an eyewitness to, and participant in many historical events. The accounts of the careers of Ah Tye's descendants are no less fascinating, as they each in their own way thrust ahead to overcome obstacles and coped with being Chinese Americans in a changing California.

The Ah Tye story provides valuable insights into the Chinese American historical experience. Hopefully it will inspire the publication of other such histories and fill in the numerous gaps that still exist in this field today, thus leading to deeper understanding of Chinese American historical development.

Him Mark Lai
Asian American Studies Department
San Francisco State University

PREFACE

In many ways, the Ah Tye family (pronounced Ah Tie) symbolizes the history of the Chinese in California during the years of 1850 to 1945. Their story parallels the experiences of other immigrant families: the arrival in a strange, new land and the difficulties that must be faced; then the gradual integration into society and eventual acceptance by a country which the family comes to call their own.

This story had a simple beginning in the summer of 1971 in Stockton, California. I'd often visit my paternal grandmother, Rose Ah Tye, and admire a family album of beautiful old photographs that were unlabeled. I said, "When you're gone, Grandma, no one will know who is pictured in these photographs." I offered to label the album, and, as my grandmother identified each photo, she shared some of the family oral history . . . and I started taking notes.

My younger sister, Doreen Ah Tye, accompanied me to city halls, libraries, courthouses, and museums to find data chronicling our family's history. We scoured through huge leather-bound deed, tax assessment, birth, and death books that were written in beautiful script. Some of those books, dating back to the late-nineteenth century, had not been touched for decades. They listed a rainbow of ethnic names, revealing the diversity of people who had tried their luck in the northern California mining towns.

Doreen became a research technician at the National Center for Electron Microscopy at Lawrence Berkeley National Laboratory. Her Berkeley apartment provided a base and afforded me the opportunity to do thorough research at the Bancroft Library, which is renowned for its collection of Californiana.

This book completes a circle of self-knowledge that began in my college days at California State University, San Francisco, in the late 1960s. In those days of searching for my identity, I would ask myself, "Who am I? Am I Chinese or American?" My father, Edward Ah Tye, had given me stability and deep American roots, and my mother, Blanche (Chin), had passed on a love and understanding for my Chinese heritage.

In 1968, a strike at the University centered around the issue of whether ethnic studies should be added to the school's curriculum. I was only an observer during this tumultuous period, but I came to realize that I knew very little about my own Chinese American roots. American education had taught me mainly about European history.

Over the years, I have come to know that I am a hybrid of both Chinese and American cultures, striving to blend the best qualities of both. After researching and writing this book, I now understand why I feel more American than Chinese.

I hope this book will encourage those who search for identity to seek it among their family's roots, and will give readers a better understanding of Chinese American thought, history, and culture.

A traditional Chinese burial in Lone Mountain Cemetery, San Francisco, 1882. *Left to right:* Paper money and incense burning on sticks atop grave; mourners with food offerings; musicians with gongs, cymbals, and horns; priest with bells; roast pig; paper road money scattered over sheet-wrapped bodies; carriage waiting in background; Caucasian visitors; mourners with trays and baskets of food. Woodcut by Paul Frenzeny, *Harper's Weekly,* January 28, 1882. Mountain House Books.

Chapter One
THE END AND THE BEGINNING

Most Chinese came to America as sojourners, hoping to make their fortune and return to China as rich men and die among their people. If they should die in America, rich or poor, they made sure of one thing: their bones must be returned to the land of their ancestors and be buried there, so their spirit would not wander forever in the darkness of a foreign world.

But Yee Ah Tye was different. He astonished his family and friends with his last request. Just before passing away, he spoke to those around him:

I am old. Nearly seventy-three years have passed over my head. I have lived in this land since I was a young man. My wife lives here, and this land is the home of my sons. Now let my old body be buried here and my bones lie undisturbed for all times in the land where I have lived.[1]

Several of those nearby urged Yee Ah Tye to follow the customs of his people and have his bones sent back to China, but he was unwavering. "I have voiced my wish. My bones must lie in the land where I have lived. Let none interfere."

Yee Ah Tye died on April 20, 1896. A wagon carried his body from his home in the northern California mining town of La Porte to a funeral parlor in Marysville. His funeral in San Francisco was held almost two months after his death, honoring his request to wait for his eldest son, Sam, to return from China.

An American Band
Yee Ah Tye was given a funeral "with all possible ceremonies of his native land and the addition of an American band."[2] His body lay in state in the rooms of the Kong Chow Association on Pine Street, while on Brenham Place, near Clay Street, the usual Taoist religious ceremonies took place.

Five kinds of cooked and uncooked animal food, cakes, vegetables, fruit, wine, and tea sat on tables to feed Yee's spirit in the world beyond. The food also appeased other spirits that were believed to be hovering over his body. Whole fowl, fish, and hogs, roasted to a golden brown, also burdened the tables.

The *San Francisco Chronicle* obituary stated that Yee Ah Tye came to America in the early 1850s, and for years was prominent among the Chinese in San Francisco. He was president of the Kong Chow Association, one of the Six Companies, and "personally advanced the standing and wealth of that organization."[3]

Ah Tye secured from the United States government a piece of land near Point Lobos and gave it to his association for a cemetery. He also gave them the property on Pine Street near Kearny, which was used as the association headquarters. He lived in Plumas County and owned mining properties and a general merchandise store in La Porte. Interestingly, the obituary described Ah Tye as "not a very rich man, though well to do," perhaps reflecting the caution of a Chinese miner who struck gold yet remained quiet about it.

The *San Francisco Chronicle* reported that Yee Ah Tye "was buried with the greatest honors on account of his good deeds of the past and his good standing with his business associates." Nearly every Chinese merchant in San Francisco attended the services. Women (some hired) wailed in sorrowful tones. The eulogies were punctuated by outbreaks of sobbing and wailing against the steady background of Chinese funeral music. Friends and relatives viewing the body moved haltingly, as each person stopped to bow three times in respect for the deceased.

At one o'clock the funeral cortege started for the cemetery, and in the line were more than forty carriages carrying relatives and friends. Headed by an American band, the procession went to the

The **Call**

SAN FRANCISCO, SUNDAY MORNING, JUNE 14, 1896—THIRTY-TWO PAGES.

HIS BONES TO LIE IN THIS LAND,

The Strange Request of an Aged Chinese Merchant.

He Did Not Want His Body Sent
Back to the Flowery
Kingdom.

The Funeral Was Postponed Until His
Eldest Son Could Return
From China.

A newspaper article in the *San Francisco Call,* 1896,
detailed Yee Ah Tye's strange deathbed request and
formal funeral.

mal conversation, Chinese commonly use the sound "ah" to precede a given name to maintain the rhyme, rhythm, and flow of the Cantonese language.

In everyday conversation, Yee's family and friends called him *Ah Dy.* Hearing this, Americans thought his last name was Ah Tye. He adopted this American version of his name, but the misunderstanding was not limited to him alone. In the 1870 United States census of La Porte, the enumerator listed Ah Chuck, Ah Kom, Ah Ley, Ah Cue, and eighty-seven other Chinese placer miners with first names preceded by an "Ah."

As Yee Ah Tye grew older and gained prominence in his community, the Chinese began calling him *Yee Lo Dy. Lo* is a term of dignity and honor.[4]

Kong Chow cemetery. After his body was buried, his widow and children returned to their La Porte home.

Origin of the Name, Ah Tye

Yee Ah Tye illustrates especially well the coming together of two cultures, and the combinations and confusions that resulted. His original name, Yee Dy, became *Ah Tye* in America. Americans introduce themselves by saying their given name first, then their last name. The Chinese, who place primary importance on the family, introduce themselves by saying their last name first, then their given name. Hence, the name John Smith, would be Smith John in Chinese.

Yee Ah Tye's Chinese signature on an 1866 San Francisco Kong Chow deed is *Yee Dy,* meaning that his family, or last, name is *Yee* and his given name is *Dy. Dy* means "big" or "large," implying the eldest son. The genealogy shows that Yee Ah Tye was indeed the eldest of four sons, but it doesn't indicate whether his three brothers died in infancy, as young boys, or as teen-agers. It appears that none lived long enough to marry.

The Cantonese language is made up of eight or nine tones and to the Western ear sounds sing-song. In infor-

Genealogy—Mid-Eleventh Century to High Middle Ages

The Yee (Yu) family roots are from common people.[5] Like more than eighty percent of the Chinese in the United States, Yee Ah Tye's descendants originated in Kwangtung (Guangdong) Province, sometimes referred to as Canton Province.[6] This province in southern China, an area of about 80,000 square miles, is approximately the size of the state of Oregon.

Yee Ah Tye was born in the 1820s in the village of Chang-wan (Zhangwan) in the Sunwui (Xinhui) district. The village was located near the coast, where a canal meets a river.[7]

Sunwui is one of the *Sze Yup,* or "Four Districts" in the delta, a fertile plain lying between the Pearl River estuary and the sea. Most of the villages were built next to waterways and were engaged in fishing, while others were farming communities.

At Chinese funerals, paper objects in the shape of houses, money, servants, and horses were burned to provide for the deceased in the afterlife. Photograph by Willard Worden, c. 1900; Wells Fargo Bank.

The family traces its roots to an illustrious past, as far back as the Sung (Song) Dynasty in the mid-eleventh century, the period that Western history calls the High Middle Ages.

The present Yee family tree was compiled during the Ming Dynasty, A.D. 1368.[8] A translation of the narrative account of the lineage by L. Eve Armentrout Ma explains the importance of genealogy:

If a family has a genealogical account, then looking back into time one can identify the origins of one's ancestors and lineage and looking into the future, the descendants can understand their inheritance. This is why genealogies are important.

As for the saying "a tree cannot grow without roots, water cannot come forth unless it has a source," a man's original nature lies in his ancestors just as a tree has roots and water has its source.[9]

The Yee's ancestral genealogical records adhere to an established pattern followed by Chinese clans, lineages, and surnames. The records begin with a legendary origin: a direct connection to a pre-historical figure of great antiquity, a son of the Yellow emperor named Yen Hiu (Xuan-xiao).

The ancestral account reveals that more than thirty generations later the Yee surname appeared. The first fifteen generations were legendary, including figures such as Qi (Chi), the minister of agriculture to the sage Emperor Shun. Qi was invested with a feudal estate and given the rank of duke.

By the thirtieth generation, during the historical kingdoms of Chun and Jun (Chin and Jin) of the Warring States period, the ancestor You Yee (You Yu) was honored by the kings of both states. You Yee moved from the north China plain to the Shantung peninsula. A number of generations later, an ancestor actually surnamed "Yee" appeared—Yee Suey (Yu Rui). He served Chin (Qin) as a censor then moved from Shantung to southeastern Shimsai (Shensi), where he retired in obscurity near the source of the Lok (Lo) River, a tributary of the Yellow River. The clan's migratory movements under You Yee and Yee Suey reflected the general extension of Chinese culture and population expansion eastward and southward from the central plain.

Yee Jing—Sung Dynasty Scholar and Clan Forefather

During the Tang Dynasty, Chang-wan's Yee ancestors moved several more times in larger population shifts. Over a period of six to eight generations, the ancestors

The cover of the Yee family genealogy translates "Family Genealogy of the House of Heng Hop." The Ah Tye family is descended from the founder of the branch house of Heng Hop of the Yee Clan. Ah Tye Family Collection.

first went to southern Onfai (Anhui) and then during the Wong Chao (Huang Chao) rebellion, moved into Kongsoo (Kiangsu), settling near Shanghai. Later, in the Five Dynasties period, the Yee forebearers migrated further south into Kwangtung. Three generations later Yee Jing (Yu Jing) was born.

Yee Jing is honored as the forefather of the Yee family in Sunwui, Kwangtung Province. Following the footsteps of his father as a Sung Dynasty Confucian scholar in 1024, Yee Jing had a respectable but unremarkable official career. However, his accomplishments after his retirement won him the honor of clan forefather.

While he was in his sixties, a large-scale tribal uprising broke out in the provinces of Kwangtung and Kwangsi. Yee Jing raised his own army and joined forces with a military official to put down the rebellion.

The imperial court publicly honored Yee Jing and awarded him an income collected from the rent of three hundred households. After Yee Jing's death in his late sixties, the imperial court conferred upon him the posthumous position of grand secretary of the Board of Public Works and the Board of Criminal Justice and the posthumous title of Duke Xiang. Yee Jing's widow was given the title, Lady of Lu, and two groups of convicts were consigned to construct and maintain his grave site.

The Yee lineage reached its zenith beginning with Yee Jing's father and continued its prominence for three generations after Yee Jing. Many family members received official positions, several were successful at government examinations, and an even larger number received honorary titles. The Yees clearly qualified as a gentry family at this time.

During the approximately five generations after Yee Jing, many male descendants became lower-echelon officials, and lived in Kwangtung Province. In the time of the Southern Song dynasty, Yee Tong Lo (Yu Tang-lao) was the sub-clan progenitor. Yee Tong Lo's father moved his family several times to avoid rampant banditry, finally settling in the Yee village in an area that became Xinning (Sunning) County. Upon reaching maturity, his younger son, Yee Tong Lo, moved to Sunwui (Xinhui- xian), the first family member to settle in that county. Three generations later, Yee Nim (Yu Nian) founded the village of Yi-mei and later the village of Chang-wan.

Farmers and Fishermen

From Ming times (A.D. 1368) onward, the Yee lineage comes from the country rather than the court. Yee Ah Tye's relatives lived in rural regions and were predominantly farmers and fishermen. Like thousands of other families in the south China countryside, the Yees of Chang-wan were poor and its members were common individuals.

The lineage "is a mirror: a mirror of ordinary lineages in an ordinary area with an ordinary history, and, presumably, ordinary aspirations."[10] This ordinary Chinese lineage settled in an extraordinary country, however, and became part of the fabric of America's unique history.

Chinese emigrants in San Francisco were searched by agents at the Customs House before they were transported to their company house. Most of the newcomers are men except for two women in the doorway and one seated near a basket. *Left:* A merchant inspects a cargo list. *Harper's Weekly.*

Chapter Two
1850: EMIGRATION AND SAN FRANCISCO

Emigration to foreign countries was not new to men like Yee Ah Tye. Decades before the California Gold Rush, men from Kwangtung (Guangdong), Kwangsi (Guangxi), or Fukien (Fujian) provinces migrated to Southeast Asian countries—Cambodia, Laos, Vietnam, Thailand, Burma, Malaysia, Indonesia, and the Philippines. Driven by hard conditions in China, many emigrants hoped to keep their families united with savings and earnings from working overseas, then eventually return to their native Chinese villages.

In the 1840s, the Manchu dynasty began a long period of decline and decay, political corruption, injustice, and inadequate administration. In 1846 and 1848, droughts and floods ruined staple crops, leading to massive starvation and poverty. Banditry increased, and peasant uprisings and rebellions broke out, the greatest being the Taiping Rebellion (1850-1864). Local feuds in southern China added to the domestic turmoil, and forced many Chinese to consider emigration as an escape from such misery. This turbulent period created a "push" factor, leading to the emigration of thousands of Chinese to Peru, Cuba, Mexico, Southeast Asia, Canada, Hawaii, and California.

At the same time, European nations were developing their colonies and frontier regions. The growing economies and the need for laborers became a "pull" factor that attracted immigration.

The people of South China were especially inclined to emigrate. Their close proximity to the coast and ports of Canton, Macao, and Hong Kong gave the Cantonese early contact with foreigners, making them more adventuresome and open to new ideas and change than were most Chinese. The international ports of Hong Kong and Macao also facilitated their emigration to many parts of the world.

Gold Mountain
In the spring of 1848, gold was discovered at John Sutter's mill at Coloma, California. When the news reached Hong Kong, there was great excitement. Masters of foreign vessels saw the potential for profit in mass emigration. They distributed posters, maps, and pamphlets with colorful and alluring descriptions of *Gum Shan*, or Gold Mountain, as California soon became known.

Almost all of the Chinese who migrated to California during the Gold Rush period landed in San Francisco, known to them as *Dai Fow*, or Big City. When California became the thirty-first state of the Union in 1850, the *Daily Alta California* described the celebration in San Francisco as one that "touched every heart and fired every mind." A parade included military units, fire brigades, and civic groups. The German, Italian, and Spanish consuls residing in San Francisco marched in a procession, followed by a company of Englishmen bearing the cross of St. George. The Chinese, or "Celestials," as they were called, "had a banner of crimson satin, on which were some Chinese characters and the inscription, 'China Boys.' They numbered about fifty and were arrayed in their richest stuffs and commanded by their chief, Norman Assing."[1]

No Ordinary Aspirations
Yee Ah Tye immigrated to California around 1852 to seek his fortune in the gold fields. Mo-Mo Ahtye, who cared for Yee Ah Tye's widow during the last years of her life, remembers that he had one advantage over his countrymen—he had learned English in Hong Kong before coming to America. From that one fact, one can surmise that he aspired to become a merchant, not a laborer. Mo-Mo recalled this description of Ah Tye's journey to America:

> *Yee Ah Tye came to America in a junk. He was about twenty years old. The voyage started with twenty-two young Chinese men and ended with twenty.*[2]

There was no reception committee waiting for Ah Tye and his companions when they arrived in San Francisco. The men spent their first night on American soil huddled together in the doorway of a building.

District Association or Huiguan

When a great number of Chinese clan members visited another province or foreign country, they formed a district association or huiguan (meeting hall). For example, candidates of Kwangtung Province went to Peking (Beijing) to take government examinations, and formed a huiguan where they lived while away from home. Even though they spoke Mandarin, the language of the capital, they were easily identified as strangers and thus vulnerable to insults and cheating, the treatment city-folk reserved for their country cousins. The huiguans provided self-defense, much like a mutual-aid society.

Four Great Houses

The huiguan was also traditional in overseas Chinese communities. In California, Yee Ah Tye soon became an important figure in the district association for people who came from his province.[3]

For better organization in America, the emigrants divided themselves into four huiguans (commonly referred to as companies). At that time, Chinese and Americans referred to them as the "Four Houses." These grew to "Five Companies," then to the well-known "Chinese Six Companies."[4]

Each huiguan had a house in San Francisco presided over by agents or superintendents elected by its membership. The agents, membership, and Chinese origin of each San Francisco district association in 1853 were:

Gee Atai (Ah Tye) and Lee Chuen—Sze Yup Association (Siyi Huiguan)9,500 members from the four districts of Sunning (Toishan or Xinning), Hoiping (Kaiping), Yanping (Enping), and Sunwui (Xinhui)

Tong K. Achick and Lum Teen-kwei—Young Wo Association (Yanghe Huiguan) 7,500 members from Heungshan (Chungshan or Zhongshan)

Tam Sam and Chun Aching—Sam Yup Association (commonly called the Canton Company or Sanyi Huiguan)4,000 members from the Sam Yup or three districts of Namhoi (Nanhai), Punyu (Panyu), and Shuntak (Shunde)

Wong Sing and Lee Yuk Nam—Sun On Association (Xin'an Huiguan)1,000 members of the Hakka, one of the major dialects in Kwangtung[5]

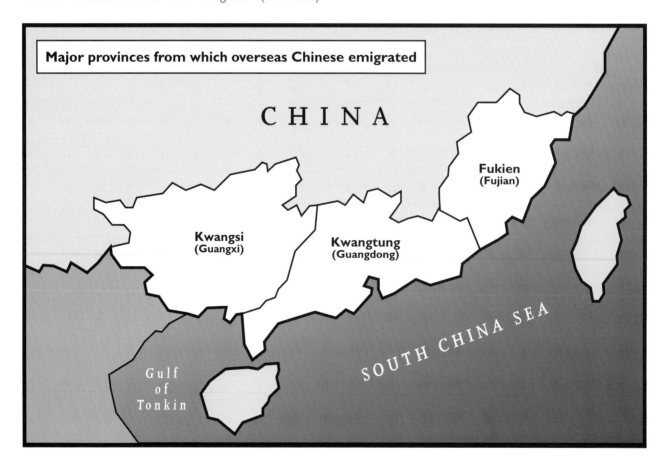

Major provinces from which overseas Chinese emigrated

CHINA

Fukien (Fujian)

Kwangsi (Guangxi)

Kwangtung (Guangdong)

Gulf of Tonkin

SOUTH CHINA SEA

During the early years of the Gold Rush, Chinese companies based in both California and Hong Kong operated a contract labor system. The imported workers sold their services for several years in exchange for passage. Because it was difficult to enforce contracts and proved to be unprofitable, the practice was discontinued. Some emigrants paid their own passage or received aid from their families or friends.

The huiguans and their leaders had an enormous influence on the nineteenth-century Chinese emigrant from the moment he set foot on American soil until he returned to China. Most Chinese laborers came to California by the credit-ticket system. The huiguan advanced passage fare to the emigrant in a Chinese port, and after he had reached his destination, the debt was paid from his earnings.

An umbrella of security was provided by the huiguan for the sojourner encountering a strange new land. Upon arriving in San Francisco, Chinese emigrants were met by representatives of the huiguans. By merely listening to each person's regional dialect, representatives were able to divide them into district groups. After they passed inspection by customs officers' searching for opium, the Chinese newcomers followed their district representative to their huiguan. The sojourners either piled into wagons or followed on foot, shouldering their belongings of bedding, matting, and clothing on the ends of bamboo poles.

The emigrants, with their shaven heads and braided queues, were normally dressed in coarse blue cotton tops, loose baggy pants, blue cotton knee stockings, and heavy, wooden-soled slippers. Most of the Chinese carried one or two broad-brimmed hats of split bamboo and huge palm-leaf fans to shield them from the burning sun in the Gold Mountains. Sometimes trips through San Francisco en route to the Chinese Quarter were peaceful, other times not. If they were lucky, the emigrants reached their huiguan without being the targets of stones, mud, or potatoes thrown by White ruffians. Some sojourners were provided with used pots, pans, and skillets if they needed them. However, many others had brought their own utensils from China so they could prepare food during their passage on board the ship. After the house had recorded his name, the emigrant paid a membership fee of ten to twenty dollars to cover operating expenses that included salaries for the agents and servants, fuel, water, candles, oil, coffins and funerals for the poor, tomb repairs, taxes, and legal expenses.

The huiguans also served as clearinghouses of business for men departing for China. It was customary for

Emigrants were often the target of ruffians. *Pacific Tourist,* 1878.

each Chinese to settle all debts before leaving America. The house made an arrangement with the sailing and steamship companies that every Chinese must show a paper from his association stating that he had paid his debts before he was allowed to purchase a return ticket to China. Most importantly, if the emigrant died in America, huiguan membership ensured the return of the emigrant's bones to the land of his family and ancestors.

Chinese Spokesmen

The huiguan heads were spokesmen for the Chinese emigrants, as evidenced by an appearance the association heads made before the California Assembly's Committee on Mines and Mining Interests in 1853. The leaders stated their grievances through agent Tong K. Achick, who served as interpreter. They complained that the testimony and statements of their people had not been allowed in court controversies because "of the color of their skin." While the state taxed the Chinese "for the privilege of working in the mines," they were at the same time denied the protection afforded by the payment of those taxes.[6]

The district heads also took responsibility for the behavior of their compatriots. On the afternoon of December 19, 1853, the chief engineer of the San Francisco Fire Department, Mr. Duane, was passing a building occupied by the Sze Yup Association on the southeast corner of Sacramento and Stockton streets.

He saw a row of twelve fires on the Sze Yup premises (probably the fires of outdoor kitchens) that were dangerously close to the adjoining house. Duane found sixty or seventy Chinese inside the building, waiting for their supper. He told a Chinese, Ching Ley, to throw a bucket of water on the fires to put them out. The Chinese cooks took offense at the fire chief's interference, and the bucket of water was poured over him instead. *The San Francisco Daily Herald and Mirror* explained that six or seven other Chinese rushed upon Duane, "who only saved himself from complete extinguishment by seizing the 'respected pig-tails' of his assailants, and swinging them round in a manner that formed a queuerious tableau."[7]

The newspaper reported that it took two days to ascertain who was the head of the Sze Yup Association. Several members were brought forward, but each one proved to be "not that man." Finally, the court recorder called Ah Tye to the stand, and he acknowledged that he was the head of the company. The complaint was therefore entered against him.

Eventually, Ching Ley (the man who had poured the bucket of water over Duane's head) was found guilty and fined two hundred dollars for his refusal to put out a fire, a violation of a city ordinance.

Mandarin Among His People

The huiguans also had a negative side. Many Chinese emigrants in the nineteenth century assumed a debt of forty dollars for their initial passage and paid a high monthly interest of four to eight percent. Expenses for papers might also be added, often leaving laborers with a total debt to their merchant creditors that could take from three to five years to repay.

The houses also provided the structure of authority within which the newly arrived emigrants had to live, and leaders did not hesitate to use force on those who opposed them. An 1853 San Francisco grand jury report voiced concerns about tactics used by the association leaders against their brethren:

> We find in existence in this community a society of Chinese called the *Four Great Houses*, established for the purpose of forcing trade to their different establishments and to prevent passengers among their countrymen from purchasing tickets from any but them-selves, and punishing with fines and the bastinado all who may transgress their laws. Several on this account were most cruelly beaten. . . .
>
> They have regular meetings, which are presided over by the heads of the four great houses, viz: Sam-

Wo, Ah-Ti [sic] and the two Ah Chings. They have posted up printed handbills in their own language, and signed by themselves, forewarning all from transgressing their laws and threatening their punishment.[8]

Referring to Ah Tye, the *San Francisco Herald* reported a great many stories "afloat respecting the misdeeds of this would be Mandarin among his people." He "inflicted severe corporeal punishment upon many of his more humble countrymen . . . cutting off their ears, flogging them and keeping them chained for hours together." Titled "Chinese Vassalage," the article reported:

> Ah Ti, the Chinese petty despot that was brought before the Recorder upon a charge of assault and battery, was convicted of the offense and sentenced to five days' imprisonment in the city prison. An appeal was made, however, and he was allowed to remain at large upon giving bail in the sum of $1000.

Various complaints had been made against Ah Tye, but he "always succeeded in evading the law, by his superior adroitness, influence, and cunning."[9]

Huiguan leaders were shaped by their culture which ranks scholars at the top of the social hierarchy. The ideal scholar exemplified Confucian qualities of benevolence, gentleness, and loyalty. These qualities kept society peaceful and orderly by winning the hearts of the common people. However, if these gentler means failed, the delicate scholar might have a suspected criminal beaten or have his fingers or ankle bones crushed.

Disputes and Arbitration

In China, people brought disputes, debts, and business differences before their clan organization to be arbitrated by titled scholars and elders. Scholars, however, rarely emigrated from China, because opportunities for upward mobility were available to them there. Therefore, the richer and more literate merchants (sometimes referred to as "merchant princes") became the dominant leaders abroad.

Committees elected from among the Chinese merchants of San Francisco acted in conjunction with association agents in all public matters relating to their people. When differences arose, association houses served as courts of justice, in which the heads of the houses sat as judges, enforced the collection of debts, and punished petty offenses.

A joint committee of the associations handled difficult cases. Only in cases of serious crime, or when people did not agree with the arbitration, was the case settled by American law. Americans did not always look kindly on this double system of justice.

On August 13, 1852, the *San Francisco Daily Alta* reported a dispute involving Ah Tye, and pictured him as an extortionist:

DIFFICULTIES AMONG THE CHINESE. . . . We understand that an A-thai [sic] has assumed the robes of a Grand Inquisitor, and is endeavoring to coerce his brethren into such measures as he may suggest and dictate. He accuses one Le a-chan of having brought the poll tax gatherer among his people, and complains of the rebellious and unloyal acts of many of his kindred. He has offered a reward of three hundred dollars to he who shall bring Le a-chan before his grand inquisitorial court, and has threatened destruction to many others. Le a-chan was before the Recorder's Court yesterday for the purpose of making a complaint that he was afraid for his life, and that he did not feel secure unless the Dictator was restrained by law. We may expect some rich developments concerning Chinese legislation.[10]

Several days later, however, the *Daily Alta* reported that the matter between Ah Tye and Le a-chan had been "satisfactorily settled outside of the (American) judicial tribunal."[11]

Chinese Madam, Miss Atoy

American courts were sometimes used in the struggles for power that increasingly occurred within the community during the 1850s. Miss Atoy, the first Chinese prostitute in San Francisco to rise to the rank of madam, became the most infamous and successful Chinese courtesan in the city. Her tea parties were attended by important dignitaries, and she was said to influence Chinese participation in the celebration of California's admission into the union.

Miss Atoy had appeared in court a number of times to sue clients who had paid her with brass filings instead of gold. And she successfully fought off Chinese leader Norman Assing's attempts to extradite her to China. She apparently made quite an impression on observers. As the *San Francisco Daily Herald* noted, she appeared in court "with flying colors, dressed in the most splendid style" and won the right to remain in America.[12]

The summer of 1852 was not a good one for Yee Ah Tye. Shortly after his dispute with Le a-chan, the *Daily Alta* reported another storm brewing, this time with Miss Atoy:

A-thai, [sic] the self-styled dictator, it seems has ordered one of his agents to summon a number of women residing on Dupont street [now Grant Avenue] and under the guardianship of Miss Atoy, to appear before him, at his headquarters on Sacramento street, and show cause why they should not pay a certain tax or contribution.[13]

The reporter assured his readers that "Miss Atoy knows a thing or two, having lived under the folds of the Star-spangled Banner for three years and breathed the air of Republicanism, and she cannot be easily humbugged into any such measures."

By now, Miss Atoy had gone before the American courts as a defendant at least fifty times and lived near the police station, so she knew where to seek protection.[14] She outsmarted Ah Tye by bringing her case to the American court, and his efforts at extortion were put to an end.

The growing Chinese community in San Francisco was full of competition and controversy. In the year after Yee Ah Tye's dispute with Miss Atoy, he found himself in court again. This time he was the defendant in an assault-and-battery and grand larceny case, accused of illegally seizing some of the Sze Yup Company's funds. The *Daily Alta California* reported "there were so many witnesses on each side, that it was proposed to count which side had the most, and let it be considered the winner."[15]

Ah Tye, the Presbyterian Church, and Idol Worship

William Speer, D.D., a Presbyterian minister, was the first pastor to practice missionary work among the Chinese in San Francisco. From knowledge gained as a missionary in Canton, Reverend Speer presented two series of lectures on Chinese culture, customs, and history in 1853. Printed in the *San Francisco Daily Herald*, the articles sought to promote a greater understanding of Chinese civilization among the general American public.

Almost every Protestant denomination established mission houses for the Chinese in California. Missionaries like Speer were almost the only Americans to speak in favor of Chinese immigration. He encouraged trade with China in his lectures and felt America needed the Chinese to work as farmers, manufacturers, servants, fishermen, and miners.

In addition to acting as a spokesman for the Chinese, Speer ministered to those in need. Many emigrants reached San Francisco suffering from scurvy and poor health, due to poor conditions on the shipboard passage.

Chinese mingled with Spaniards, Europeans, Englishmen, and South Americans in a typical saloon in San Francisco.

Changes in climate and food and a lack of immunity to American diseases caused further illness among the newcomers.

Seeing that Chinese associations and relatives could not tend to all the emigrants who needed help, Speer added a medical dispensary to his Presbyterian mission. The Chinese seemed suspicious of him at first, but in time the numbers of people seeking relief increased. During the months when Chinese ships landed, it became common to find from thirty to forty emigrants waiting for aid at the mission dispensary every Wednesday and Saturday. After Speer gave the Chinese "some service in temporal, and he trusted, in spiritual things," they "eagerly manifested their gratitude."[16]

Audiences for Speer's lectures grew larger with each succeeding speech. In the summer of 1853, he concluded his second lecture series before a large audience of Caucasians and Chinese. At the end, they gave donations to build a Chinese Presbyterian church, the first Protestant church to be formed for Chinese outside of China.

Besides a long list of generous Caucasian contributions, there were donations from many Chinese associations and their leaders. Tong K. Achick, agent of the Young Wo Association, gave $50, his association donated $100, and Chung Aching, agent of the Canton Association, also gave $100. Gee Atai (Ah Tye), agent of the Sze Yup Association, gave $50, and an additional $200 in the name of his association.

The Chinese Presbyterian Church was built on land sold to Speer for $4,500 by Ah Tye, as agent of the Sze Yup Association, and Tso Asze, agent of the Ning Yung Association. Constructed in 1853, and "dedicated to the service of God on the fourth Sabbath of June, 1854," the church was on the southeast corner of Sacramento and Stockton streets, just north of the Chinese Quarter.[17]

The Chinese first located their canvas houses on Sacramento Street in 1849, and, according to the *San Francisco Daily Herald*, stuck to this area with "remarkable tenacity," creating a barrier to improvement occurring in every other part of the city.[18] The Chinese Quarter took up nearly the whole of Sacramento Street, between Kearny and Dupont (Grant Avenue). The tenements were cheaply constructed and flimsy, with the upper stories of most houses used for gambling. Tightly crowded goods blocked passages everywhere. Every foot of the Chinese Quarter was occupied, with people packed as closely as their goods.

Speer's primary motive in helping the Chinese was his desire to Christianize them. He and other evangelists felt that the oppressive Manchu dynasty would eventually be expelled from China, leaving it open to the introduction of Christianity. In anticipation, Speer urged Americans to Christianize the California Chinese, who could then go back to China as missionaries and "plant the religion of Christ in the place of the gigantic systems of Idolatry now crumbling into dust."[19]

Although Speer's relations with the Chinese were amicable, he converted very few to Christianity. The Christian religion required the Chinese to abandon all their previous religious practices. Christian doctrine did not allow for co-existence with Chinese traditional beliefs. This lack of tolerance, as well as a condescending attitude toward traditional Chinese culture, caused most Chinese (especially those born in China) to reject Christianity. One of Speer's lectures exemplified this attitude:

> The Chinaman comes here a spiritually degraded being, trembling with a thousand absurd superstitions and horrible fears. As he bends over the toilsome spade he fancies that demons haunt those hills and watch their treasures; at whose anger, as expressed in the thunder and lightning, he is terrified, and would fain appease it with incense and offerings of fruit and cakes. . . . Unless the Gospel is speedily preached to them [the California Chinese], they will bring here their gods of the hills and rivers, and seas and skies.[20]

In spite of Ah Tye's generous support of Speer's church, it was clear that the profound differences of their cultures and religions would allow no lasting peace between the two men.

The Kong Chow Asylum had a Victorian arch cornice crowning its facade. Only the gilt Chinese characters on a marble slab identified the building as Chinese, c. 1880s. The Bancroft Library.

Chapter Three
THE KONG CHOW TEMPLE

There is a parcel of land on Pine Street with a special significance to the Chinese. According to legend, the first of their countrymen to arrive in San Francisco were two men and a woman, servants aboard the American ship, *Eagle*, in 1848. They spent their first night on the Pine Street land. Another story says that in the early 1850s, a wooden shack on a plot of land on Pine Street was given to three young Chinese by a mission-minded American who hoped to "bring the light of Christian faith to many Chinatown inhabitants."[1] The three who had recently arrived with a thirst for Western learning, did not live in the shack for very long.

Yee Ah Tye gained ownership of the Pine Street land on May 14, 1853, in a deed signed by Gay and Barbour to "G. Ah Thai," the Sze Yup Company agent. It is written in the usual form, but these words were added: "in trust for the use of a Chinese church, or place of religious worship and moral instruction," under the rules of the Sze Yup Company.[2]

A Chinese Church
Imagine Reverend Speer's reaction when he read this notice in the *Daily Alta* on July 10, 1853:

> A CHINESE CHURCH is to be built on the rear of a lot on the corner of Kearny and Pine streets. It is to be 42 by 45 feet upon the ground and three stories in height. It will be devoted to moral and religious instruction, under the superintendence of George Athei [sic], of the See Yup Company. The designs for the building are by L. R. Townsend, architect.[3]

The company built on the lot and made improvements valued at about forty thousand dollars. In his book, *The Oldest and the Newest Empire*, Speer writes that Ah Tye asked him if the Sze Yup building could be "made free of taxes, as he understood that American churches and benevolent institutions were granted that privilege."[4] Speer explained that an association or club of its kind, designed for purposes of mutual convenience, had no more right to claim tax exemption than a hotel that gave food and lodging to beggars and the distressed.

However, Ah Tye applied for tax exemption on the grounds that the building belonged to a benevolent institution. Perhaps with the vivid memory of arriving in America with no place for shelter, he hung a sign over the entrance, designating the building an "Asylum." The sign also reflected the feeling that the Chinese were aliens in a hostile environment.

To further carry out his purpose, Ah Tye convinced the Sze Yup Association to order an image of the god, Kuan Ti, from China and to dedicate a large room to its worship. This, Ah Tye told American visitors, is a "Chinese church!"[5]

Chinese Church Opposition
Controversy over the "Chinese church" was recorded in the San Francisco newspapers. The *Daily Alta* accused the new institution of being "a banking and speculative concern," and claimed that there was "a ruse being played off for the purpose of escaping assessments, which would amount to $200,000." It also stated that the church plea would enable the association "to slip through the fingers of the Custom House, with materials for this church."[6]

Four days later, a letter to the *Daily Alta* editors defended the huiguan:

The See Yup company of China . . . consists of some 12,000 Chinamen, under the directorship of respectable men, and formed into a society for charitable purposes, to support and protect each other, in case of sickness, or necessity of any kind. The church spoken of is now being put under contract—the materials and workmanship of this country's labor. So much for 'slipping through the Custom House with materials for this church.'

Several articles have been published in newspapers of this city, prejudicial to this company, and particularly against one of the employed, named Atei [Ah Tye], who is simply a clerk of the company. It would appear from representation of the parties, to be an attempt at levying upon these Chinamen a system of black mail, as any threat of publishing them in any way, greatly alarms them, for fear they may lose favor, and appear degraded in the eyes of the public. This persecution has been attempted and prosecuted for some weeks past. E. Cany[7]

Speer voiced his opposition to the Chinese church in a lecture. He praised the efforts of one of the Chinese who had been of "great service in preventing the execution of the project for erecting a heathen temple" in San Francisco.[8] Speer furnished "the assessors with an exact account of the purposes of the company," and "the tax was laid upon the house," much to Ah Tye's disgust.[9]

Harmony With Cosmic Breath
In the 1850s, Pine and Kearny streets were not far from the edge of the San Francisco Bay. The temple faced the water, not so much for its marine view, but to have good *feng shui*, or harmonic balance between the building and nature.

The literal translation of *feng shui* is "wind and water." The significance of wind and water is that they move energy, and many Chinese believe that energy in motion is essential to good health, happiness, and prosperity. The flow of waterways, wind directions, terrain, and even the placement of doors and windows were taken into consideration before construction of the Sze Yup Association building. The Kong Chow temple's official master of divination ruled that the *feng shui*—"the art of adapting the residence of the living and the dead so as to co-operate and harmonize with the local currents of the cosmic breath" surrounding the place—was exactly right.[10]

Kuan Ti—God of War and Peace
In 1856, a spring festival was held in the Sze Yup Associ-

ation building, which now proudly bore on its front a Chinese inscription and the words "See Yup Asylum, 1853." A reporter for the *Daily Alta* wrote that the asylum was a credit to the Chinese residents of the city. "It is built of brick, large, substantial and commodious, and will compare favorably with any public institution in our midst."[11]

The new statue of Kuan Ti had been placed in the temple, located in the upper part of the building. Kuan Ti is the red-faced god of war—not a god who takes pleasure in fighting, but one who can avert and protect people from war. Known also as Kuan Kung (Guan Gung), he is one of the most popular gods of China, embodying right action, integrity, and loyalty. Kuan Ti is also one of the three gods of literature. Chinese Buddhism adopted Kuan Ti as one of the three divine protectors of monasteries.

Kuan Ti's real name was Kuan Yu, an historical figure who lived from A.D. 165 to 219. Kuan Yu's chivalry forced him to flee from his home after he killed an official who had made unwelcome advances to a young lady. To escape, Kuan Yu had to travel through the T'ung Kuan mountain pass. He stopped to drink from a spring and consider how to manage this without being recognized. As he knelt down to drink, he saw in the reflection that his face had turned red, which enabled him to get through the pass unrecognized.

A Chinese spring festival was held to dedicate Kuan Ti's statue. Although Ah Tye had moved to Sacramento around 1854 and lived there at this time, he was on the committee that issued this invitation:

You are invited to attend the Religious Festival of the Chinese, at their Asylum, on Pine street, between Kearny and Dupont streets, commencing on Friday, April 4th, 1856.
Committee of Arrangements—G. Athai, Ahing.[12]

Editors of the *Daily Alta* felt it necessary to comment on the Chinese celebration described in their paper that day. They wrote, "It certainly appears singular, to persons born and reared as Christians, in a Christian land, to witness on their own soil and beneath the very shadows of their church spires, the worship of an idol of wood."[13]

One witness who recorded his impressions of "this display of Idol-Worship in San Francisco," was an Episcopal minister, the Right Reverend Bishop Kip. According to him, the only religious Chinese ceremony that the Caucasians were aware of "seemed to be one in the

Wood engraving of Chinese temple in San Francisco, 1871. Worshipers light incense and burn paper messages to their gods as Caucasian visitors look on. *Harper's Weekly.*

spring, in commemoration of the dead." Chinese, "clothed in their richest dresses," walked in procession to the cemetery accompanied by a wagon of musicians.[14] Another wagon was filled with food, and a whole, roasted goat with gilded horns occupied a prominent place. After services at the graves, the procession returned to partake of the food at their houses.

Ching Ming—Chinese Memorial Day

The ceremony that Kip had observed was the springtime festival called *Ching Ming* (literally "Clear Brightness"). Like the rites of spring of many cultures, it is celebrated by Chinese around the world when the air and light become clear and pure, marking the rebirth of nature and a period of new beginnings.

Similar to America's Memorial Day, Ching Ming is a traditional day to commemorate the dead. It is not a mournful day. After people visit ancestors' graves and tend to their upkeep, the day turns into a spring holiday. The dead are intimately connected with life. Sacrifices of food and paper money are made to keep the ances-

tors in good humor so the living will receive abundant blessings.

In 1856, the Ching Ming festival began on the fourth of April. After the ceremony of visiting the graves at the Yerba Buena Cemetery, the public was invited to attend services dedicating the statue of Kuan Ti. Kip wrote that it was not previously known by Caucasians that the Chinese had any place of worship in San Francisco.

By early morning, avenues and passageways that led to the main building were crowded with Chinese and curious White spectators. Only on rare occasions had the Chinese held public worship. The doors were opened at ten a.m., and more than fifteen hundred people (a large number of whom were women) rushed toward the doors.

According to Kip, visitors entered a large reception room on the first floor of the Sze Yup building. Emblems and pictures decorated the hall. Seats were covered with red satin and richly embroidered with golden flowers and were placed against the wall on both sides of the room. Next to each seat was a carved ebony table for serving refreshments. The Chinese hosts, all male, were dressed in holiday attire. As Kip observed, they made every effort to be polite and attentive to their visitors, serving them "tea in very diminutive cups and without sugar or milk."[15]

A long passage led visitors to kitchens, storerooms, and various conveniences for a hospital. Through another door, a dozen Chinese were seated, smoking, while two others lay on a raised lounge with pipes in their hands. Prevented from entering further, the visitors smelled smoke that they identified as opium.

Religious Ceremonies

Reverend Kip described the statue of the mighty warrior, Kuan Ti, who was seated on an elevated throne, as "a superbly carved, painted and gilded wooden figure, life size . . . surrounded with all the decorations which Chinese ingenuity could devise."[16] Its face was brick red in color, with a long, horsehair moustache on its upper lip. It was clothed in rich garments, and its knees were adorned with jewels and precious stones.

Colored boards inscribed with sacred maxims in Chinese writing hung on the sides of the room. In front

Kuan Ti is depicted in his dual roles as a deity of war and literature. Scroll painting, c. 1800s.

of the statue stood a high altar, covered with offerings of food. Huge red candles covered with emblems burned upon the altar. Amid these were three metallic urns, the central one decorated with a dragon from whose mouth streamed incense smoke.

At the center of the room was another long table covered with every conceivable Chinese delicacy, including dried and fresh fruits, cakes, wines, and tea. Fish were cooked whole, their heads gilded and their fins and tails painted in gaudy colors. A whole roasted pig filled the center of the table. A ram was set on the table, dressed, but uncooked, and decorated with flowers and colored papers. Once the spirit had consumed the "essence" of the food, worshipers ate it.

The religious ceremonies began at noon. Officials and festival participants were dressed in expensive silk robes that reached the floor. One of the high priests began a musical song or recitation, and a dignitary walked around the room, occasionally kneeling on cushions and bowing many times to the idol. At a signal from an official, a small cannon fired in the yard below, while those in the banquet hall maintained perfect silence.

A kneeling high priest received various articles, which he raised to his forehead and offered to the god. Most of the articles were presents sent in congratulation from wealthy Chinese, who were members of the different huiguans. The reporter observed that everyone "seemed to be in high glee and enjoying the festivities remarkably."[17]

Outside Barbarians

According to Reverend Kip, the temple was filled to such capacity the first day that there was no room for the Chinese priests' processions and kneelings. So "all strangers" were asked to leave the temple when the services began on each of the following nine days. Doubtless, there were other reasons for the closure.

In a letter to the editor of the *San Francisco Daily Herald* an observer wrote that although he was opposed to the "encouragement of Asiatic emigration to America," he felt the Chinese, as a class, "the most outrageously abused and well-deserving people" in San Francisco. The observer had witnessed the "idolatrous ceremonies" at the asylum and cemetery, noting that he had never seen such "shameful depredations on decorum and decency" by those who "claim to be citizens of civilized and enlightened America!" He continued:

With their accustomed civility, they (the Chinese) gave our people a general invitation to come and witness their doings, and it is fair to suppose they expected their visitors would allow them to go through with what they believed to be their religious duties, without interruption; but they were greatly mistaken; for no sooner did they commence their evolution of supplications, than they were greeted with a perfect avalanche of "hi-yahs!" and the most filthy, profane, and obscene language it has ever been my lot to hear. I was there one hour, and during that time they (the Chinese) were compelled to suspend their devotions no less than four times. . . . One gentleman (!) more daring than the rest took a quid of tobacco from under his very moustache and threw it at their "god" just "to see if he couldn't put his eye out." Another lank-jawed specimen of Territorial civilization, "kicked John to see if he would do anything about it."[18]

The observer felt these outrages were the thanks "John Chinaman" received for his civility from those Whites who were facetiously called (and he thought very appropriately) "outside barbarians." The Chinese stood aghast at seeing their idol subject to such abuse, "their ceremonies were prematurely but effectually broken up; sacrilege reigned supreme," and the writer left in disgust. He ended his letter by asking: "I am an American, and as such, I would ask, why is it, that such humiliating and disgraceful depredations can be committed without the interference of the police, when 'John Chinaman' is the victim?"

Nevertheless, the services were held every morning during the ten-day festival. These ceremonies, said to be the first in California to which the White world was invited, attracted an estimated ten thousand Caucasians.

A busy street in Sacramento; Chinese in the foreground. *Frank Leslie's Illustrated Newspaper,* May 4, 1878.

Chapter Four
SACRAMENTO: SECOND CITY

Sacramento was called *Yee Fow*, or Second City because it was the second largest city in California, and in many ways, it was the second most important. To reach the gold country in the hills, emigrants in San Francisco gathered the necessary mining supplies, boarded a sailing ship, side-wheeler, or paddle-wheeler, and traveled to the inland river port of Sacramento.[1] From here the routes led in all directions, and the city soon became a vital center of commerce, shipping freight to hundreds of towns and camps in the mountains.

Perhaps tiring of the continuing internal conflicts in San Francisco and desiring to start anew in a town closer to the gold fields, Yee Ah Tye moved to Sacramento. In the *City Directory of Sacramento For the Year 1854-5*, the "See Up Company" listed "A. Thei" as "Consul, office I between Fifth and Sixth."[2] The Sze Yup Company seems to have been the main huiguan in Sacramento during this period, formed in late 1851.

By 1854, the Chinese were firmly established on I Street between 5th and 6th streets. Known as "Little China," the district was the main thoroughfare and center of trade for Chinese miners and residents. It included numerous Chinese stores, gaming houses, lodging houses, a butcher shop, a doctor's office, and a theater.

Destructive Fires

On July 13, 1854, Little China was entirely destroyed by the second most disastrous fire in Sacramento's history. The thermometer stood at one hundred degrees in the shade when the alarm sounded. Buildings as dry as tinder caused the fire to spread rapidly and fiercely. No lives were lost, but there was estimated damage of $350,000. The *Sacramento Union* reported:

> The Chinese are literally left homeless. They had taken almost exclusive possession of I Street, between 5th and 6th, which they had built up almost solid of materials calculated to make a flaming fire. Had they been made of cotton, they could not have burned with more feverousness. The fire seemed to lick them up as it passed.[3]

The fire didn't reach the Chinese quarter until three p.m., so the Chinese were able to move much of their goods to safety on an island in the slough. The greater portion of Sacramento was prevented from going up in flames by light winds, fireproof buildings, and an abundance of water.

The Chinese rebuilt immediately. Within four months at least eleven licenses were issued to businesses on I Street between 5th and 6th, including five markets, a merchandise store, a bar and boarding house, and four gaming houses. Sacramento Chinatown started anew, as did Yee Ah Tye.

Less than a year later, Little China was partially destroyed by fire. The Fourth of July, 1855, edition of the *Sacramento Union* described a "destructive fire in Chinadom," that probably directly affected Ah Tye, then head of the Sze Yup Company.

The fire was discovered in the second story of the Sze Yup building. With the first cry of fire, a drayman named Henry Bliven, standing near the house watering his horse, rushed up the stairs with his half-filled bucket. Discovering that the canvas lining of one of the rooms was ablaze, he threw the water on it but was unable to stop the flames. The drayman felt that if the bucket had been full, he could have put the fire out completely. The fire spread so rapidly that in less than half an hour the entire block of Chinese frame tenements was aflame. Several fire companies arrived promptly, but could only try to prevent the fire from crossing the nearby streets. Engine Company Number Three used water from the slough in the rear of the Chinese Chapel to save it from destruction.

Chinese merchants, butchers, barbers, and

The great Sacramento fire of November 2, 1852 destroyed most of the town, including every public building except the courthouse and the Presbyterian church. Little China, located on I Street between 5th and 6th streets, was entirely destroyed. *Illustrated News*, January 1, 1853.

restauranteurs suffered the greatest losses, estimated between $65,000 and $100,000. It was thought that a large number of Chinese invalids perished in the Sze Yup house, which also served as a hospital.

About a month later, the *Sacramento Union* noted "grand improvements" on the site of the fire. The main floors of the buildings were raised to the grade of the street, "whereas, under the old arrangement, it was wholly below the level, and excluded from the free circulation of air."

A more strictly enforced fire ordinance prohibited the erection of wood-framed structures in Chinatown. In lieu of "unsightly shanties," six substantial brick buildings were erected—"safe, commodious, convenient and comfortable." The *Sacramento Union* commented that "John must move along with the community generally." He had proven in many ways to be "inoculated with the spirit of progress."[4]

Weaverville War

Problems among the Chinese were not limited to natural disasters. Conflicts among Chinese in California were often based on village and clan feuds that had originated in China. In the northern California mining town of Weaverville, there were four separate Chinese companies (or district associations): Young Wo (Yanghe), Sze Yup (Siyi), Ning Yung (Ningyang), and Sam Yup (Sanyi) Companies. The Young Wo Company members were from the Heungshan (Chungshan or Zhongshan) district and called themselves "Hong Kong men," while members of the Sze Yup, Ning Yung, and Sam Yup Companies called themselves "Canton men."

In the spring of 1854, the four companies became joint owners of a public gaming house in Weaverville. Several months later, while a Hong Kong man was playing against the bank at a table owned by a Canton man, a dispute arose over the winnings. The Hong Kong man snatched the money from the gaming table and ran into the street, pursued by the owner of the table. The Young Wo Company sided with its member, and the other three companies sided against him. The stake had amounted to less than a dollar, but the squabble provided the spark that escalated into an armed conflict involving all four companies.

In a letter to the *Shasta Courier*, a correspondent wrote:

> The Chinese were preparing for a general fight—the cause for such preparation is the same here as in other parts of the State, a sectional hatred and clannish difference, brought from their native land; from day to day these differences have increased, although numerous attempts have been made by their leaders and Americans to settle them, but all endeavors were in vain. Patience, with them, ceased to be a virtue on Saturday last, when they met to fight out their "pent up wrath—and a bloody fight it was.[5]

Up to the last hour, the sheriff did everything in his power to stop it, but "fight they would and fight they did." Public sentiment was mixed. Some Whites wanted to prevent the battle, while others felt it was an excellent opportunity to get rid of "these pests of California."

The *Sacramento State Journal* stated, "as they are desirous of killing each other, we see no reason why we should interfere in their social relations. Fair play and plenty of room is our motto. Let 'm fight."[6]

A Weaverville correspondent sent the *Shasta Courier* a description of the May 20, 1854 conflict. "The parties met in all of their accustomed modes of warfare" —banners, shields, lances, and helmets. One hundred and forty Hong Kong men overpowered the four hundred men. At three o'clock in the afternoon, in front of a thousand White spectators, the smaller Chinese party charged the other in a short but destructive conflict. The Hong Kong men drove their opponents away and captured their flag as a trophy of war. Eight Canton men and two Hong Kong men were killed, and a dozen men on both sides were severely wounded. One White man interfered by shooting his pistol at one of the Chinese parties, then another spectator shot the White man dead.

Canton Defense

In a letter to the editor of the *Shasta Courier*, Ha-Sing, Ah Tye, and Ah-Ching—agents of the Canton companies in San Francisco—told how they came to Weaverville immediately after hearing of the difficulty. Numerous obstacles made mediation difficult.

The Chinese of Weaverville went to battle carrying shields of tightly-woven straw, and armed with 15-foot pikes, five-foot swords, and large pronged spears. About 550 men engaged in this tong war, July 15, 1854. *Hutchings' California Magazine.*

Ah Tye and the other San Francisco company leaders voiced the Canton view of the dispute. If the fight had been conducted according to the plan agreed upon between the Chinese parties, there would have been little bloodshed, and the matter would have been settled. However, because of misconceptions passed on by the Hong Kong men, White spectators sided with them and rushed in between the Canton men, thus leaving about seventy-five Canton men entirely cut off from their companions.

The White spectators hurled rocks and fired revolvers at the Canton men, not knowing that it had been agreed upon by the opposing parties that no firearms would be used. The contest thus became more than just a "trial of skill" . . . "leaving the parties further from reconciliation than at first."

The Canton leaders wrote that all the men of the three companies were eager to settle the dispute by a fair contest. "They are anxious that each party shall be permitted to select an equal number of men, say 50, 100, or 150, as shall be agreed, and let the whole difficulty be settled by a fair contest, without interference from any source, and they will faithfully abide the result."[7]

The *Shasta Courier* described the burials:

On Sunday the large party collected their dead together and burnt them, in the same manner as do the Indians of this country, and then buried their ashes. The small party buried theirs with all the imposing ceremonies of war—they all turned out in funeral procession and followed the bodies to their graves, accompanied with music, as white men would. The white man killed was also buried the same day. It was a day of funerals. Long will it be remembered by the people of this town.[8]

Eight days later the excitement of the Chinese fight had passed away. Weaverville returned to its usual quiet summer months. In an effort to stop further "wars" of this nature, a sheriff confiscated all the swords, pikes, lances, and Chinese weapons he could locate. Called the "Chinese Armory," the weapons were sold a few years later, and the proceeds were placed in the county treasury.

Chinadom Disturbances

As in San Francisco, Yee Ah Tye did not find harmony and peace in Sacramento. On the night of September 6, 1854, Ah Tye and about twenty-five other Chinese were arrested on I Street during a disturbance in "Chinadom." "They were subsequently arraigned before the recorder, charged with disturbing the peace, had a jury trial, and were convicted and fined in sums averaging from $10 to $100. The appeal was dismissed with costs."[9]

As a leader in the Sacramento Chinese community, Ah Tye continued to be embroiled in conflicts. In November 1854, three Chinese were convicted of a "breach of the peace" before the recorder's court and fined. They were found guilty of creating a disturbance at the Sze Yup Company's house on I Street "and threatening Ah Tai with all sorts of bodily injury."[10] Two of the Chinese were fined $20 and costs, while the other, Chock Chung, was charged $30 and costs, because it was the second time that day he had been fined for a similar offense.

More than a year later, another Chinese named Ah Woh was fined $30 and costs for disturbing the peace. He was "threatening and seeking to flog Yu Atai (Yee Ah Tye), the reported leader of one of the rival companies, at the theater."[11] Perhaps in the cases of Chock Chung and Ah Woh, the inability of Chinese to redress their grievances in American courts and the autocracy of the Chinese leadership led them to strike out in frustration at company leaders such as Ah Tye.

Chinese Festivities

The monotony and restraint of work-filled days were relieved by Chinese festivals and entertainment. The *Sacramento Union* described Chinese New Year celebrations as "a constant scene of hilarity." The explosion of firecrackers resembled "a distant and continued discharge of musketry."[12] Chinese believed that firecrackers drove away evil spirits and ushered in good omens. With the close of the year, the Chinese paid off old debts.

According to the *Sacramento Union*:

The Celestials, male and female, remained up the night previous, dressed in their best suits, and promptly, at sunrise, went the rounds, delivering at the residences of acquaintances slips of red and orange paper, appropriately inscribed in gilt and otherwise with congratulatory salutations. At every domicile a table was spread with edibles—delicacies—for the dead—the living fasting through the entire day. Today they will enter upon the consumption of the viands that were thus displayed.[13]

The grand feature for the Chinese New Year of 1855 was a puppet theatre. In the rear of a gambling establishment, the "Thespian Temple" contained seats for about one hundred guests. The puppets were simple busts on sticks, between three and four feet in height, clothed to represent human figures. The puppet heads represented both males and females "fully marked with Chinese characteristics." The diverse costumes were "made of different colored silks, satins, fur or fringe and illuminated with tinsel."

Flexible only at the arms, the puppets were controlled by puppeteers hidden from view by a screen. The puppets "were made to go through all the appearances of singing, dancing, conversation, devotion and occasionally of battle."[14] Chinese instruments provided background music.

During the spring of 1855, a group of Chinese kite flyers gathered on the corner of I and 5th streets, attracting a crowd of "outside barbarians." One of the kites resembled a bird, another the rising sun, while a third "emitted musical sounds similar to the Eolian harp." The *Sacramento Union* advised: "Gentlemen who wish to fly kites scientifically could not do better than visit Chinadom on any afternoon, and take observations of the most approved method."[15]

Chinese dragon boat painted on greeting card. Ah Tye Family Collection.

The Dragon Boat Festival (fifth day of the fifth month) was held in commemoration of Wat Yuen (Qu Yuan), a poet who served as a loyal Chinese minister in the third century B.C. When he threw himself into a river and drowned, a great reward was offered for the recovery of his body. This incited some of the most dramatic boat races in Chinese history, and since that time, the day has been marked by regattas and boat races.

In the late 1850s, the Sacramento Chinese transplanted this holiday to their waters. Six boats were entered in the race in 1858, a contest between the Sze Yup and Sam Yup Companies. Four oarsmen manned each boat on a circular course in the slough, going around the course eighteen times. The boats of the Sam Yup attracted great attention, and took first and second prize out of the four offered.

A large crowd lined the levee to watch the race. American reporters expressed surprise at the "remarkable grace, nerve, skill and precision displayed by the Sam Yups in the management and propulsion of their crafts," who "appeared as fresh when they came in on the fourteenth turn as on the first." Contestants were all thought to be Sacramento Chinese men of the merchant class, and the reporters noticed that "considerable money changed hands among their countrymen on the result."[16]

Clan Feuds Continue

One month after the Weaverville War of 1854, another conflict seemed to be brewing in Marysville. A Canton spokesman informed the *Marysville Express* about "Hong Kongites" preparing weapons and "anxious to get up a fight with the Cantonians," who preferred not to go to war. The article described the Hong Kongites, members of the Heungshan company, as men "engaged in business avocations."

While appearing more pacifist, the Cantonians (men from Ah Tye's Sze Yup Company and the Ning Yung and Sam Yup companies) were not viewed as kindly by the newspaper. It described the Cantonians as frequenters of "houses of bad repute" and, after nightfall, provokers of fights and "perhaps robbing or stealing."[17]

Several days later on September 9, 1854, a battle began in Sacramento. The Sacramento Chinese had started preparing for conflict as early as May, manufacturing a "large quantity of pikes, lances, iron swords, and various other weapons."[18] One Sacramentan had a contract for making eight hundred dollars' worth of implements of war. The *Sacramento State Journal* described the battle as the "Great Chinese War."

Between 10 and 11 o'clock last evening the Chinese of this city, to the number of 500 or 600, collected on I street, between 5th and 6th, to do battle. They were armed with tin hats, bamboo shields, tin and iron swords and cutlass a la pick handles, and proceeded at once to business. They were not separated into different armies, but pitched in generally, every man apparently on his own hook. Every one behaved in the most Ishmaelitish manner, and raised his hand against every body and every body's hand was against him. They fought some half hour or so, when the police interfered in the sport and quelled the row in Chinadom. Of all the wounded, and there is no telling their number, only one is supposed to be injured sufficiently to cause death.[19]

Chan Shee was Yee Ah Tye's third wife, beloved for her sweet and gentle disposition. Ah Tye Family Collection.

The *Sonora Herald* reporter described the battle as "a curious kind of backing and filing arrangement" and guessed that it was "probably conducted according to Chinese tactics." The leader of the Hong Kong party, "who valiantly undertook to draw the enemy from their ground by a feint," was shot in the leg and fell.

Then, according to a White witness, the enemy surrounded the Hong Kong chief and "pierced him until he was entirely dead, after which they disemboweled him. His heart and liver were tossed for some time in the air and caught upon the points of their pikes, while his carcass was swung upon a pole and carried from the field." Another man was also killed. Deputy Sheriff Cogswell and some citizens eventually arrived and commanded that the fighting stop; finally it did.

The following day the Sacramento Cantons had a celebration in honor of the victory in Chinese Camp. They obtained permission to fire off firecrackers from four to eight p.m. and "partook of an elegant national supper at the Chinese restaurant on I street, between 5th and 6th streets." In answer to a reporter's query as to the cause of the jubilee, a Chinese replied, "Big day—big fight (pointing in the supposed direction of Tuolumne)—big man killed—all same as Fourth July— sabe?"[20]

These were more than just regional conflicts. During the 1850s, the Chinese were fighting for territorial spheres of influence and the spoils that included control of gambling. The disputes were largely settled by the 1860s, and the fighting decreased.

Ah Tye's Three Wives

Around 1857, Yee Ah Tye married for the third time. Following Chinese tradition, Ah Tye was probably betrothed to his first wife, Sech Shee, before immigrating to America. Mo-Mo Ahtye recalls that Ah Tye was planning to return to his Chinese village to visit his first wife and their baby girl, when he received a letter saying that his wife had died.[21]

Ah Tye was matched to another bride in the United States named So Shee (a lady from the family of So). This second wife also died at a young age, and had no children.

Yee Ah Tye's third and final wife, Chan Shee, is the one from whom the California Ah Tye family is descended. Ah Tye was in his early thirties when he married his sixteen-year-old picture bride in Oroville. Chan Shee was introduced to her prospective husband through correspondence and a picture. She was tall for a Chinese woman—five feet, three inches in height. She and Ah Tye, who stood five feet, ten inches tall, had five daughters and two sons, all of whom were tall like their parents.

Approximately twenty of the Chinese leaders and the most "riotous," were taken to the station house and locked up, where "their belligerent blood" could "cool down below fever heat."

Two years after the Sacramento battle, in the fall of 1856, another "grand battle" was fought between the "Cantons" and the "Hong Kongs" near Chinese Camp in Tuolumne County. The *Sonora Herald* newspaper reported that "a feud had existed between these two factions for some time past, growing out, it was thought, of a dispute about mining claims. Both parties armed and equipped themselves, and drilled like regular armies" several days before the fight. The forces on each side were estimated at about four hundred. "One party was armed with fifty muskets and bayonets, besides side arms; the other was armed with spears, rifles, revolvers, etc. . . . The two armies took positions on two hills, separated by a little valley, and commenced reconnoitering and watching each other's movements."

Boundary People

According to archaeologists Mary and Adrian Praetzellis, the early Sacramento Chinese merchants and leaders functioned as "boundary people" between Chinese and American society. They were financially successful, well-traveled, and busy in civic endeavors. They entertained White American friends, organized festivals, funerals, feasts, and other community activities; represented the Chinese in legal matters; and kept the press and politicians apprised of events in their community.

As a leader in the Sacramento Chinese community, Yee Ah Tye probably was always on the lookout for ways to gain influence and control. Nelson Pike approached Ah Tye with documents, claiming that he was associated with reducing the monthly mining license tax to $4 per person by an act of the Legislature. He had supposedly rendered this service on behalf of several Chinese and Japanese companies, and was now charging them $2 per person. Pike claimed that the original bond had been destroyed by fire and produced another document that he said was its replacement. Ah Tye was unsure whether Pike was authentic or not, but was willing to try to buy some influence. He gave him $39 as a small retainer and ordered another Chinese to give $5. Pike then tried to sell the same claim to an intelligence officer for $2,000, but was arrested and taken to the station house.

It was unusual for Chinese to own property at this time; yet, in 1856 and 1861, the Sze Yup Company was assessed for a parcel of land on the north side of I between 5th and 6th streets. Ah Tye's experience in purchasing land in San Francisco was no doubt valuable to him in Sacramento.

Chinese New Year's Dinner —1861

The early Chinese merchants and leaders carefully shaped their ethnicity to cultivate connections with influential people in White society. For example, a dinner was given in the winter of 1861 by several prominent Chinese merchants and Ah Teen, a chief member of the Sze Yup Company. Ah Teen probably asked Ah Tye to help host the annual dinner because of his proficiency in English and his leadership in the Sze Yup Company.

The merchants had previously invited an ex-justice of the peace, who was presently a federal official, to dine with them annually. This year, the federal official sent invitations to friends of his choice. The small party included an elected county judge, a physician, an ex-officer of the regular army who was now at West Point, a lawyer, and two newspaper reporters from the *Sacramento Daily Bee*.

The reporters wrote that Ah Teen and Ah Tye met their guests at the door of the Ye Chin Restaurant on I Street punctually at three o'clock. Ah Teen and Ah Tye led their guests behind the restaurant to a room decorated with Chinese paintings and calligraphy.

"The table was set with cloth, knives, forks, plates, spoons and napkins, very much like ordinary tables, with celery in glasses and salt in cellars," wrote the reporters; "but there was no bread, or butter, or potatoes, or chopsticks to be seen." The reporters had hoped to have "the rare pleasure of eating with chopsticks," as had the previous year's guests.

Ah Teen and Ah Tye sat down with their guests, and there were "any number of waiters in attendance." Previous guests had cautioned the reporters that there would be a great number of dishes, and they must eat sparingly "or they would not at one sitting be able to go through them all."

In the excitement, the reporters forgot the caution, and their plates "at the end of each course looked as clean as if both Jack Spratt and his wife had been at it." They asked Ah Teen for stationery "for the purpose of marking down the courses as they came." The result of their "notes and queries" was this listing of each Chinese course (as nearly as they understood the names and descriptions):

1st dish: Lichequom—nuts of a glutinous vegetable —saccharine substance.

2nd: Laqunquow—nuts much like the first, only not so palatable.

3rd: Numichow—rice whiskey, tastes and looks like Mexican pulque, and is almost equal to, though not so palatable to Americans, as "old rye."

4th: Tingmuchow—rice rum, very like Jamaica.

5th: Moiquelow—rice rum, like Santa Cruz. (These two were set in large goblets, one of each, on the table, and every man took his little China cup, covered all over with flowers and gold, and of the size of the smallest liquer glass, or lady's large thimble, dipped into the general reservoir, and drank as he chose.)

6th: Yunna—birds nests, with eggs hard boiled, the royal dish of China, and worth $40 to $50 per pound. It is a glutinous substance, and said to be very good for sick or appetite-seeking people, because, perhaps, they can't get much of it in other words, because of its scarcity. Those present could have eaten more of this dish if it had been pressed upon them, but there were others that came after, which they preferred even to the famed birds' nests.

7th: Quichl—fishes gills, fishes tails, fishes bones, and a little Chinese parsley jellied and intermixed.

8th: Champagne—Mumm.

9th: Tuyungki—chicken fricassee with Chinese sauce the sauce is a regular Soyer article.

10th: Ap—fricassee duck.

11th: Champagne—Sillery.

12th: Bougee—date fish with mushrooms.

13th: Champagne—Mousseux.

14th: Thinmi—a kind of sea weed hashed, sauced and cooked.

15th: Goieow—eyes, gills, and flesh of fishes.

16th: Champagne—Heidseick.

17th: Lunni—rice-cake, or ground rice cooked with butter.

18th: Aploo—fried duck, a la Chinese.

19th: Chingoo—fried pork, or "pork for the million," a most delicious dish.

20th: Yunminhep—sweetmeats.

21st: Champagne—Cliquot.

22nd: Ling-Kou-Kong —fish soup.

23rd: Tea—the real Chinese article.

24th: Pinlong—sweetmeats, something like dates without the taste or stone.

25th: Champagne.

26th: Cigars.

The reporters wrote "that each course was served in quantities of two to three tablespoonfuls to each person and every course with its own plates" and utensils. Fish, fowl, and seaweed made up the main courses. Pork was served only once, and there was no beef, mutton, or venison.

"In place of bread or potatoes there was rice cake, a rich and palatable food. . . . Although champagne was brought on several times, the brands were all different and all first class." The newsmen concluded, "Chinese dinners consist in variety."[22]

Mary and Adrian Praetzellis observed that in the Sacramento merchants' role as boundary people, the banquet exhibited an "intentionally exotic, yet subtly altered and thereby unthreatening, face to boundary types from White society. . . . These (Chinese) men were not politically naive."[23]

Tapestries with intricately embroidered designs decorated the restaurant walls. The crane and peaches on this panel symbolize long life; c. 1800s.

Many people, regardless of their nationality, did not own horses or could not afford stagecoach fare. They traveled on foot by "shanks mare." Chinese, Indians, a South American and others on trail to mines, 1855. *Hutchings' California Magazine.*

Chapter Five
1860: ROUTE FROM SAN FRANCISCO TO LA PORTE

Chinese miners bound for La Porte continued their journey from Sacramento, up the Sacramento and Feather Rivers to Marysville, called *Sam Fow*, or Third City. From Marysville they rode a stagecoach to La Porte. The route was rough and very steep in places, and the trip lasted from twelve to sixteen hours, depending on the weather and road conditions. Passengers sat in spaces not occupied by baggage, express, or mail, and the Chinese were made to ride on the top. At the end of their long journey, they climbed down off the stagecoach and looked for a place to camp among their countrymen.

The Settlements

There were two types of Chinese settlements in the mining areas of California. The first were numerous camps—separate Chinese communities which were generally located on the banks of rivers and streams. Chinatowns made up the second type—distinct Chinese settlements that formed sections of American towns.

Before 1851, Chinese mining was done individually. These early miners, being relatively few in number, did not attract much attention. California's first foreign miners' license tax, enacted in 1850, was directed toward Mexicans and other Hispanics. But by 1852, Chinese had replaced Mexicans as the most numerous foreigners in the mines. In Plumas County, Chinese miners lived in shanties, tents, and patched-up cabins. They owned little property other than mining claims, and occupied a small place on the tax list.

The California legislature passed another foreign miners' license tax in 1853, this one directed especially toward Chinese miners. In Plumas County they paid four dollars per month, collected by the sheriff. He received twenty percent of the revenue, and the remainder was equally divided between the state and county. This was an important tax; it provided one-fourth of the state's entire revenue until it was declared unconstitutional in 1870.

Chinese Camps

A sharp increase in Chinese immigration in 1852 coincided with the beginning of the formation of Chinese camps along rivers, often on diggings already worked over by Whites. These camps con-

sisted of small tents and brush houses, and followed the Chinese custom of grouping together to carry out cooperative undertakings. J. D. Borthwick, a traveler through the California mining camps during the 1850s, noted a distinguishing characteristic of the Chinese:

> They did not venture to assert equal rights so far as to take up any claim which other miners would think it worth while to work; but in such places as yielded them a dollar or two a day they were allowed to scratch away unmolested. Had they happened to strike a rich lead, they would have been driven off their claim immediately.[1]

Compared to others, Chinese were slow but thorough miners. They were so thorough that it was said to be a waste of time to work over any mining ground that had been previously worked by a Chinese company, for they had gotten all of the gold.

Mining Techniques

The simplest form of placer mining was panning. The miner scooped sand, gravel, and water into a shallow pan and with a circular motion, washed out the gravel and sand. The gold, heavier than most rocks and dirt, settled to the bottom of the pan.

A step toward larger production, and an implement that proved to be a favorite of the Chinese, was the "rocker." Resembling a child's cradle, it was a box with a screen to separate rough gravel with a series of bars (riffles) underneath to catch the gold. Pay dirt (the earthy matter containing the gold) was

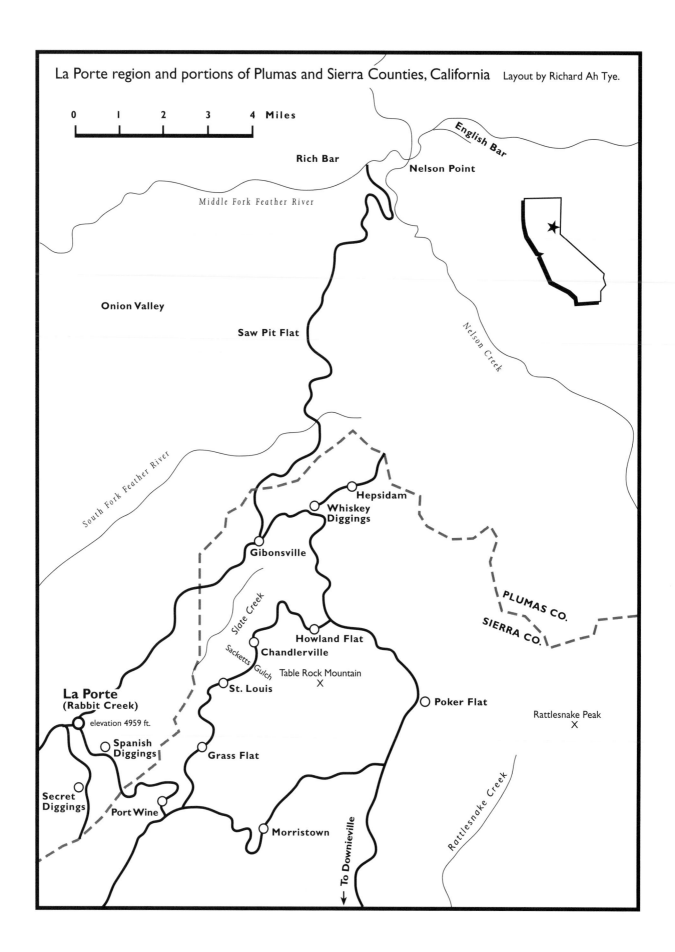

La Porte region and portions of Plumas and Sierra Counties, California   Layout by Richard Ah Tye.

0   1   2   3   4 Miles

Rich Bar

English Bar

Nelson Point

Middle Fork Feather River

Onion Valley

Saw Pit Flat

Nelson Creek

South Fork Feather River

Hepsidam

Whiskey Diggings

Gibonsville

Slate Creek

Howland Flat

Chandlerville

Sacketts Gulch

Table Rock Mountain
X

PLUMAS CO.

SIERRA CO.

St. Louis

La Porte
(Rabbit Creek)
elevation 4959 ft.

Poker Flat

Rattlesnake Peak
X

Spanish Diggings

Grass Flat

Secret Diggings

Port Wine

Morristown

Rattlesnake Creek

To Downieville

shoveled into the top, then washed through with water. Lighter materials were washed away, and the gold collected on the riffles.

A single man could operate a rocker, or he could join forces with other men to increase production. One man rocked the cradle and poured in water, a second man hauled the dirt and loaded the hopper, and others would shovel and dig. The rocker enabled workers to change jobs from time to time. Although some of the finer gold slid over the riffles and was lost, the rocker processed a larger quantity of dirt and brought a higher profit than a pan.

River bottoms were often the sites of the richest deposits of placer gold. The most practical way to get at the river bottom was to build wing dams to divert the water's flow to a fraction of its channel and work the exposed bottom. Shaped like an "L," a wing dam extended from the shore to the middle of the river. At the river's midpoint the dam turned at a right angle and went downstream back to the same side, thus leaving one half of the riverbed bare. The sand and gravel were washed for gold, exposing the bedrock. Miners frequently found gold dust and nuggets in the depressions, cracks, and crevices of the bedrock.

While living in Sacramento, Yee Ah Tye tried his luck in the gold fields. Ah Tye and Company had mining claims listed in a deed book for the Brown's Valley Mining District, an area north of Marysville.

Notice is here by given that we the undersigned claim three hundred feet of this Bar and Bed of the River for Mining Purposes in 1860 & 1861. Said Claim Commences at this Notice and runs down stream 300 feet.

Ar Tye & Co
Mo - Bar, October 7th 1860.[2]

Chinese with rocker on poles. Nevada Historical Society.

J. D. Borthwick's observations of a Chinese camp might well have described Ah Tye's mining operation on Scott's Bar:

There were about 150 ... living in a perfect village of small tents, all clustered together on the rocks. They had a claim in the bed of the river, which they were working by means of a wing dam....The Chinamen's dam was 200-300 yards in length, and was built of large pine trees laid one on top of the other. They must have had great difficulty in handling such immense logs in such a place; but they are exceedingly ingenious in applying mechanical power, particularly in concentrating the force of a large number of men upon one point.[3]

La Porte Chinatown

The La Porte Chinatown was an example of the second type of Chinese mining settlement, a section of an American town.

John Bidwell's gold discovery at Bidwell Bar near Oroville brought throngs of miners to the Feather River during 1849 and 1850. Discoveries at Rich Bar, Nelson Point, and Onion Valley soon followed. La Porte was founded in 1850 as a result of a gold strike. The town was located on a ridge between the north fork of the Yuba River and the south fork of the Feather River. The diggings were profitable and at times rich, and the camp of tents and shacks grew. In 1851, Jim Beckwourth, a noted hunter, trader, and guide, discovered a pass over the Sierra, later called Beckwourth Pass, which made the area accessible from the northeast.

La Porte was first named Rabbit Town, because it was unusual to find so many rabbits at such a high elevation. Later, the town assumed the name, Rabbit Creek, after the stream that meandered through its limits. In 1857, the town's name was changed to La Porte, after the Indiana hometown of its respected town banker and expressman, Frank Everts.

La Porte is approximately sixty miles from Marysville, twenty miles from Downieville, and thirty-five miles from Quincy. Placer mining communities such as Howland Flat, Poverty Hill, Grass Flat, Scales, Morristown, St. Louis (or Sear's Diggings), Gibsonville, Whiskey Diggings (or Newark), Sackett's Gulch, and Poker Flat surrounded La Porte. These settlements later provided Bret Harte inspiration for the short stories, "The Gentleman of La Porte" and "The Outcasts of Poker Flat," among others.

By 1858, the Chinese of La Porte had a Chinatown within the town's limits, between the business district and residential section of the town. In 1860, La Porte's total population was about one thousand, with males outnumbering females four to one. One hundred of the 136 La Porte Chinese were placer miners.

In contrast to the California Mother Lode area, the Chinese in the Northern Mines experienced less persecution. La Porte's newspaper, the *Mountain Messenger*, printed an editorial in 1863 expressing a strong dislike for Chinese, yet voiced the concern that persecution went against the American spirit of democracy.

We never had any particular liking for Chinamen; in fact we have always regarded their presence in the State as little short of a curse; and therefore we have constantly advocated the adoption of measures for their entire exclusion from our borders. . . .

We trust and believe that the instances are rare where men descend to the level of barbarians by interfering with these people wherever they are quietly and industriously disposed; but we are sorry to say that we have observed numerous cases in the State of thoughtless and ill-mannered boys abusing Chinamen, by pelting them with stones and other missiles as they passed through the streets. . . .

If our laws are such that we cannot help tolerating the presence of this despised race, we should at least, while they dwell among us, allow them to do so in peace, remembering that persecution is neither sanctioned by our political system nor by the religion which we profess.[4]

White Exodus

By 1863, La Porte's White miners had excitedly flocked to the new gold mines of Montana's Reese River. La Porte's newspaper reported that every camp in the mountains, "so far as heard from," had lost enough of its population to cause "a general stagnation of business and a paralyzing influence" upon future mining enterprises.[5]

A White prospector wrote to the *Mountain Messenger*:

Another year and the Chinamen will have undisputed possession of the whole river from its junction to its source, with two or three exceptions. . . . True, there is left some pieces of ground that will pay good wages yet, but the cost of working will more than cover the sum received. Such diggings don't pay. Many of our best men have left for the different "lands of promise" that are being reported almost daily, and many more are preparing to follow shortly.[6]

White miners were all too happy to sell what they thought were "worked-out" mines in order to relocate in new areas. This White exodus gave the Chinese an opportunity to live in one place and progress from the portable rocker to more permanent and sophisticated mining techniques.

"Chinamen with their bed and board," reported the *Mountain Messenger*, continued to pour into La Porte.[7] To the White man, there appeared to be no end to their coming.

Mining claims give their possessors the right to use the land, rather than ownership. On August 19, 1864, Ah Tye and Company paid Joseph A. Denson $175 for several mining claims on Slate Creek. The deal included a cabin, a ditch conveying water to the claim, an arrastra and wheel, and all the sluice boxes and appurtenances.[8]

An arrastra was an ore-processing device that originated in Mexico. A bed of big, flat stones was arranged in a circular track with a low retaining wall built around it. A mule was tied to a long, horizontal pole attached to a pivot in the center of the track. The mule walked in a perpetual circle, dragging heavy boulders over the gold ore and reducing it to a fine powder which was then washed out by the usual method in pan or rockers.[9]

The sluice was a long, wooden trough, through which a constant stream of water ran. Usually, sluice boxes were fitted end-to-end, extending for several hundred feet. Riffle bars (cross-cutting ribs) in the bottom of the sluice were large enough to trap the gold from the stream of water but small enough to allow waste material to pass through the sluice. Miners frequently used

An arrastra was powered by mule or water to grind the gold-bearing ore.

mercury to catch small flakes of gold that would otherwise be washed away.

The sluice box was an improvement of the long tom, which consisted of only one riffle box. One advantage of the sluice was that it could be run for a week without the hazard of the gold washing away. Another benefit was that cleanup could be done weekly, rather than daily, but it was necessary to guard the gold that had accumulated in the riffle bars. Dirt shoveled directly into the sluices allowed large masses of pay dirt to be washed. Five to twenty men could profitably combine their efforts.

Rugged Times

The Chinese had a difficult time in the 1860s, according to the La Porte newspapers. The Chinese miners' success and their tendency to save their gold dust made them easy prey for robbers. On the other hand, Chinese were often accused and found guilty of "doctoring gold" and robbing sluices. Doctored gold was created by mixing and heating silver or brass filings with very fine gold dust so that they became thoroughly coated with gold. The result could deceive even the most expert buyer.

In 1863, the *Mountain Messenger* reported that there was "another Chinaman" attempting to sell doctored dust at the banking house of John Conly and Company in La Porte.[10] Tests showed that brass and silver filings were mixed with genuine gold dust. The Chinese man said that a fellow countryman had entrusted the package to him to sell. One of the Chinese merchants vouched for the good character of the accused, and he was allowed to go free. But later the man fled from his camp, leaving behind tools for filing brass and silver, along with a piece of a partially melted silver spoon.

"Skirmishing among the Celestials," reported the local newspaper in 1864, was becoming one of La Porte's "institutions." For several weeks, Sunday clashes between members of different Chinese companies had occurred, but without injuries more serious than a broken head or bloody nose.

One Sunday, a skirmish started in the early afternoon and "continued with slight intermission until nearly dark. A lively pitched battle took place between a Chinese belonging to the Sze Yup Company and another belonging to the Hung Wo Company, in which the former was cut in the groin with a knife, and died during the night." The belligerent Chinese was jailed with two other supposed accomplices.[11]

Members of the various Chinese huiguans were scattered throughout mines and mining towns such as La Porte. Unlike the great battles in Weaverville and Sacramento in 1854, these district allegiances nevertheless continued to cause frequent, although brief, skirmishes.

A sluice consisted of several, long interconnecting wooden boxes about a foot wide with high sides. The bottom of each box had "riffles" or wooden ribs, which resembled an old-fashioned washboard. California State Library.

Samuel Auerbach, a successful Jewish merchant in La Porte during the 1860s, wrote in his "Reminiscences" that there was considerable robbing of sluice boxes in La Porte and nearby camps, and the Chinese were frequently blamed. Auerbach wrote, "While the Chinese did oftentimes resort to sluice robbing, as did many Mexicans and Whites, more often than not they were wrongfully accused."

Sluice robbery was a serious crime and often resulted in cropped ears for thieves, or in a "hanging bee." When the circumstances did not seem to warrant hanging, the culprits received a number of lashings. If the evidence of guilt was uncertain, the suspects were sometimes banished from the town.

In the nearby mining community of St. Louis, a Chinese man was caught robbing a sluice. He was held until morning, "handsomely flogged," then invited to leave town within a certain time or "take the consequences." Preferring to take the consequences, the Chinese man remained in town for several days, "when the citizens turned out and burned all the Chinese cabins in the place."[12] Apparently his guilt had implicated his countrymen, too.

In the autumn of 1864, a gang of Chinese thieves were arrested and there was great excitement in La Porte. The thieves had been stealing from cabins, and it was thought that threats of a lynching should be used to "quiet such rascalities."[13]

In this atmosphere, Chinese became likely targets of crime. Two gangs of Chinese, comprised of about thirty men, were robbed on Slate Creek by a gang of seven White men in disguise. They tied up the Chinese, threw blankets over their heads, and stole approximately $650 in gold dust. There appeared to be organized bands of White thieves prowling through the mountains committing crimes on defenseless Chinese and robbing their isolated cabins.

Chinese emigrants received some legal protection in 1868, when the United States and China signed the Burlingame Treaty, agreeing to reciprocal trade, travel, and immigration. It also implied that citizens of either country would be treated as equals if they chose to immigrate. It permitted Chinese to become "permanent citizens" of America, but not true citizens. The Burlingame Treaty brought a second wave of Chinese immigrants, even larger than that of the Gold Rush. Despite this treaty, Chinese miners continued to be treated unequally.

In 1868, the *Mountain Messenger* reported "a batch of robberies of Chinamen in the vicinity" by the same gang of three men who had committed robberies on Chinese throughout the county the previous year at the same season.

There were several robberies committed on Slate Creek, below Secret Diggings, a short time ago. The villains being unable, after a thorough examination of the premises, to find the money or dust belonging to the China company, and threats proving equally unavailing, the Chinamen were finally hung up by the neck and one or two were dangerously stabbed. They were at last brought to confession, and the result was several hundred dollars, mostly in dust. . . . In the Slate Creek robbery, the Chinamen were taken by surprise, and the arms with which they were expecting to defend themselves were first secured by the robbers, and afterwards taken away.[14]

The editors thought it strange that the legal authorities made no effort to catch the thieves. It was believed that the robbers continued to prey on Chinese camps because they offered "the best chance for booty with the least chance for detection and punishment."[15]

Even though Chinese could identify their robbers, the oath of a Chinese in court was worthless against a White man. In 1854, a statute prohibiting Indians and Negroes from testifying for or against a White person was extended by the Supreme Court to include the Chinese. The statute was not repealed until 1872.

Lincoln Assassination

The 1860s were rugged years for the Chinese in La Porte and for the nation as a whole. The Civil War continued from 1861 to 1865, and La Porte stood staunchly behind the United States government.

President Abraham Lincoln issued the Emancipation Proclamation in 1863, paving the way for the Thirteenth Amendment of the Constitution which prohibited slavery in the United States. That same year, President Lincoln delivered his Gettysburg Address.

In 1864, editors of the *Mountain Messenger* heartily endorsed Lincoln for re-election and Andrew Johnson for vice president.[16] The editors felt that Lincoln, as head of the American government, had "dealt with the question of rebellion with almost divine ability." He had proven himself "an able, honest and great man."[17] Lincoln won the re-election.

At noon on April 15, 1865, a rumor spread through La Porte that Lincoln had been assassinated. People left their businesses to gather in groups along the streets, hoping it was not true.

By four o'clock that day, the telegraph brought details

Main street of La Porte, 1858. Jann Garvis Collection.

confirming Lincoln's death. Soon after dark the *Mountain Messenger* issued an extra edition, finally convincing the citizens of the sad truth.[18]

Businesses throughout the Union draped their buildings in mourning. In San Francisco, the *Daily Alta* reported:

The mourning was confined to no race, kindred, or class—it was universal. Every foreign consulate displayed its flag at half mast, as did the French war vessels and other foreign shipping in the harbor; and it was noticed as worthy of especial remark that the Chinese residents of our city, who usually take no part in our public demonstrations, were prominent in displaying tokens of grief, and doing honor to the memory of our Nation's illustrious head.[19]

Every building in San Francisco occupied by Chinese —from temples (such as the Sze Yup Association) and fine mercantile houses to the humblest wash houses—was draped in black and white.

When the Chinese merchants were informed that there was a place reserved for them in San Francisco's procession of mourning, in less than ten minutes $170 was paid, more than the required amount. This led the *Daily Alta* to conclude that the Chinese merchants were "proverbial for their liberality."[20]

Hop Sing Merchandise Store

Tax assessment rolls of La Porte show that Ah Tye became a partner in a Chinese merchandise store named "Hop Sing and Company" in 1866. It was not customary for Chinese to name a partnership after its owners; instead, the store was given a motto which denoted good luck. In Chinese, *Hop* means "unite," and *Sing* means "victory."

Merchants like Ah Tye, who had Sze Yup Association affiliations, probably telegraphed their San Francisco headquarters when there was a need for laborers in their area.[21] When Sze Yup emigrants arrived in La Porte, their first stop was no doubt the Hop Sing store.

In the early days, Chinese emigrants' social and economic activities centered around a merchandise store operated by one of their group. Huiguan clerks in San Francisco kept a record of the location and movements of the main groups of Chinese, so that letters from China could be distributed to those in the outlying mining areas.

Chinese merchants were the wealthiest men in La Porte's Chinatown. By 1866, Hop Sing and Company was the richest of the four Chinese merchandise stores, with property valued at $1,500. This included $1,000 in goods, and two houses on China Alley worth $500. Competing merchandise stores followed closely; Hop Kee and Company and Gee Chung and Company each had property valued at $1,200. Hop Sing and Company owned ten times more than Hong Lee, the owner of a wash house, and twenty times more than the druggist, Win Chuck.

However, Hop Sing and Company had moderate wealth compared to White businesses. The banking house of John Conly and Company had assets of $21,750, and French hotelkeeper Madam Cayot was twice as rich as any of the Chinese merchants.

In late 1866, the *Mountain Messenger* reported two incidents involving Ah Tye and his company. One incident involved Old Louis, an Italian watchman, and some Chinese of the Hop Sing Company, who had purchased some old claims. The claims were disputed a year earlier, and the Chinese men had paid for them twice. Old

Louis ordered the Chinese company to stop working these claims. When the Italian fired his double-barreled shotgun and wounded one of the men in the shoulder, the Chinese left. The next morning another Chinese sent to the claim by the company was "shot dead in his tracks."[22] Louis hid until evening, then he was arrested.

That same year, the *Mountain Messenger* reported that a great commotion had "boiled over" in La Porte's Chinatown. Goods of all kinds had been stolen from American stores and diggings. Jacobs lost gloves worth approximately $100; Koppel lost mercury and cigars; Wheeler and Thomas were missing boxes of tobacco and cutlery worth $300; and Orr and Gard lost $300 in picks, drills, and sledges from their diggings. In addition, mercury had been stolen, and three pairs of boots were taken from Mr. Kingdon's shoe shop. A gang of regularly organized thieves had taken property amounting to $3,000, leading people to believe that there must be a big storehouse somewhere.

As the 1866 *Mountain Messenger* reported:

There was no trouble in finding three of the gang by applying to Gee Ah Ty, of the Hop Sing company, as he knew all the gang, where they lived and to whom they sold the boots for $35, another China storekeeper being the purchaser. Other property, tobacco etc., has been sold to the China stores, the keepers of which encourage thieves by patronizing them in the purchase of their stolen wares.

One of the three caught was the leader of the gang, and was tied with his hands behind him to a post in front of the Post office, and Mr. Kingdon and Gee Ah Ty "cupped" him in the face and other parts of the body, for half an hour, which procured a confession, but only to a slight extent, after which Ah Ty offered to become responsible for a small part of the goods, which only showed (more plainly than he had been induced to say it) that he knew more than he had revealed.[23]

The gang leader was turned loose "to return again, no doubt, to the old avocation," after publicly acknowledging "that he had employed six others in carrying on his extensive business."[24] The thieves were warned that if the robberies continued, they would be hanged.

Ah Tye again found himself acting as mediator between two peoples. By pointing out the guilty Chinese culprits and getting a confession (albeit "slight") from the gang leader, Ah Tye satisfied the Whites' demands that the thieves be apprehended. Ah Tye would not reveal the names of the Chinese businesses

Fred Auerbach and his brother, Samuel H. Auerbach, emigrated from Germany and were merchants in Rabbit Creek (later renamed La Porte), c. 1862. Around 1864, the brothers moved to Nevada, then to Salt Lake City, where they established a great mercantile company with close ties to the Church of Latter-day Saints. Jann Garvis Collection.

that had purchased the stolen goods, but did claim responsibility for a portion of the losses, thus pacifying the White businessmen's demands for compensation.

Jewish Merchant—Samuel H. Auerbach

The "Reminiscences" of merchant Samuel H. Auerbach include comments on the Chinese of La Porte in the 1860s. There was a large colony of 300 to 500 Chinese in La Porte, and many more came from the surrounding country to gamble and purchase supplies imported from China.

To Auerbach, the Chinese were "inveterate gamblers" and their quarters were "very interesting if one could stand the weird and awful odors of the place." Auerbach's merchandise store had many Chinese

customers, "some of them very high grade men." At Chinese New Year, they gave him generous presents of Chinese candy, nuts, and water lilies.

There were many Chinese wash houses around La Porte. One Chinese "boiled" Auerbach's shirts and did his washing. "Although his sign proclaimed him to be Chin Lee," Auerbach observed, "I never heard him called by any other name than 'John.'"

Another washerman was entrusted with much of the laundry of La Porte in preparation for a big dance. On the day before the dance, "John took French leave, accompanied by sundry boiled shirts comprising practically all the holiday linen of the camp." On the night of the festivities, "the dancers appeared in grey, red and blue flannels and rough everyday work shirts, and the absent Chinese laundryman was easily the main topic discussed."

Auerbach wrote:

After the whites had abandoned a digging, the Chinese coolies frequently worked it over, and as they were content with small wages and worked like slaves, they usually did very well. They frequently averaged $3-$6 per day, but they were very canny and if I asked how they were doing they would reply: "Muchee gravel. No gold."

Minted money was rather scarce, according to Auerbach, and a large part of the business was transacted by means of credit, trade, or barter. Paper money was frequently used, but not worth its face value. One saw occasional large nuggets, or "gold slugs." Gold dust was widely used, and every merchant had a pair of gold dust scales on the counter. "A piece of the Brussels carpet," wrote Auerbach, "was usually placed under the scale. From time to time the carpet was burned and its gold contents saved."[25] A pinch of gold dust consisted of as much dust as could be held between the thumb and index finger. It was worth about two bits, or twenty-five cents.

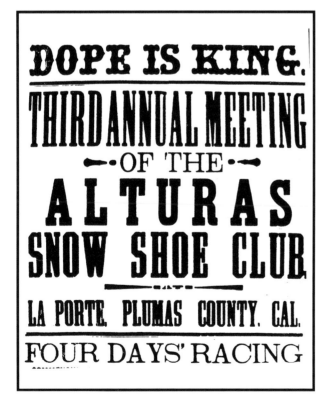

A poster announced the third annual meeting of the Alturas Snow Shoe Club, February 22, 1869. The original document is approximately 2 x 3 feet in size. Yuba Feather Historical Association.

Snowshoe Races

La Porte is part of the Sierra Nevada mountain range, situated at an elevation of five thousand feet. Snow reaches depths of up to twenty-four feet, with snowfalls beginning as early as October, and remaining on the ground well into April or May.

The introduction of Norwegian "snowshoes" by early Scandinavian miners made survival through the long winters in La Porte easier. A single leather strap held each foot in place on the snowshoe. Larger than modern downhill skis, Norwegian snowshoes were twelve feet long. One pole, rather than two, propelled or retarded the skier's speed.

La Porte has the distinction of being the birthplace of American skiing. In 1867, it established the first organized ski competition in the world. The second ski club was organized in 1878 at Christina, now Oslo, Norway.

Dope

The snowshoes were polished to a smooth finish then the bottoms were coated with a special preparation called "dope" to increase the speed. The base of dope was spermaceti, mixed with many kinds of oils, rosins, and tallow. These included beeswax, bear fat, deer tallow, snake oil, camphor, and the oils of cedar, turpentine, or spruce. There was an infinite variety of ingredients and an endless number of methods of combining them.

Each skier had his favorite dope recipes—one for hard snow, one for soft, and some specialists even had a recipe for each hour of the day. When the sun was hot, the snow was called "hot snow," and on cloudy days it was "cold snow." Then there was new snow, wet snow, dry snow, crusty snow, and many other kinds. A person with well-doped snowshoes could sail across the slopes with exhilarating speed like an arrow shot from a bow.

In 1867, the Alturas Snowshoe Club in La Porte held its first tournament, with some racers reaching speeds of eighty miles per hour. Participants in these early competitions came from nearby mining communities, including Whiskey Diggings, Poker Flat, Port Wine, and Onion Valley. Idled by the winter snow, miners scheduled races during every week of the ski season. One week the races would be in Howland Flat, another week in Gibsonville, and thus involved every town.

Chinese Snowshoe Races

After the main races, the competitions for women, boys, girls, and Chinese were held for minor purses. In an 1869 *La Porte Union*, an article titled "The Funny Races" described Chinese participation in skiing, after the snowshoe races at La Porte's third annual meeting of the Alturas Snowshoe Club:

On Saturday the Chinamen had permission to use the race track. Purses amounting to $60 were raised and about twenty celestials entered to contend for the premiums. . . . La Porte, Howland Flat, Poker Flat and Saw Pit were all represented and the rivalry between the riders was as great as it had been among the 'Melican men. Upon the track it was truly a rich, rare and racy scene. Chinamen acted as judges both at the starting and coming out poles. In several of the squads every rider fell and not more than two came through at any time. Talk about grand and lofty tumbling by a circus troupe—it is nothing when compared to a Chinamans snow shoe race. . . . The La Porte Johns were badly beaten, Howland Flat and Saw Pit were the victors. . . . We shall not be surprised if Chinese races prove quite a feature in racing in this facility hereafter.[26]

The Chinese merchants raised more money the next day, and another race was held. The La Porte Chinese were beaten again. Chinese from Howland Flat and Poker Flat won every race and all the prize money.

Two weeks later at the Howland Flat races, seventy dollars were raised for prizes in the Chinese competitions, and twenty men entered the contest. The *La Porte Union* reported that "the riders with few exception, managed to stick (to) their shoes and did good running."[27]

Auerbach wrote that a White miner, Charley Littick, once disguised himself as a Chinese man and won the Chinese race. Littick walked over to the Chinese who should have won the race, removed his disguise, then took the real winner to the judges and gave him the purse. Auerbach observed that "from the chatter of the Chinaman and his excited gestures, he was not overjoyed at the trick which had been played on him. However, the crowd thought it a huge joke and bought so many drinks for the Chinese impersonator that he soon passed out into dreamland."[28]

Old-timers called snowshoeing "More Than Just a Sport—But a Way of Life" in Plumas County's "Lost Sierras."[29]

Kong Chow Land Dispute

Controversy followed Ah Tye to La Porte in the 1860s.[30] Like most large organizations, the Sze Yup Association in San Francisco had internal rivalries and power struggles. When several groups broke away and formed a new

Snowshoe racers at the starting line. A "dope man," right, stands ready with his box of specially formulated dope waxes for any kind of weather or snow conditions.

association, the Yee clan was split in two. The Sze Yup Association reorganized as the Kong Chow Association and they inherited the land and building of the Kong Chow Temple.[31]

According to family oral history, a hired assassin was sent to La Porte to kill Ah Tye because he would not give the land exclusively to the Yees. He missed killing Ah Tye, but slashed his face with a knife. Ah Tye bore a ghastly scar on his left cheek and never had his photograph taken while he was alive. The miss cost the assailant his fee of three hundred dollars. With no money and no place to hide, the would-be assassin was stranded in tiny La Porte, so Ah Tye gave him the money to return to San Francisco.

Ah Tye went before the Chinese Six Companies tribunal in San Francisco and argued that the Kong Chow Association owned the land that he had donated to the Sze Yup Association. He found his word "naught in his own guild."[32] Some friends rallied to Ah Tye's side and formed the Suey Sing Tong (Cuisheng Tang), a secret society, for future protection and assurance that the land would remain with the Kong Chow people.[33]

The Kong Chow Association became an organization that received tax-free property rights in San Francisco, fulfilling Ah Tye's desire of fourteen years earlier.

Eight to ten thousand Chinese, mostly ex-miners, helped construct the Transcontinental Railroad. The work was done entirely by hand with wheelbarrows, one-horse dump carts, and black powder blasting. Dynamite had been invented, but was not yet in general use. Sierra Point, 1867. The Bancroft Library.

Chapter Six
1870: ANTI-CHINESE MOVEMENTS

Transcontinental Railroad: When Congress approved funds to build the Transcontinental Railroad, it awarded contracts to two companies and rewarded them for each mile of track they built. The Union Pacific Railroad hired predominantly Irish crews to build westward. The Central Pacific Railroad had the job of recruiting workers from the sparsely populated West to build towards the East.

The Central Pacific began construction on January 8, 1863, filling its labor needs with difficulty. After almost two years of construction, the Central Pacific found that White laborers were so scarce and unreliable that as a last resort, it hired fifty Chinese workers as an experiment. To the surprise of many doubters who felt Chinese incapable of performing heavy construction work, the new men proved to be excellent railroad workers.

The railroad's labor problems coincided with a period of recession. Chinese ex-miners, such as those from La Porte, sought employment anywhere for almost any wage. Mining and railroad work were similar in that they involved picks, shovels, and the moving of materials. Railroad routes often required tunnels and ditches, and ex-miners were likely to be experienced in this type of work.

Agents for the Central Pacific scoured the towns of California for Chinese laborers, and after the local supply of workers was exhausted, they began recruiting in the Far East. By the time the Transcontinental Railroad was completed, ten thousand Chinese workers, mostly ex-miners, had helped in its construction.

Chinese merchants in La Porte thought that after the railroad's completion large numbers of Chinese would flock to Plumas County in search of work. The *La Porte Union* commented that if Whites were "obliged to tolerate" the Chinese presence, the fact that they gained four dollars a month foreign miner's tax was "some consolation."[1]

On May 10, 1869, Governor Leland Stanford drove the golden spike, signifying the completion of the Transcontinental Railroad. Five days later, Chinese passed through La Porte in droves almost daily. So many Chinese congregated in and around the small mining town that the *La Porte Union* warned its readers to "Watch Out":

> There is bound to be a large number of professional thieves, and knowing that it is a part of their religion to steal anything and everything they can from white men, it will be necessary for our citizens to be a little cautious about leaving their hen roosts open, or other property exposed so that they can reach it.

On May 18, 1869, an agreement was made between George Lawrence of Port Wine, Sierra County, and Hop Sing and Company of La Porte. For five hundred dollars, Mr. Lawrence sold Hop Sing and Company the right to work tailings for gold in Pat's Gulch near Port Wine. Stipulations were:

> Keep claims in good order and not in any way damage walls or timbers in said claims—and if damaged by accident to replace them in a good and workman like manner—and further agree to blast three or four large boulders and to save and lay by in a safe place all rocks suitable for paying.
>
> And it is further agreed that the said parties of the second part shall have all the old Sluice Boxes [sic] on and belonging to said Tailing claims provided that they shall leave new lumber in their place—said new lumber to be piled on a certain Dam after working said Tailings.[2]

This is a fine example of stipulations required of lessees and contractors by land owners. Walls of the tunnel, timber, and all of the mining equipment were to be maintained and preserved in their existing conditions.

It made perfect sense for Hop Sing and Company to try mining the claims for only two months. The month of May was the height of the snow melt, and the runoff provided plenty of water for mining.

In 1870, La Porte had a population of 640 people—392 White and 248 Chinese. The large population of Chinese miners lived in dwellings that housed an average of three to six men. The miners' basic needs were met by La Porte's Chinatown community, and included a barbershop, three restaurants, a laundry, a physician, a carpenter, an opium dealer, four houses of prostitution, three gambling houses, and three merchandise stores.

Yee Ah Tye, now age forty-six, lived in back of the Hop Sing and Company store with his wife and two daughters. Emma was born in La Porte in 1867, and Annie was born in 1870. Two other merchants named Ah Mook and Ah Wah, two store clerks (La Man and Ah June) and a teen-age cook named Ah Quern also lived with them. The custom among merchants was to sleep in the rear to protect the store and its merchandise.

Chinese Boss

In 1870, the *Mountain Messenger* reported that Mr. Kingdon, a miner from Poverty Hill, intended to employ about three hundred "Celestials" to build a ditch capable of carrying two thousand inches of water into Slate Creek. Kingdon's diggings were in "fine working order," and "a rich reward" was expected.[3]

It is very likely that Kingdon went to the Hop Sing store to ask Ah Tye for help in hiring the three hundred Chinese workers. A contract between an American employer and a Chinese merchant for laborers carried the general understanding that the laborers would patronize the merchant's store. The benefit to the merchant and the laborer was mutual. The Hop Sing store gained profits by selling more goods, and the laborer got work more easily.

Because most of the Chinese laborers did not understand English, an interpreter was necessary when a large number of Chinese worked together. All communications between Kingdon and the Chinese laborers were made through Ah Tye, who spoke both English and Chinese. To some, this line of command from American employer to interpreter to Chinese laborers gave the impression that the laborers were "slaves" controlled by a Chinese "boss."[4]

Chinese road gangs must have given a similar impression. The wagon road near Sierra City (northeast of Downieville) was built in sections, and contractors were hired to construct each portion. Four miles of it were "sublet to Chinamen for $1,000 per mile."[5]

A mining deed from Emory L. Willard to Hop Sing and Company was written in both Chinese and English, November 3, 1869. Chinese writing is from top to bottom, right to left. The first two Chinese characters phonetically spell out "Willard," the second two characters mean "Doctor," and the last three characters mean "living place papers." Jann Garvis Collection.

Chariot of Fire

Chinese usually formed partnerships when investing in business ventures to pool their resources and spread out the risks. Besides its merchandise store, Hop Sing and Company invested in mining and tailing claims. Most of its claims were on Slate Creek near La Porte and ran thirty-five hundred feet in length. By 1874, the Plumas County tax assessment book described the Hop Sing and Company property as follows:

House & Lot in La Porte known as Hop Sings on China Street; Mining claims on Slate Creek between Borings & Kirk known as Hop Sings; Debt, $200; Goods, $1500; Liquor, $170; Arms, $20.

The fortunes of the Hop Sing and Company partnership were dealt a catastrophic blow in the summer of 1874. The fireworks of the Fourth of July were still fresh in the minds of La Porte residents when, as the *Mountain Messenger* reported,

About midnight of the sixth and seventh, China Town ... went up in a 'charriot of fire.' ... One heathen surmises that some Chinamen sleeping in the rear and upper part of Ah Ti's [sic] store, went to sleep with their light burning in some place where it caught the furniture.[6]

The blaze illuminated "the country round" and threatened to sweep the whole town. The newspaper reported that H. G. Weston had the only loss among the "White folks," with one end of his stable badly charred. However, "Chinatown was licked up clean, and nothing but a fireproof cellar or so was left. Ah Ti suffered the most loss—about fifteen hundred dollars in addition to his buildings." Forty or fifty houses were consumed and one young Chinaman perished in the flames, unable to escape from the room where the fire supposedly started.

Two months later the La Porte Chinatown was rebuilt, though not as extensively as before the fire. Hop Sing and Company actually showed an increase in property assets the next tax year. They added another tailing claim at the head of Rabbit Creek, 160 gallons of liquor worth $160, and nine hogs valued at $100 to its property assets in 1875. The Hop Sing and Company store also gained a stable and a gambling house.

Gambling—Favorite Chinese Pastime

Transplanted from a culture where athletic sports were considered child's play, Chinese adults gambled as a favorite pastime. It was a welcome diversion from the laborious mining and the long, snowbound winter months.

Yee Ah Tye made investments as head of Hop Sing and Company and also entered business ventures on his own. After the gold rush of the 1850s, Oroville experienced another short boom in 1874 in the rich diggings called the "lava-beds." Following the usual pattern, White miners sold worked-out claims to the Chinese, who continued to work them laboriously for returns that the original owners did not consider worthwhile. The Chinese flocked to the lava-beds in great numbers. It has been estimated that five thousand Chinese were working in these mines at one time.

In the autumn of 1873, Ah Tye purchased property in Oroville's Chinatown for $150. The lot was bounded on one side by a brick building and on the other by the saloon of Sarah Johnson, and may have been the site of a gambling house. He sold this holding just a year and a half later for $100, perhaps because of the played-out lava-beds in Oroville and his losses in the Fourth of July fire in La Porte.

Hydraulic Mining

Hydraulic mining began in La Porte around 1855. It was the most efficient process, washing more dirt, and requiring more water and a larger sluice than any other kind of mining. The number of workers needed in a hydraulic claim was small, from three to six, with the water doing nearly all the work. A nozzle at the end of the hydraulic hose was similar to the pipe of a fire engine hose, but usually larger, and one or two men were required to hold it. The force from the stream of water was so great that it could kill a man instantly and tear down a hill more rapidly than could a hundred men with shovels.

The pipe concentrated powerful jets of water on a specific area, and washed gold-bearing earth or gravel down into a sluice that trapped the gold. Mountains of earth then passed into creeks and rivers. Progressive for his times, Ah Tye was one of the few Chinese who utilized this method. An 1876 *Mountain Messenger* reported:

Ah Ty & Co. at Chandlerville [above St. Louis] hydraulicing. Have run off, several claims, & do good work. Present indications—a clean-up of about $10,000.[7]

Sierra County tax assessments show that Ah Tye and Company had claims using a hydraulic pipe and tools at Chandlerville from 1876 to 1880.

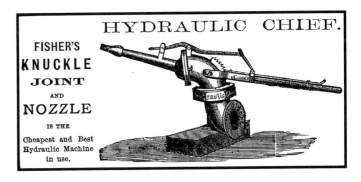

Advertisement of hydraulic equipment from Dutch Flat and the town of Nevada. After a new state took the name, residents renamed their town Nevada City.

Hydraulic hoses hooked to huge nozzles or monitors could wash away a whole mountain slope in one day. Golden Flower Trading Company and Museum.

Kearney's Sandlot Speeches

The United States economy suffered a depression in the 1870s. To add to the setbacks of the Civil War and Reconstruction, a shortage of rainfall during the winter of 1876 led to a serious drought. Wheat and fruit crops failed, thousands of cattle died, and the output of gold also declined due to the lack of water.

Miners, as well as farm hands, were left without work. Clerks, laborers, and washerwomen who had speculated on highly inflated stocks, lost their savings when the stock market fell. Business failures resulted in thousands of unemployed workers.

In 1870, ninety-nine percent of the 63,000 Chinese in America lived on the West Coast. Their large numbers, their strange physical appearance, their odd language and customs, and their lack of assimilation into White society made the Chinese easy scapegoats for the misfortunes of the times.

Dennis Kearney was an Irish sailor who became bitter after he invested his money in mining stocks, then lost it all in the stock market crash. Kearney was a drayman (a puller of a low, heavy cart without sides) when he took to the sandlot soapboxes of San Francisco, delivering fiery speeches attacking two great evils: monopolies and the Chinese. With support and publicity from the *San Francisco Chronicle*, Kearney became a spokesman for the White working class, who shouted with him, "The Chinese Must Go!"[8]

Chinese were assaulted, murdered, stoned, and robbed. People could attack them with impunity, because they knew the Chinese had no voting power and no voice in the courts. There was an attempt to burn the Red Bluff Chinatown, and Chinese were ousted from Rocklin.

In 1877, three White bandits were acquitted of the murder of ten Chinese miners in Oregon's so-called Snake River Massacre. The anti-Chinese movement started in California and gradually spread to other states. By 1877, Kearney's Workingmen's Party of California had brought the Chinese question to the national level.

Verily, the Chinese Must Go

Ripples of the anti-Chinese movement reached La Porte. On June 7, 1873, the North American Company at Hepsidam (fourteen or fifteen miles from La Porte) was hiring a large force of Chinese, but were "turning them off and putting White men in their places as fast as they could be procured."[9] In Howland Flat, about six miles from La Porte, the *Plumas National* reported "Chinamen Hung." "The (White) boys," it reported, "are getting tired of having their sluices and cabins robbed every time they turn their backs & have concluded to put a stop to it."[10]

On June 7, 1873, the *Plumas National* reported that Chinese companies in San Francisco had sent dispatches to China advising against any further immigration to California "on account of the late demonstration against those already here."[11]

Three years later, in the spring of 1876, an anti-Chinese demonstration in Gibsonville led to the burning of its Chinatown the next day, and the miners in La Porte were also developing very strong anti-Chinese sentiments. Hundreds of Chinese were employed by large companies in the area, and the feeling that they were "usurping the place of the White laborer" became stronger every day. An outburst was anticipated, and the Chinese appeared to be arming themselves.[12]

An anti-Chinese club formed in St. Louis, a mining community on the outskirts of La Porte. The bylaws of the Alturas Anti-Coolie League read:

Each member of the League shall pledge himself not to employ Chinese labor; not to purchase goods, wares or merchandise from any person who employs Chinese, and not in any manner to sustain, foster, or encourage either the Chinese themselves or those who employ them.

By 1879, the Chinese had been banished from Quincy, the seat of Plumas County. Howland Flat had few White miners, and it was hoped its new mining company would not hire Chinese. In La Porte, a four-horse team arriving with seventeen Chinese passengers prompted the comment, "Verily, the Chinese must go."[13]

The new California Constitution contained many provisions against the Chinese, including the prohibition of further immigration of Chinese laborers and their removal from within the limits of certain cities and towns. In La Porte it was thought unnecessary to organize a club to enact the state's new prohibitions against the Chinese. Fuel for hostility towards the Chinese in the La Porte area existed, but generally failed to ignite.

The slogan of the Workingmen's Party, "The Chinese Must Go!," was widely published and frequently quoted and chanted at anti-Chinese rallies.

Plenty to Go Around

The first reason for this failure lay in La Porte's prosperity in 1879. Miners were in good humor, because the season was "panning out splendidly."[14] The Bank of La Porte made its largest bullion shipment of the season —$43,000. La Porte gravel mines were paying well. Several new drift and hydraulic claims were recorded. "La Porte," reported the *Plumas National*, "may yet be as thriving a camp as it was in the early days."[15] In these times, there seemed to be plenty to go around.

The second reason was the White mining companies' dependence upon cheap Chinese labor. Many mining companies hired Chinese "for all the rough work" and only employed "a few White men to look after the 'Heathen.'"[16]

Furthermore, although La Porte's general voting populace favored doing away with Chinese laborers, it did not approve of the sacrifice of law and order to accomplish it. "The policy of the shotgun and the revolver, of murder and arson, will always and in every cause fail. It has been tried often, but ineffectually, as the truths of history attest," noted the *Mountain Messenger*.[17]

During this anti-Chinese period, Hop Sing and Company started its first partnership with a Caucasian. During the years of 1878 and 1879, Hop Sing and Company joined with surveyor Charles W. Hendel to purchase the Slate Creek tailing claims, previously owned independently by a Chinese company.

Charles (C. W.) Hendel, an elected supervisor of Plumas County, was born in Saxony, Germany, and educated in Dresden. A graduate of Zchocko Technic Institute, he immigrated to America in 1852, briefly living in New Jersey and Connecticut before arriving in California

Surveyor Charles (C. W.) Hendel wears surveyor's field jacket and carries his case of surveying tools; binocular case is strapped across his chest. California State Library.

in 1853. Hendel was elected Plumas County surveyor in 1860, served two terms, and moved to La Porte in 1871.

Despite the strong prejudice against the employment of Chinese, Hendel knew the value of their labor. In an 1878 mining report Hendel stated that, where manual labor was required, Chinese compared well with White labor and were "very apt to learn in matters requiring skill."[18] Chinese tunnel miners received $1.50 per day while skilled White labor earned $2.50 per day.

Forty-Niner Slug

Mining companies owned by Chinese partners also flourished at this time. In 1876, Ah Tye entered into partnership with Ah Mook, one of the merchants who lived with the Ah Tye family behind the store. They bought the English Bar claims on the Middle Fork of the Feather River. The *Plumas National* reported that the joint stock company worked one hundred men and that its claim was rich in spots.

Two years later, Ah Tye and Ah Mook's company was reported to have picked up a "regular old-fashioned 49er slug." The gold nugget weighed over a pound, eliciting the comment, "That's the kind of 'pellets' that old 'played-out' Plumas produces."[19]

In 1879, "lots of Chinamen" worked the river bed of the Middle Fork.[20] Ah Tye and Ah Mook's company was making money at a lively rate, bringing into town $600 in gold dust. Another Chinese company had worked below the bar for a short time and had already paid up its debts of $400 to $500. This led a *Plumas National* reporter to surmise that there remained a rich spot in the old river bed, and it was surprising that White miners "let the 'Heathen Chinee' get the first chance at the gold."[21]

Business Letters and Ledgers

LeRoy Post, born in La Porte in 1890, remembered that Ah Tye leased sections of the creek that the Chinese worked on. "Of course," said Post, "the White man had worked the creek before that, but it was just like taking the cream off the milk. . . . The Chinese could make a living where the White man couldn't."[22]

A Chinese miner in La Porte rarely talked openly about his good luck at gold mining. LeRoy Post said that, "instead, people could tell how well his mining was going by the food he bought." When the Chinese miner was not doing well, he ate simply foods such as rice with salt fish, fresh or preserved vegetables, and boiled tea. But when the miner did well, he ate fresh chicken and pork. Chickens and pigs were raised by almost every household in the countryside of China and similarly in California.

A few copies of some Hop Sing and Company business letters still exist in a La Porte Bank copybook. The letters are carbon copies of the bank's correspondence from 1876 to 1880.[23]

Bank president Dixon Brabban wrote Ah Tye's letters. Two letters were written to Robert Hall, a drover who brought pigs, sheep, and other domesticated animals to market. Notice how Hop Sing and Company had become synonymous with Ah Tye, the firm's head.

April 9, 1878
Robert Hall, Esq., Oroville
Dear Sir,
Find enclosed check in your favor for $600, for which amount give Hop Sing & Co. Not having got any more than this amount from the North America (mining company) this time, he cannot send you more. He wants you to bring him up as soon as possible sixty head of good hogs—and by that time he will have some more money for you.

Truly yours,
Dixon Brabban

March 14, 1879
Robert Hall Esq., Oroville
Dear Sir,
Hop Sing & Co. wishes me to write and tell you that if you can bring him Hogs at seven cents (per pound) he will take thirty head. If you cannot bring for that price, he cannot take any.

Truly Yours,
Dixon Brabban

The following two ledger entries list the goods bought by Hop Sing and Company and tell us much about the needs of the miners:

1877 Howland Flat Ledger Book entry
1877 Hopp Sing & Co. [sic]

July 22 30 # Nails	3.00
" 29 10 # Nails	1.00
" " 5 # Nails	.50
" 30 2 pr. Butts	.75
" " 10 # Nails	1.00
Aug 12 1 Sauce Pan	1.50
" " 1 Lock	1.15
" 22 1 Lamp	1.30
" 25 Tin Pan	.30
" " 1 Saucer	.13
Oct 5 1 Stove	6.00
" " Joint Pipe	.60
	17.23 [24]

The long nails were probably used as spikes for mining, while shorter nails were used for building flumes and sluice boxes. The butts might have been used as door hinges; the lock was for the door. The joint pipe was to join the cast-iron stove, which was probably fueled by wood.

La Porte December 9, 1884
Gold Gravel Hydraulic Mining Company
To Hop Sing Company

Receipt issued December 9, 1884, by the Gold Gravel Hydraulic Company for $29.20 "in full for Labor and Material to date. (Including barley since October 1883.)" Signed: Hop Sing Co. Jann Garvis Collection.

Punk	.35
Ground Barley	2.15
Brooms for cleaning bedrock	.75
Nitric Acid	.50
Ground Barley	4.25
Rice flour for white wash	.50
Ground Barley	1.95
Ground Barley	14.25
2 cans oil for tunnel cars	6.00
	30.70
4 as labor at $2 per day	+8.00
	38.70
By 316 ft. lumber at 3 cents	-9.48
	$29.22

Punk was used to light the fuse for dynamite in mines. The ground barley was feed for mules, the animals most favored for mining work. The sure-footed mules were able to go places that horses found difficult to traverse. A broom made of little strips of bamboo about one foot long was used to scrape dirt left in the cracks of the bedrock. After the dirt was swept into a mining pan, the gold would be separated from the gravel. Lead from a shotgun or iron from a nail was often mixed with gold. Nitric acid dissolved the lead and iron, and removed impurities from the gold. Rice flour had multiple uses for chores such as painting the inside of pigpens and chicken houses. Castor oil (made of castor beans) was spread on the axle of a tunnel car to lubricate its bearings. The labor of four men was added to the Hop Sing and Company bill, and credit for 316 feet of lumber reduced the bill to $29.22.

Sze Yup Association Strength

Two incidents in areas north of La Porte illustrate the continuing strength of the district association in Chinese immigrants' lives in the 1870s. The Sze Yup Association took its responsibilities seriously, especially when it came to returning a Chinese member's remains to China.

In 1876, a member of the Sze Yup Association who mined on Nelson Creek went to Onion Valley to get a load of rice. Travel was difficult because the snow was very deep, and the miner disappeared. There was rumor of an inquest performed on a body found on a hill in the area, however, no official report of the inquest was ever filed.

The agents of the Sze Yup Association thought that perhaps the "spoils gathered on that occasion rendered it impolitic for the parties, who held the inquest, to make publicity of the transaction."[25] The association offered a reward to anyone who would designate the spot where the body was buried so that the bones could be recovered.

News of the association's diligence in tracing the remains of its member's body probably spread through the Chinese population. The guarantee that in the event of death his remains would be returned to the roots of his homeland was an important reason an emigrant maintained membership in his district association.

Chinese cabin, c. 1800s. Drawing by Raymond Ah Tye.

There were other reasons. A Chinese woman, Tue Lin, lived alone in a small house in the Chinatown of Silver Creek, in nearby Quincy. Ah Shune, the "boss Chinaman" of that section, gave a supper that was attended by nearly all the Chinese in the neighborhood. The supper broke up around midnight. A Chinese who lived near Tue Lin's heard a scream around two o'clock. He recalled sitting up and listening, but it was not repeated, so he thought no more about it.

Tue Lin was found dead the next morning, stabbed in fifty different places—literally hacked to pieces, apparently with a pocketknife. She reputedly had considerable money and jewelry and these were missing. A Chinese suspect, King Wing, was arrested and jailed to await a grand jury trial. Wing had thirty dollars in his pockets when arrested, and the missing jewelry was found buried near a fence.

The *Plumas National* reported that King Wing refused to talk to White men, but made a full confession of his crime to the Chinese. He apparently went to Tue Lin's house on the night she was killed and asked her for fifty dollars. She refused, offering him twenty dollars instead, and in a dispute over the difference, they began to fight. Wing struck and killed her.

A meeting of several of the principal men of the Sze Yup Association—to which Wing belonged—convened in Oroville. The Chinese tribunal condemned King Wing to die, saying that if he was released from the American jail, he would be executed.

The grand jury failed to indict King Wing. The *Plumas National* reported that he was freed from jail, but "he seemed to dislike the idea of coming out, and was evidently afraid of the balance of the Heathen. Reckon his chances are slim."[26] King Wing stayed in town for some time, then left to work in another town. Nothing further was ever seen or heard of him. The supposition was that he was watched and assassinated by other Chinese while on the road.

"Verily," commented the Quincy newspaper, "the Heathen are a queer people."[27]

Chinese merchants tallied sales with an abacus and recorded them in ledger books with ink-and-brush calligraphy. Their merchandise included clothing, hats, cooking utensils, tea, dried fruit and meat, herbs, games, grooming supplies, writing paper, brushes, and ink, among many other goods.

Chapter Seven
1880: CHINESE EXCLUSION

Nevada City Ordinance: Jerry Brady, the son of an Irish miner in Nevada City, California, remembers that his father described "Ah Tie" as "the rich Chinaman dressed in white."[1] Yee Ah Tye apparently went to California's Nevada County in the 1870s to oversee Hop Sing investments.

There were more than one hundred Chinese in the vicinity of the town of Washington in the 1870s. Mostly engaged in mining, they outnumbered the White population. The *Nevada City Daily National Gazette* reported that the Chinese seldom made the news with any quarrels or unlawful acts.[2]

While living in La Porte, Yee Ah Tye presumably oversaw the Hop Sing investments in Nevada County. Nevada County assessment books for the years 1876 and 1877 list Hop Sing with general merchandise worth two hundred dollars.

In 1878, Charles Foran sold to "Hop Sing & Company Chinaman" a mining claim known as Brass Wire Bar, opposite Washington. For the price of $250 the claim included "a dam site and dam about 600 feet … with a ditch and flume conveying water from said dam … for the purpose of mining."[3] In 1879, records show that Hop Sing and Company paid a tax assessment for improvements on the claim.

However, these investments were short-lived, perhaps due to anti-Chinese attitudes that were far more severe than those in La Porte. In response to the California Constitution of 1879, Nevada City enacted an ordinance in 1880 that removed the Chinese from its city limits.[4] The presence of the Chinese was said to be "dangerous to the well-being of the community and injurious to public health, safety and public morals." All Chinese were removed from Nevada City within sixty days of the ordinance's passage. Any Chinese who failed to comply was either fined $15 to $100 or imprisoned for no more than ten days; sometimes they faced both penalties. Failure of a Chinese to move within forty-eight hours after a conviction constituted a new offense. Perhaps this ordinance prompted Hop Sing and Company to sell the Brass Wire Bar mining claim to Ah Fat in 1881.

Anti-Chinese Leagues
An image of La Porte's Chinatown in 1880 can be glimpsed in the 1880 United States census of Plumas County and its listing of trades or professions:

six merchants
one clerk in store
one barber
one house of prostitution
one prostitute
one laundry
one opium den[5]

The main merchandise store in La Porte Chinatown was Hop Sing and Company, headed by fifty-seven-year-old Ah Tye. Two other merchants, Li Wo (age forty-nine) and Sam Ting (age fifty-two), were listed as partners with Shok (age forty-eight) as the store clerk.

Hop Sing and Company built a boarding house for twenty-five Chinese miners, with three additional outhouses. Three of the boarders were married, and the others were single male miners.

By 1880, La Porte's Chinese miners had dwindled to twenty-seven. This number, however, failed to account for the Chinese laborers who had gone to work in nearby mining communities; they were listed in other counties. For example, in St. Louis, a mining community about four miles from La Porte, 150 Chinese were employed to finish a ditch from St. Louis to Grass Flat.[6]

That same year, "Ah Tye and Company" paid $11,500 for 2,300 feet of mining property at Rattlesnake in Sierra County. Included in the purchase was a cabin, a blacksmith shop, a reservoir, sluice boxes, and flumes.[7] This mine probably had another sizable Chinese work force. The partners in Ah Tye's firm were two La Porte merchants, Ah Wah and

Ah Tie, a gambler named Ah Fook, and placer miners Ah Chuck, Ah Sing, Ah Chung, and Ah Sam.[8]

By 1880, Ah Tye's family had grown to four daughters and one son: eldest daughters, Emma and Annie, Ah Tye's first son, Sam, and two more daughters, Charlotte and Alice. As an elder in the Chinatown, Ah Tye's family and economic roots were well-established. This may have been the time when Chinese started calling Yee Ah Tye "Yee Lo Dy," to denote dignity and honor.

Once the major railroads in the West were completed, there was no longer a labor shortage. Chinese went

Dilly Ah Tye, August 17, 1888. Ah Tye Family Collection.

Alice and Charlotte Ah Tye were photographed in Yokohama en route to Hong Kong where they continued their education. Ah Tye Family Collection.

wherever they could find work, even working as strike-breakers in labor disputes in Massachusetts, New Jersey, and Pennsylvania. In 1882, the Democratic and Republican parties were in a close battle for control of Congress. They concluded that support of the anti-Chinese stance would secure crucial Western votes.

With minimal opposition, Congress passed the 1882 Chinese Exclusion Act, the first United States law to restrict immigration on the basis of race. It suspended the immigration of Chinese laborers, both skilled and unskilled (including those engaged in mining), for ten years. Only teachers, students, merchants, and travelers were allowed into America. It also prohibited naturalization of the Chinese in America. In 1884, the act was clarified to ensure that wives of Chinese laborers would also be denied entrance to the United States.[9]

This exclusion act was a severe blow to the miners in the Hop Sing lodging houses. The three married miners could not send for their wives in China, and the twenty-two single male boarders were virtually condemned to lives as bachelors. Under the exclusion act, a Chinese laborer who left America to find a bride could never return, and California's anti-miscegenation laws prohibited workers from marrying White women.[10]

Merchant's Family

As the family of a merchant with a business establishment in America, the Ah Tyes were free to leave the United States and to return. On December 19, 1884, Ah Tye's wife, Chan Shee, and her younger children sailed on the S.S. *San Pablo* from San Francisco to the Orient. Yee Ah Tye was sending his American-born children to Hong Kong to further their education.

Broad-minded for his time, Yee Ah Tye believed in educating his daughters. He also was strongly against the practice of foot-binding, a symbol of high class, gentility, and beauty in nineteenth-century China.

Countless young girls, whose bones were still soft and pliable, suffered excruciating pain as their toes were permanently turned under and their feet were tightly wrapped until the arches were broken. The large toe was left extended to produce a sharp, pointed appearance. The ideal length of a foot was only three inches. A woman with bound feet stood and walked with difficulty; it was impossible for her to work, an indication of her leisure and affluence.

Mo-Mo Ahtye remembered that Ah Tye told his wife that if she allowed their daughters to have their feet bound while in Hong Kong, she needn't return home.[11]

The S.S. *San Pablo* left port bound for China and Japan, carrying a cargo valued at over $100,000—30 cases of arms and ammunition, 7,631 barrels of flour, 120 packages of fish, 10,527 pounds of butter, and over $250,000 in gold bullion. There were five White cabin passengers and 681 Chinese in its steerage, including the Ah Tyes. Many of the Chinese passengers were returning to their homeland to enjoy the Chinese New Year.

An 1872 proclamation listed provisions for Chinese passengers according to the following dietary scale:

Rice—1 1/2 lb. per day
Salt Beef, Salt Pork, Salt Fish, Fresh Beef or Mutton in
  tins—1/2 lb. on alternate days
Salted Vegetables, Pickles, Fresh Vegetables, yams,
  pumpkins, etc. —1/2 lb. on alternate days
Water—3 Imperial quarts a day
Firewood—2 lbs. a day
Tea—1/3 oz. a day
Lime or Lemon Juice and Sugar—2 a week[12]

Evidently, the Chinese passengers were amply fed.

During the Christmas season, the principal topic in San Francisco's Chinatown and commercial circles was the overdue steamer *San Pablo.* Her last run from San Francisco to Yokohama had been made in sixteen and a half days, the fastest on record. The average time was twenty-five days at that season of the year, and now she had been out thirty-nine days.

Yee Ah Tye must have been greatly distressed at the news that the ship was fourteen days overdue and had not been sighted by any other sailing vessels. Others must have worried over the treasure and valuable merchandise shipped by Chinese firms and insured by their own companies.

After forty-eight days at sea and twenty-three days overdue, the *San Pablo* finally arrived. Delayed by a machinery breakage, the steamer had met with a series of heavy gales, which had caused her to run short of coal.

The ship had sought refuge in a harbor on Peel Island, a small Japanese island in the west Pacific. There was never any danger of a lack of provisions. Since there was little timber among Peel Island's volcanic rocks and no coal, the crew used a portion of the ship's cargo for fuel. With this improvised fuel, the *San Pablo* steamed into Yokohama with everyone on board well.

Ah Tye's eldest daughter, Emma, met her mother and siblings in Yokohama. She had married a Chinese Christian, Koa Cheong, an executive for a Japanese steamship line. The second daughter, Annie, was also married to a Chinese Christian, Mr. Lee, a Hong Kong banker. The third and fourth daughters, Charlotte and Alice, would attend an English school in Hong Kong.

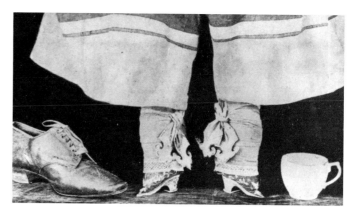

Bound feet, known as Golden Lilies, compared to a man's shoe and a tea cup.

Charlotte remembered another factor that may have led Yee Ah Tye to send his family off: as a child in La Porte, her family had had to pull the shades down for fear of people attacking them.[13]

Miners' Anti-Chinese Association

La Porte seemed to have escaped the extremes of anti-Chinese agitation in the 1870s, but the 1880s were a different story. The 1882 suspension of immigration was only the first, albeit large, step against the Chinese population in America. The exclusion movement gained momentum in the 1880s, reaching the hinterlands of La Porte in the form of anti-Chinese leagues.

Adding to the town's distress were frequent fires. In the summer of 1884, La Porte experienced its worse conflagration in over twenty years, the eighth fire since its first settlement. Only Chinatown, a small number of dwellings, and some fire-proofed buildings escaped the fire.

A high wind rapidly spread the flames over the town and there was no fire department to stop the devastation. La Porte's citizens energetically began to rebuild amid the charred ruins. Only a year later, fire nearly destroyed La Porte again, making it truly an "afflicted town."[14]

The first Miner's Anti-Chinese Association meeting was in Howland Flat at Corbett's Hall on February 14, 1886. Citizens from the neighboring areas of Poker Flat, Gibsonville, St. Louis, and La Porte attended. Committees reported that most mining companies had agreed to replace their Chinese laborers with White workers. Mr. M. Schofield, of the North America claim, said he had had no Chinese at work for a month. He "recognized the evils done by them and would not hire any Chinese if others did the same."[15]

Some mine owners expressed dissent. Harry White

In 1885, twenty-eight Chinese were massacred in Rock Springs, Wyoming. They had been hired by contractors to replace the workers in Union Pacific's coal mines who were on strike for higher wages. This was one of the worst outbreaks of violence in the West. Federal troops were brought in to protect the Chinese workers, and many of their attackers were arrested. *Harper's Weekly,* September 26, 1885.

of the Empire Company said his mine could not afford to hire White labor. However, the local newspaper questioned White's statement by reporting that his mine yielded large dividends, indeed, that gold could be seen in the dirt.

The La Porte committee reported that there were no Chinese employed in their town. The league adopted a declaration which promised that miners would not employ Chinese laborers and would boycott Chinese goods in "preference to the products of White labor." League members also took an oath to "unite in good faith to accomplish the peaceable removal of the Coolies, Chinese or Pagans" from their midst.[16] Fifty-one members signed the declaration at the first meeting in Howland Flat. The league adjourned to reconvene in La Porte a week later.

Feelings against Chinese immigration grew stronger each day in the Eastern part of the United States. "In the meantime," warned the *Mountain Messenger,* "Californians should be careful to use no violence. Let us keep the law on our side and we will soon be relieved of the Mongolian incubus."[17]

The Miner's Anti-Chinese Association meeting in La Porte was the largest gathering that had been held

there for some time. Large delegations from Howland Flat, Gibsonville, St. Louis, and Port Wine elected permanent league officers. The secretary prepared a list of those who refused to comply with the league's wishes, the so-called "Boycotted List."

Upon his election as permanent president, R. J. Sinnott of Gibsonville proposed that "in order to protect our League from slanderous accusations . . . we imperatively discountenance any unlawful means of ridding ourselves of the Chinese."[18] Sinnott's speech reflected the community's sentiments that were mild in light of the violence occurring in other areas of California and the United States.

West Coast Inflamed

In 1885, shortly after a riot which killed a score of Chinese in Rock Springs, Wyoming, the entire West Coast became inflamed almost simultaneously. Tacoma, Washington, burned its Chinese quarter. The Seattle, Olympia, and Portland Chinatowns were saved from a similar fate by quick official action. Truckee, California, expelled its Chinese and held a torchlight procession to celebrate the event.

In other California towns, the actions ranged from

new ordinances of regulation to the burning of Chinese quarters and the expulsion of their inhabitants. Among those localities were Anderson, Auburn, Carson, Chico, Cloverdale, Dixon, Gold Run, Healdsburg, Hollister, Lincoln, Los Angeles, Merced, Napa, Nevada City, Oakland, Pasadena, Petaluma, Placerville, Red Bluff, Redding, Sacramento, San Buenaventura, San Jose, Santa Barbara, Santa Cruz, Santa Rosa, Sonoma, Vallejo, Wheatland, and Yuba City.

Boycott List

In Scales, an outlying community of La Porte, White men now had work instead of the Chinese. The motto was "No Chinese need apply! The Chinese must go!!!"[19]

Members of the Anti-Chinese League of Howland Flat wrote the *Mountain Messenger* to ask where they could get board and lodging in Downieville where Chinese were not employed. The newspaper was "obliged to reply" that both hotels employed Chinese cooks.

"The excuse the proprietors" gave was that they could not "get steady, reliable, and competent White cooks." White cooks had been tried several times, and in each case during a rush, the White cook was found "blind drunk." The newspaper concluded that both hotels would make the change if the owners could get reliable White help at prices they could afford to pay and boarders in either hotel would not "kick" against such a change.[20]

Some La Porte area miners opposed the anti-Chinese movement because they felt their mines could not afford to hire all-White labor. One foreman said he could not ask a White man to work in his mine for less than three dollars a day, because it was quite wet. He also felt his mine could not be prospected unless by cheap labor. Chinese laborers in the La Porte area averaged about $1.50 a day, while White miners averaged about twice that amount.

Harry White was on the boycott list of the Miner's Anti-Chinese Association. In a letter to the local newspaper he complained that some men had come to his saloon requesting him to dispose of "the Chinamen working in the Empire [mine] and work all White men." White told them that "the mine would not pay to hire all White men," but that he was "trying to work all the White labor he could." He had twenty-three White men on the payroll and intended to hire more if the mine would pay enough.

At a company stockholder's meeting a few days later, White proposed a trial plan to work White men only. He would charge the men seventy-five cents a day for the use of the water and, if they made three dollars a day, they could have the profit; if not, the White miners would have to be content with what the mine paid.

The stockholders all agreed with White's proposition, and "it was drawn up and pasted in the saloon for two days." But the agreement did not suit the White workers: "They wanted more flume and a monthly settlement." White increased his offer, only to have it turned down by the company's stockholders.

At another "large and enthusiastic" meeting of the Miner's Anti-Chinese Association in St. Louis, F. A. Gourley, president of the Nevada Gold Mining Company at Gibsonville, wrote the following plea:

> *I cannot sign your test [declaration]. I have my money in mining property and must get it out. My mines will not pay to hire all white labor. . . . I have $12,000 in these mines, and if there is a profit in Chinese labor I wish to get it.*[21]

Gourley said that some members of the league "suggested violent means of reaching the desired result." The league chastised Gourley by saying that his "sympathies and intent" were adverse to the anti-Chinese movement. Gourley and his company's interests were labeled as selfish and caring "nothing for the condition" of their fellow man. The anti-Chinese league adopted a plan of action which resulted in the "peaceable and lawful discharge of the Chinese" from Gourley's mining company. At the next meeting Gourley was warned that if he didn't discharge his Chinese, the league would order his mines to do so.

Dissenters were under heavy pressure to conform. In the case of White, a committee asked shareholders to force his mining company to release its Chinese by May first. Finally succumbing to the pressure, White reported that he had only two "Chinamen working on repairs and would discharge them by the first of May."[22]

Other dissenters followed White's example. By springtime, a local newspaper reported that everybody was working and confidently expecting success. "Not a son of Confucius" was employed in the vicinity.[23] For greater effectiveness, the anti-Chinese league changed from an area-wide association to several local leagues.

Dissenters

While the majority of the La Porte residents used the boycott to muscle people into an anti-Chinese stand, a few men successfully resisted the tactic. French-born Frank Cayot of La Porte's Union Hotel was on the boycott list. He retained his Chinese cook throughout the difficult times. His daughter, Claire Cayot O'Rourke,

Frank Cayot II (inset). The Union Hotel, c. 1896. *Left to right:* Frank II, his wife Claire, A. V. Rugg, Annie and Margaret Spencer, Annie Sherman, and Dolly and Hattie Trescott. Jann Garvis Collection.

remembers her father had raised his children not to feel superior to the Chinese and "not to be anti-anything." Satisfied with his Chinese cook's work, Cayot felt that everybody had a right in this world and "a right to live just the same" as he did.[24] Efforts by the townspeople to boycott the Cayot restaurant proved ineffectual, because his business was not dependent upon them; most of them ate at home. Travelers were the crux of his business.

Known as one of the best-kept hotels in the mountains, Cayot's Union Hotel also served as headquarters for La Porte's stage companies. His saloon and office had been "re-fitted in elegant style" and "graced with a billiard table" that equaled those "used in the most aristocratic club rooms." For the "entertainment and instruction of his patrons," Cayot spread his tables "with the leading periodicals and journals of the country, for the cost of which not a cent" was begrudged.[25] Even the stage driver regularly stayed at the Union Hotel.

One of the tactics used by members of the Miners' Anti-Chinese Association was to accuse dissenters of caring "nothing for the condition of his fellow man."[26] Dr. Mussey, one of the most respected doctors in La Porte, was the target of such an attack. At one meeting, it was recommended that members secure the services of a reputable physician who had at heart their interests. The ploy proved ineffective, however, because Dr. Mussey cared for many patients without compensation. O'Rourke remembers Dr. Mussey as a big, broad-shouldered man with light-colored hair, a mustache, and blue eyes, a man who was respected for his knowledge and skill. At a Miner's Anti-Chinese Association meeting, Dr.

Mussey approved of getting rid of Chinese by all fair means, but he did not sign the declaration promising to boycott them.

Growing up in La Porte, O'Rourke felt that the little towns functioned by themselves, as separate entities. O'Rourke said, "Outside of a dance every once or twice a year, women didn't have opportunities to socialize or have outside interests."[27] Thus, the women's participation in the Miner's Anti-Chinese Association meetings added an interesting sidelight. Newspaper accounts of the meetings told of women serving refreshments and eventually signing the league's anti-Chinese declaration. A total of 191 people signed the declaration, including sixteen women.

Chinese Strength

The Plumas County tax assessment books provide evidence that the La Porte Chinese merchandise stores, Hop Sing and Company and Hop Kee and Company, were strong enough to continue their businesses independent of Whites. They paid their taxes faithfully from the early 1860s through the early 1900s. Moreover, both Chinese stores paid high taxes, indicating that this was a stable and profitable period for them, despite the anti-Chinese leagues.[28]

Along with the Chinese merchants' prosperity came an increase in the wages of the Chinese workers. Frank Cayot handled the account books for many mines and businesses in addition to operating the Union Hotel. One of his entries for Ah Tye showed that the average daily wage of a Chinese worker in 1885 increased from $1.50 to $1.75 per day.[29]

Charles W. Hendel, a partner with Hop Sing and Company during the anti-Chinese years of the 1870s, was again a partner in the turbulent 1880s.

On November 18, 1881, members of the "Hop Sing Company & Pike & Company" from La Porte sold some Slate Creek mining claims to the Gibsonville Union Water Company, et. al., for two thousand dollars in gold coin. The La Porte partners who signed the deed were:

*Ah Tie for Hop Sing—58 year old merchant,
  La Porte Chinatown
Henry Buckley—53 year old Irish hotel keeper
Charles Pike—47 year old carpenter from New York
Frank Steward—46 year old mine superintendent
  from Maine
Dixon Brabban—52 year old banker from England
Charles Hendel—40 year old civil engineer from
  Saxony*[30]

During the heat of the anti-Chinese leagues in 1886, Hendel again became a co-owner in the tailing claims on Slate Creek, known as the Hop Sing and Company's claim.[31] Hendel, a respected United States deputy mineral surveyor, was acquainted with "most every trail, ravine and hill" in Sierra County's vast mining regions. Much in demand as a surveyor and familiar with all the mines and mine owners, Hendel was one of the best-known men in Sierra and Plumas Counties. He was nicknamed "Quicksilver" because quicksilver (or mercury) had the ability to attach itself to gold.

Yee Ah Tye had lived and worked in La Porte for over twenty years. As the leader of Hop Sing and Company, he had become partners and friends with prominent La Porte businessmen. From this intermingling, Ah Tye gave the Chinese a well-respected "face," which resulted in less violence and greater tolerance toward his people.

Mohawk Railroad

A few months after the Miners' Anti-Chinese Association dispersed into local leagues, labor opportunities opened up for the Chinese again. In Sierraville, southeast of La Porte, twelve White men were at a saloon looking for work. The Mohawk Railroad Company, anxious to employ White labor, offered work to the men, but none would accept. The *Plumas National* newspaper warned, "So long as White men would rather 'bum' around saloons than work, the Chinese are bound to get employment."[32]

By the winter of 1886, Moy Foot, a Chinese storekeeper and labor contractor from Sawpit Flat (eighteen miles from La Porte), had a contract with the Mohawk Railroad to work approximately sixty Chinese men. Work seemed plentiful in general; about 250 White and Chinese men were already employed as timber men and graders.

Moy Foot and Charley Tone, partners in a Chinese merchandise store, advertised in the *Plumas National*, June 27, 1891.

Dilly Ah Tye was about nine years old when he posed for this 1894 photograph with his friends. *Seated, left:* Cleveland O'Rourke, the son of an Irish gold miner; *Standing:* Bill Pike, the son of a widowed milliner and grandson of a La Porte boot and shoe merchant. Dilly's queue is barely visible coiled on top of his head. Jann Garvis Collection.

Chapter Eight
A NEW HYBRID CALLED CHINESE AMERICAN

The Ah Tyes were the only family in the La Porte Chinatown; most of the other residents were single male miners. La Porte native LeRoy Post remembered Ah Tye as the "big head man," who took care of all the Chinese business in the community.[1] The Hop Sing and Company store sold Chinese items, including dishes, rice, clothing, slippers, pipes, tobacco, salt fish, and Chinese brandy.

Typical of La Porte-area dwellings, the Hop Sing building was a long, narrow structure with a forty-five degree shake roof to allow snow to slide off. Sierran residents learned early that if the angle of a roof was not steep, the weight of a heavy winter's snow could break the rafters.[2]

As soon as La Porte children walked, they were on snowshoes—the only way to get around in the wintertime. When they were adults, Dilly and Bessie Ah Tye often reminisced about their skiing days in La Porte. Bessie always talked about her prowess as a skier and all the secret waxes she had rubbed onto her snowshoes. In fact, her eldest son, Bola Lowe, remembered hearing that she skied so well that boys enviously tried to wangle secret dope recipes from her.

Snow often covered La Porte buildings, making the town look like a huge snowball with a house top sticking out here and there. Whites who lived in two-story homes were often forced to exit through their upper-story windows. Sometimes they had to climb out through the chimney after punching a hole through the snow above.

Great Snowfall of 1890

The great snowfall of 1890 would long be remembered as one of the most severe winters in La Porte history. Streets piled high with snow were broken by tunnels leading down to the doorways on either side. All business was conducted with the aid of lamps and candles.

Being snowbound and living in darkness for seemingly endless months often brought on depression. To get a glimpse of daylight, people climbed up the inclined tunnels and looked upon the vast expanse of silent and beautiful snow.

On February 25, the snow measured about twenty-three feet on the level, and snow was still falling. Many families ran out of wood, and it was feared that if the snowstorm didn't stop long enough to give people a chance to get in a new supply, there would be considerable suffering.

Some businesses, such as the Union Hotel and the Hop Sing store, had cellars for storing food for the winter. But this winter proved to be so severe that the Ah Tye household was running out of food. Beulah (Ah Tye) Jung remembers hearing that all eyes turned to her father's pet lamb. Dilly's beloved pet was finally slaughtered, which left him so heartbroken he couldn't even take a bite.

The dreariness of the winter was broken by two things: mail and talk of snowshoe racing and dope. Enterprising citizens managed to get their mail out with the aid of Gus Berg, who carried the mail to Nelson Point, and Mr. Schofield, who continued his regular trips on snowshoes. The pungent smell of oils of tar, cedar, spruce, and other secret dope ingredients filled each home. Everyone made dope and talked dope. They talked of snowshoes and races, and the gatherings that brightened their lives and would get them through yet another long winter.

Value of a Daughter

Most Chinese men deemed a daughter less valuable than a son, because once she married she was considered a member of her husband's clan. Why raise a daughter for the benefit of another clan? The low value of daughters in China in the 1880s is illustrated in a story told by a Baptist missionary. A Chinese man went to market with five baby girls in his basket, saying he hoped to get as much as forty cents each for them.[3]

The only way in or out of this home in La Porte was through a second-story window. When the snow reached the eaves it could no longer slide off the roof and if allowed to build up, the roof would collapse. The men have just finished shoveling the entire roof, and their jackets have been tossed aside; their snowshoes are stuck in the snow, and a woman is nearby with her dog. Yuba Feather Historical Association.

Bob Cook leads a horse from the barn through a snow tunnel. The horse, obviously thin from the long hard winter, is equipped with iron snowshoes and may be ready to harness to the stage company's sleigh. Because of the enormous work and care keeping animals in deep snow and the difficulties of stocking enough feed, only work horses, the family milk cow, chickens, and other livestock that would provide food were kept in La Porte through the winter. The rest were sent to pasture in the lower hills. Jann Garvis Collection.

The Chinese children on snowshoes were members of the Quock family who lived in Howland Flat. *Third from left:* Poy; *sixth from left:* Etta; *second from right:* Ginn. Jann Garvis Collection.

Bessie Ah Tye graduated from a young ladies' finishing school in San Francisco and became a talented pianist. Chang Family Collection.

Contrary to tradition, Yee Ah Tye valued his daughters. He hired a tutor, Ah Que, to educate his girls in their La Porte home. Then he even bought a piano for his youngest daughter, Bessie, and had it transported to La Porte by horse and wagon from San Francisco. His more traditional Chinese friends thought he was crazy to spend so much money on a daughter.

In the summer of 1892, the *Mountain Messenger* reported that three of Ah Tye's daughters had returned to La Porte to visit their ailing father, who was being treated by a Chinese physician from Marysville. Emma arrived from Yokohama. Annie lived in Hong Kong with her husband, who held a "lucrative position in the Charter Bank of that city."[4] Charlotte was teaching in the English public school at Hong Kong. Ah Tye apparently recovered and his children returned to their homes.

In the winter of 1892, a fire broke out in the lower end of La Porte's Chinatown at three p.m. It swept through the whole street, leaving only two buildings standing. Fortunately, the wind drove the fire away from

town, protecting half of La Porte from going up in flames. Several buildings narrowly escaped the fire, saved by people who nailed wet blankets to the roofs and sides of buildings exposed to the intense heat. The fire was supposedly caused by a faulty stovepipe; losses were confined to the Chinese section.

The *Mountain Messenger* reported that "Ah Tye, the President of the Hop Sing Company, was probably the heaviest loser, his loss being estimated at between $16,000–$18,000, and no insurance." Neighboring Hop Kee and Company had an estimated loss of $1,000. Although Ah Tye was discouraged, he immediately "commenced to rebuild."[5]

Yee Ah Tye also had a legal problem. In 1892, he sued the Union Consolidated Drift Miners Limited corporation in Sierra County's Superior Court over a debt they owed him. In a non-jury trial, the judge ruled in favor of Ah Tye and also awarded him attorney's fees of $300, as well as court costs of $21.25.[6] This case demonstrated Yee Ah Tye's ability to use the American judicial system to redress his grievance. Furthermore, it showed that the rights of Chinese litigants were increasingly acknowledged by and enforced in the California courts.

From 1890 to 1895, Hop Sing and Company mined in tailings and mining claims at Saw Pit Flat, on Hopkins Creek and Onion Valley Creek. Hop Sing and Company sold Chinese merchandise valued more than three hundred dollars at Grass Flat in 1895 and 1896. From 1897 to 1900, Hop Sing and Company worked in placer and tailing claims in Gibsonville.

Just one month before Yee Ah Tye's death in 1896, the *Mountain Messenger* reported that "The English Company leasing a tailing claim at Slate Creek," had re-let about five thousand feet of the claim to Ah Tye.[7]

However, a month later, Ah Tye sold the lease to P. Doray and D. Corbett of Gibsonville. This was deemed by the local newspaper as "a very commendable move" by Doray and Corbett, as it would "furnish employment to a large number of men."[8]

Death of Ah Tye

On April 20, 1896, Yee Ah Tye died in La Porte at about age seventy-three. LeRoy Post recalled that in La Porte the Chinese never carried their dead through the front door, but instead, always went out through the back door, or through an opening cut especially for that purpose. Coins were placed in the deceased's mouth for his travel to the world beyond.

A stagecoach transported Ah Tye's body to Marysville. Seated beside the driver was a man who threw small, rectangular-shaped papers into the air

The *Plumas National-Bulletin* reported Ah Tye's death April 23, 1896.

every hundred feet or so. Each strip of paper had a hole in its center in imitation of Chinese coins as "road money" to purchase the "right of way." The papers were bought for the funeral service from the joss house priest and scattered along the route to buy off any bad spirits that might be lurking, thus preventing any interference with the deceased's spirit as it proceeded to its final resting place.

Yee Ah Tye's body was taken to Coroner Bevan's Undertaking parlors in Marysville, where "all of the embalmer's arts were brought out to preserve the body" until his eldest son, Sam, arrived from China.[9]

Ah Tye had never allowed his picture to be taken because of the scar left on his cheek by his assailant's near miss. Now, after his death, his body was propped up for a photograph, and the photographer drew in the eyes using Charlotte as his model.[10]

Four weeks after Ah Tye died, Sam returned to America, and his father's remains were brought to San Francisco. Ah Tye was buried on the land that he had donated to the Kong Chow Association for a cemetery.

A New Hybrid

Yee Ah Tye was one of the first of a new hybrid called Chinese American. Because he had learned English in Hong Kong as a young boy, he could communicate with both Chinese and Caucasians and absorbed elements of both cultures. He seemed to have an openness to Caucasians, creating greater mutual understanding.

Ah Tye held on to the stability of the Chinese world by retaining the dress and food of his roots. Yet he adapted to American business practices and recognized the importance of documentation and the American judicial system. He adopted the Americanized name, Ah Tye, and even assumed the first name, George, for a short time.

During his early years in America, he led his people in the autocratic style he had learned in China. But in the end, he evolved into a business leader highly respected for his honesty and generosity by Chinese and Caucasians alike. The *Mountain Messenger* described him as "wealthy and liberal to a fault."[11]

Ah Tye entered into partnerships with White Americans, reflecting a mutual trust unique for the times. His strength, independence, and harmonious relations with Caucasians guided the Plumas County Chinese through their hardest times during the anti-Chinese leagues of the 1880s.

Known as a progressive man, Ah Tye was one of the first Chinese to engage in hydraulic mining. He applied his advanced ideas to his family as well, when he invested in the education of his daughters.

Yee Ah Tye emigrated from a Chinese village of farmers and fishermen, led his people in the shaping of a vibrant American frontier, and carved a niche for himself as a respected gold mining merchant and labor contractor in the Sierra.

Ah Tye was neither a sojourner in life nor in death. He could have easily returned to China as a wealthy man to live out his days. Instead, he lived in California for over fifty years and died at the ripe age of seventy-three. In all that time, he never visited China. At the end, Ah Tye made the astonishing deathbed request to have his bones lie in America, reflecting the unique belief that he was now more American than Chinese.

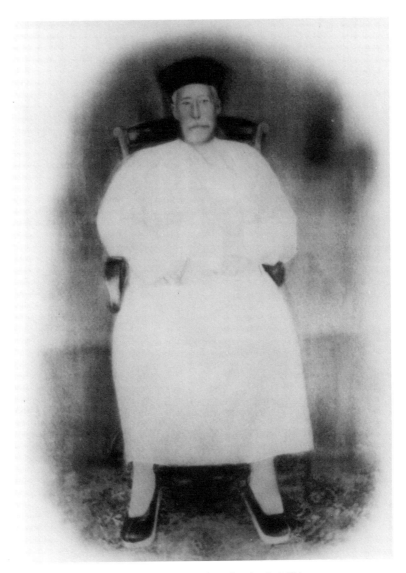

The only photograph of Yee Ah Tye was taken after he died. This was a common practice in the nineteenth century, and many times the photographer was the first person called when there was a death. It was unusual, however, to have eyes painted on the portrait. Ah Tye Family Collection.

T. Watanabe　　東京淺草公園
　　　　　　　　　渡邊製

Yee Ah Tye's eldest daughter, Emma, was born in La Porte in 1867. Chang Family Collection.

Chapter Nine
TURN-OF-THE-CENTURY LA PORTE

Ah Tye's Eldest Daughters: Before 1870, only a small number of Chinese women were born in America. Emma was the first child of Yee Ah Tye and Chan Shee, born in La Porte in 1867. She married a Chinese Christian named Koa Cheong on July 19, 1889, and lived a life of luxury and wealth in Yokohama.

During this time, China did most of its business with England and Japan. Cheong was an executive in a Japanese steamship line, and handled its Chinese accounts. His wife, Emma, traveled back and forth to America annually. She loved to go out, and when she went to dinner in Japan, a rickshaw boy waited outside to take her home.

Two years after Emma's birth, Annie was born in La Porte, but very little is known of her. According to Mo-Mo Ahtye, Annie was tall, slim, and pretty with beautiful skin and was educated in both English and Chinese. Annie married a Chinese Christian from the Lee family, and they lived in Hong Kong, where he was a banker.

Both women's good luck did not last, however. Emma became a widow early in life, and Annie died at a young age in Hong Kong.

La Porte Chinatown—1900
In accordance with Chinese custom, Yee Ah Tye's eldest son, twenty-four-year-old Sam, inherited his father's assets. By 1900, Ah Tye's widow, Chan Shee, had moved from La Porte to San Francisco with her younger children, Alice, Bessie, and Dilly.

Sam married Ko Shee, who was born in Los Angeles in 1874. The only members of the Ah Tye family living in La Porte at the turn of the century were Sam, Ko Shee, and their children, Sidney (age three) and Wallace (age one).

Many vivid impressions of La Porte in the early 1900s came from the keen and perceptive eyes of LeRoy Post.[1] He recalled that Sam's wife, Ko Shee, was called "little foot" by the La Porte Whites, because her feet had been bound and were about half their normal size. "She was kind of crippled," remembered Post, "and she didn't get around much." Rose Ah Tye remembered that Sam paid three thousand dollars for a concubine, who also worked as a servant, caring for Ko Shee and the children.

Post recalled that in 1900, all Chinese buildings in La Porte were single-story and separate from each other. The Hop Sing building was eighteen feet wide and twenty feet long. The Ah Tye family lived in back of the store.

Like most La Porte homes, the outhouse was in the woodshed at the building's end—a big pit surrounded by stacks of wood. Hogs were slaughtered and skinned behind the Hop Sing woodshed. Mules were kept in the barn. The back yard was extended with pens of chickens, ducks, and pigs.

Aging Bachelor Society
La Porte's Chinatown in 1900 was an aging bachelor society. Post estimated that about 100 Chinese miners lived in and around La Porte. According to the United States census, 67 Chinese miners between ages 40 to 60 boarded in the Hop Sing lodging houses. The majority had arrived in America during the 1870s, and had lived in America for more than twenty years.

Post recalled that each of the Hop Sing boarding houses, rebuilt after the fire of 1892, measured about eighteen feet wide and thirty to thirty-six feet long. Each one-story house had a woodshed in back, with an attached indoor outhouse. The inside of the houses were sparsely furnished, with stools and tables made by hand. The men never used mattresses, but always slept on boards with pads and blankets for warmth. They did their own laundry and cut each other's hair.

The Chinese miners lived in the Hop Sing lodging houses year-round and gambled during the winter months when the weather was most severe. When they left to mine during the summer, they moved to vacant or abandoned cabins or houses.

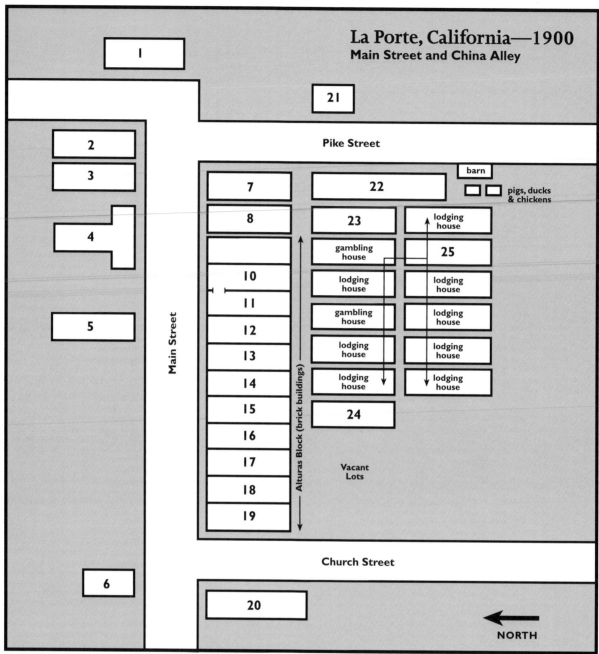

La Porte, California—1900
Main Street and China Alley

Pike Street

1	
21	

Church Street

20

NORTH

Alturas Block (brick buildings)

Main Street

barn

pigs, ducks & chickens

lodging house

gambling house

lodging house

lodging house

lodging house

lodging house

lodging house

lodging house

Vacant Lots

Map and descriptons drawn from: Interviews of Leroy Post by Jann Garvis; 1900 Plumas County tax assessment; Plumas County Hop Sing deed—1904; 1880 and 1900 United States manuscript censuses.   Layout by Fred Cheung Jr.

KEY

1. Livery Stable; Henry Buckley (Ireland).
2. Post Office; Annie Greeley, Postmaster (California).
3. Blacksmith Shop; John Hillman (Anglo-American).
4. Hotel; Moses Burrel (French-Canada).
5. Tin Shop; Aaron Harris (Russia).
6. Union Hotel stage barn; Cayot family (France).
7. Butcher Shop & barn; William Canny (Ireland).
8. Photography & Notions; Gustav Schubert (Germany).
9. Boots, Shoes, & Dry Goods; Hugh McNeill Sr. (Ireland), Hugh McNeill Jr. (Irish-American).
10. Wells Fargo agents & Dry Goods; N. Gard, owner; leased to Julius Rosenberg (Prussia) and James Jones (Anglo-American).
11. Groceries; Rosenberg & Jones.
12. Vacant building; Aaron Harris, owner.
13. Groceries; Aaron Harris, owner.
14. Saloon; Manuel Miguel (Portugal).
15. Saloon; James Jones (Anglo-American).
16. Burned out store.
17. Warehouse (closed) Rosenberg & Jones, owners.
18. Drugstore; John H. Thomas (Maine).
19. Drugstore & Notary Public; Henry Washington (Virginia).
20. Union Hotel; Cayot Family (France).
21. Hop Sing Hospital; Sam Ah Tye (Chinese-American).
22. Hop Sing Store, home, & barn; Sam Ah Tye.
23. Hop Kee Store.
24. Ah Duk's house.
25. Lodging and gambling houses; Sam Ah Tye.

The Slate Creek Mining Company at French Camp (four miles from La Porte), owned and operated by William S. Packer and Son and C. W. Hendel, c. 1903. Packer and his son had invented a unique style of mining. Buckets passing on an endless chain were filled by men; the buckets then continued to revolve and emptied into a sluice box. As Packer expressed it: "We move the machinery to the dirt." Jann Garvis Collection.

Their supplies were delivered by mule packers from the Hop Sing merchandise store.

Post said that the Chinese miners kept mostly to themselves. They generally worked independently in creeks and rivers, using labor-intensive techniques. In later years, they used sluice boxes rather than rockers. After depleting an area of gold, they slid their sluice boxes along to the next site.

Jokesters

Whites tended to perceive the Chinese as superstitious and tried to play on their beliefs. Post remembered a man named Beau; after dinner, he would say within his Chinese cook's earshot, "Hear that man up there? I hear him." It only took three or four times before his cook threatened to quit.

A man named Archie once fastened a long string to the window of a Chinese man named Gook. Archie rattled Gook's window so much that Gook returned to China. "Luckily," remembered Post, "Gook had money and a lot of gold teeth."

Post told of jokesters who would place a pan over the stovepipe of a Chinese building to smoke out its inhabitants. Lottery was played in two gambling houses in La Porte. When the Chinese players collected their lottery earnings from one gambling house and proceeded to the next, they were often tripped by a wire stretched across their path.

La Porte native Richard O'Rourke recalled hearing about a prank played on Chinese fan tan players.[2] The Chinese had high gambling tables and wore big, loose-bottomed trousers. Pranksters put a yellow jackets' nest in a barley sack and sneaked into a gambling house where a fan tan game was in progress. The jokesters threw the barley sack under the table, ran out, and held the door shut. The Chinese players nearly tore the house down trying to get out, stung by the yellow jackets up their pant legs.

Chinese Celebrations Observed

The Chinese miners continued to observe many Chinese customs and festivals in America. Chinese New Year was celebrated for three and four days with firecrackers ignited by the hundreds, in the belief that firecrackers drove away evil spirits and ushered in good omens. "Firecrackers, firecrackers, firecrackers," said Post, "outside, it'd be two inches deep with firecrackers."

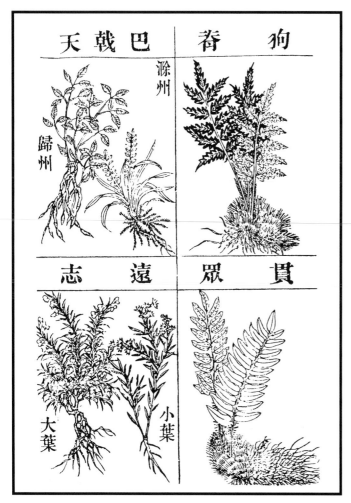

A page from a Chinese herbal book illustrated plants used for various remedies.

The Chinese were especially fond of gambling during these festivities, because it tested their luck for the coming year.

Post told about the La Porte Chinese celebrating the festival of the harvest moon. In south China, this event marked the completion of the second harvest of rice. Similar to America's Thanksgiving holiday, it was a day for the Chinese to enjoy the fruits of their hard work and thank their gods for their blessings of food. The full moon at this time was the brightest and most beautiful of all the full moons of the year. In south China homes, dishes of food would be placed on the family altar as offerings to the family's ancestors.

"Every year at a certain time of the moon," recalled Post, "they'd set out a meal for the moon . . . right outside of their house. They also put out Chinese brandy in bowls. It was quite a ceremony. Of course, the moon never ate it. As long as there were quite a few Chinamen, they kept that up. Hobos would eat the food."

Herbs and a Chinese Hospital

A Chinese man listed in the United States census as a "physician" was a doctor trained in the art of herbal medicine. He would have his patient describe the symptoms, feel his pulse, then prescribe an herbal remedy. Post remembered the Chinese used oil of cloves for toothaches. The cloves came in long bottles, the size of a man's little finger.

Prescriptions for herbal medicines were filled and sold in the Hop Sing store. A mixture of herbs soaked in three or four cups of water would be boiled down to one rice-bowl's worth of herbal tea. Many of the herbs boiled down to thick, bitter, and unpleasant-tasting brews that would cure physical imbalances.

The 1900 La Porte census listed Tue Far as a thirty-six-year-old single nurse who was a boarder in the Hop Sing lodging house. She probably brewed medicinal herbs and cared for the elderly Chinese miners in La Porte's Hop Sing hospital. Aged and ailing miners went to the four-bed Hop Sing hospital only if they were very, very sick and thought they were dying. The Chinese didn't want a person to die in their home for fear that their ghost might come back to haunt them.

As the representative of the Kong Chow Association in La Porte, Sam Ahtye handled arrangements for the shipment of miners' bones back to China. When a miner died in the La Porte area, his body was temporarily buried in the local Chinese cemetery. The graves were generally left untouched for at least three years, giving the flesh time to decay and deteriorate.

A Chinese tong that specialized in exhuming bodies, traveled from town to town, gathering bones for reburial, and carefully marking them with identification tags. When enough bones were accumulated in San Francisco, they were sent to Hong Kong, then on to China for reburial in the miner's original district or village.

Sackett's Gulch Mine, eight miles from La Porte, c. 1905-1910. At the turn of the century, Chinese miners wore ordinary hats or no hats at all, like their Caucasian counterparts. *Back, left to right:* Bill Hayes, Dan McDonnell, Milt Proseus, Jim Hayes, unknown Chinese miner, Bill Schwering, unknown Chinese miner. *Front:* George Hayes, Billie McKenzie, ?, ?, Jack Costello, and ?. Jann Garvis Collection.

Chinese gold scale used by the miners in You Bet, California. In China, this type of balance was used by money changers, gold-smiths, and silversmiths. Jerry Brady Collection.

Chapter Ten
ELDEST SON

Yee Ah Tye's eldest son favored spelling his last name together as one word, but like his father, Sam Ahtye's knowledge of both English and Chinese contributed to his success. In the spring of 1895, the La Porte townspeople anxiously followed a murder story in the *San Francisco Chronicle*; the newspaper arrived by stagecoach each day. Theodore Durrant had hacked a woman to death, then murdered her girlfriend whose body was discovered in the belfry of Emanuel Baptist Church.[1] LeRoy Post, then age five, remembered listening to Sam discuss the murder with other townspeople in La Porte and noticing that Sam had "no . . . accent not a bit when he spoke English . . . perfect."[2] Sam was, after all, a graduate of Queen's College in Hong Kong.

As a native Californian, Sam Ahtye registered to vote in 1896. When he was a twenty-five-year-old merchant in 1899, the tax description for his property included the Hop Sing lot, house, and store in La Porte's Chinatown; a mining claim at Secret Diggings; waterworks at La Porte; fur worth $100; groceries worth $1,200; and a piano worth $150.

Sam was a typical mining town merchant who bought the miners' gold as a convenience for them and to encourage them to spend money at his store. It was not always easy to gauge the worth of gold ore because it contained silver and other foreign minerals. However, a skillful old-time merchant could estimate the gold's value and sometimes tell from which creek the gold was mined.

After Sam had collected several thousand dollars' in gold, he sent it to the mint by horseback or stagecoach, and a messenger rode shotgun next to the strongbox. Merchants often grubstaked miners by providing them with supplies for a share of their profits.

Partnerships with Caucasians
Sam was co-owner of the Hop Sing Placer Mine with Charles W. Hendel, carrying on a business relationship which began with his father.[3] The two men were required to record proof that work had been performed on their claim in order to retain it. Chinese lessees worked the primary gravel and placer tailings deposited in the bed, bars, and banks of Slate Creek by building dams, wing-dams, ditches, and ground sluices. The gravel and tailings were worked and washed with rockers, prospect pans, and sluices.[4]

In 1897, Sam entered into a partnership with La Porte butcher, W. Canny, and photographer, G. H. Schubert. They claimed sixty acres of placer mining ground at the abandoned property formerly known as the Spanish Flat Placer Mine. That same year, Sam also placed a notice of water location to bring clear, spring drinking water from the reservoir above La Porte and the Marysville Wagon Road for the Hop Sing store and lodging houses.

Farmers Versus Miners
In the early days of placer mining, miners worked with a pick, shovel, pan, and rocker, and disturbed only moderate amounts of earth. Debris from such placer techniques polluted the streams for a short distance, but was soon deposited along the river's course.

However, when the easily accessible gravel in the beds of creeks and rivers was worked over, the gold was sought in the bowels of the earth with tunnels, quartz veins, shafts, and hydraulic claims. Hydraulic mining was a profitable technique, but the resulting debris pitted miners and Central Valley farmers against each other in a long-lasting conflict.

When the hydraulic miners were in full operation, hundreds of hoses were aimed against the ancient gravel beds, filling the streams with boulders, gravel, sand, and mud. This soon increased to enormous proportions. Heavy boulders lodged in canyons, gravel and sand were deposited in the

The Riffle Mine in Grass Flat, owned by Sam Ahtye, 1917-1924. *Far left:* An adit house was built at the mine's entrance; the miners' residence was in the upper story; a track for ore cars ran through the lower story. A snow shed sheltered the ore cars and tracks, permitting year-round operation. *Far right:* Testing and processing of gold was done in the dump house; debris was dumped at the track's end. Pam Kitley Collection.

small valleys of the mountains and foothills, and the finer silt was carried down the river channels, then into the San Francisco Bay and Pacific Ocean. This debris caused streams to overflow their banks, depositing silt on the valley farmlands. As the rivers became clogged, navigation was also hindered.

Hydraulic Mining Banned

By the late 1870s and early 1880s, the protests of farmers had increased in intensity. In 1884, a decree by Judge Lorenzo Sawyer of the United States Circuit Court banned the dumping of mining debris into waterways, thus making hydraulic mining illegal. Injunctions based upon this unpopular decision closed mine after mine.

Then in 1893, after studies by the Biggs Commission, federal legislation somewhat eased the decree with the imposition of the Caminetti Act. Under rigid rules and regulations that protected streams and rivers, some hydraulic mining could be approved.

In 1902, Sam Ahtye applied to the California Debris Commission to hydraulically mine the Secret Diggings Mine near La Porte. He planned to deposit tailings in worked-out pits that drained into Clark or Slate creeks.

Filing an application such as Ahtye's was no easy process. At least two inspections were necessary. The first, by the Debris Commission, applied to the dam site and resulted in permission to build. The second inspection came after construction of a restraining dam.

Several days' travel was often required to get to the widely scattered mines. Furthermore, snow, ice, and mud made many mines nearly inaccessible during winter and spring. Several weeks could elapse before an inspection was made and sometimes a whole season of mining would be lost. Mine owners thus had to submit their applications long before they were ready to build.

Many miners waiting for inspections and approval by the Debris Commission could ill afford the cost in both money and time. They secretly engaged in hydraulic mining or ground sluicing at night. Miners might turn their water on to mine at ten o'clock in the evening, then turn it off at four o'clock in the morning, in time for the muddy water to clear up and conceal the night's activities.

Sam was not above using this method. In 1905, the *Mountain Messenger* reported:

> *A Chinaman named Sam Ah Tye has been arrested by a deputy United States Marshal for illegal hydraulic mining at Scales in the northern part of the county.*[5]

The stoppage of hydraulic mining by court decrees in the early 1880s and by rigid legislation in the 1890s was a severe blow to Plumas and Sierra counties. With the resulting decline of gold production in the La Porte area, many Chinese miners moved to the valley to work on ranches and farms.

Plagued By Fires

Adding to the La Porte's woes was the constant threat of fire. Except for a few brick buildings on Main Street, the town was built of wood. A fire in 1900 destroyed many stores on Main Street, but failed to spread to China Alley. However, five years later, the La Porte Chinatown was not so fortunate.

In September 1905, the *Mountain Messenger* reported that a fire started in the Chinese quarters and, aided by a heavy wind, gained great headway. Few of the dwellings remained. The only business saved was a large brick and stone store owned by Rosenberg and Jones. The Chinese also lost heavily.

This was the seventh or eighth time that La Porte had been nearly or altogether destroyed by fire, but after each fire the townspeople rebuilt. A correspondent to the *Marysville Appeal* from La Porte reported that all the available carpenters and builders were employed, and that lumber and other building materials could not be secured fast enough to meet the demand. Immediately after the fire, Ed Metcalf restarted the sawmill in the Bernard Diggings, and every plank was taken as fast as it came from the saw. People were anxious to replace their buildings before winter.

Although much of the White sector of town was rebuilt, the 1905 fire was the death knell of La Porte's Chinatown. The only Chinese structure rebuilt was the Hop Sing store. Hop Sing and Company's stock of merchandise valued at $1,783 in 1896, declined to $650 in 1904. This was the year Sam Ahtye sold the Hop Sing store, cellar, hospital, lodging houses, woodshed, and barn to James Jones and Samuel Rosenberg of La Porte. Rosenberg also bought a half interest in the Sam Ahtye Waterworks.

According to LeRoy Post, many of the remaining Chinese miners who had managed to save about two thousand dollars, fulfilled their sojourners' wish of returning to China to die.

Sam's Return to Nevada County

After Sam Ahtye sold his holdings in La Porte, he tried his luck mining in Nevada County. Yee Ah Tye had overseen Hop Sing investments there in the 1870s, and paved the way for his son's return in 1910.

Knowledge of Sam's mining activities stems from the oral history of the Brady family, Irish miners from You Bet, California. Eight miles southeast of Nevada City, the name "You Bet" is said to have originated in 1857 from a favorite expression of Lazarus Beard, a saloon keeper from Kentucky. Beard built a small cabin and stocked it with the best liquor available. It became a popular gathering place and a little settlement grew around it.

Sam was known to be a very well-dressed, distinguished-looking gentleman. An anecdote told by Thomas W. Brady seemed to capture Sam's nature. One warm afternoon Ahtye looked for a shirt to put on for travel on the trail. One of his people said, "What do you put your shirt on for? It's warm out here; you don't need a shirt." Sam replied, "No, I might meet a lady; I'll wear my shirt."[6]

According to Jerry Brady, Sam Ahtye listened to miners talk about their successes and from these stories gained the keen ability to sift the "gravel from the gold." With hydraulic mining stymied by anti-debris laws, Ahtye turned to drift mining.[7]

In drift mining, a tunnel was run into the bank follow-

Advertisement for dynamite supplies.

ing the gold-bearing pay gravels. Black powder for blasting was purchased in twenty-five-pound kegs made of iron. Large quantities of the powder were placed in drifts that were then filled with dirt and packed down. Fuses running from the powder chambers were lighted, exploding the powder. This shattered and loosened the gravel, dirt, and rocks in the tunnel, making it easier to wash the paydirt down into the sluice boxes. Many miners were injured and killed by cave-ins in the gravel banks and tunnels.

Ahtye's Bonanza

Sam Ahtye's bonanza in gold took place around 1909 in the Brown's Hill area of You Bet. Ahtye leased land from a large land owner, Jerry Goodwin, and his silent partner, Nichols. Goodwin and Nichols had two groups of Chinese lessors, one in You Bet (under foreman Ah Sam) and another in nearby Red Dog (under Buck Sing). Each group was composed of about twenty to thirty-five Chinese.

Ahtye, head of both groups, had a relative who did some drift mining. After a few years, he ran into very rich ground and Ahtye took over. In the course of a short time, Ahtye sent nuggets and dust valued over $400,000 to the San Francisco Mint.

The continued receipts of gold of similar, high degree

Tong man in San Francisco wearing traditional apparel, closely followed by his body guard. Photograph by Arnold Genthe; California Historical Society.

of fineness from widely scattered areas led mint authorities to investigate. To the eye of an expert, raw gold has characteristics that reveal the origin to within a quarter to a half-mile distance, and Mint workers recognized that these gold shipments had originated from the same area.

Mint authorities concluded that Ahtye had feared losing his lease and had concealed the richness of his bonanza by distributing the gold among his fellow Chinese miners. In all probability, the bonanza yielded over $800,000. Seeing Ahtye's success, Goodwin canceled his lease then hydraulicked the same location. It was rumored that the area brought Goodwin an additional $200,000.

Ahtye's Last Stand

Around 1910, Sam Ahtye gained another lease from Jerry Goodwin in the You Bet diggings area. The shaft, the mill, and the superstructure for the hoist were already in place. Sam's Chinese crew went into the shaft about one hundred feet and tunneled out from that point. The gold was so thick that, whereas miners were accustomed to cleaning up the sluice boxes for amalgam and gold every one to two weeks, they were cleaning up every day.

The diggings yielded so much gold that the Chinese worked around the clock. Word got out fast. Once when a night shift was busy, an explosion ripped through the mine shaft. According to miners' lore, numerous Chinese workers were trapped and died in the tunnels. Knowing that White opposition would only get stronger and unwilling to sacrifice more men, Sam withdrew from the You Bet mining area and made San Francisco his permanent home.

The Brady family lived in the old Goodwin house for many years afterward. Chinese gold scales, and camp utensils such as a large metal wok, bowls, and spoons, were stored in the basement, ready for the miners' return. But no one ever retrieved them. However, even at a distance, Sam kept his finger in the mining pot; he owned the Riffle Mine from 1917 to 1924 in Grass Flat, about six miles from La Porte.[8]

San Francisco Fighting Tongs

The 1910 San Francisco Great Register listed Sam Ahtye as a thirty-nine-year-old Republican merchant living at 720 Jackson Street on the first floor.

Sam settled permanently in San Francisco at a time when the tongs enjoyed their greatest period of power. Unlike family district associations, tongs were secret organizations open to members of all clans and home districts. The tongs controlled gambling, prostitution, and drug trafficking within Chinatown and were often associated with criminal activities.

The Chinese Six Companies had been the real power in San Francisco's Chinatown until they were challenged by the fighting tongs in the 1890s.

Chinese Exclusion Acts

More than 40,000 Chinese immigrated to America in 1881, the year before the passage of the Chinese Exclusion Law. Only ten entered in 1887.

The exclusion of Chinese laborers was reaffirmed by another congressional act on September 13, 1888. Less than three weeks later, the Scott Act was passed. It barred the re-entry of Chinese laborers to the United States even if they left the country only temporarily. At that time, about 20,000 Chinese had gone home to China for visits. Even though they had re-entry permits, they were trapped outside the United States. Almost six hundred Chinese, on board ship on their return passage to America, were refused re-admission.

The Exclusion Law was so effective that American workers successfully pressured Congress into extending it for ten more years with the Geary Act of 1892. This act required all Chinese to obtain certificates of residence within the year and to carry a photo passport at all times. A Chinese could be stopped at any time and forced to show his certificate. If he could not produce it, he would be detained until someone could bring his

Residence certificate issued to the Chinese had to be carried at all times. Ah Tye Family Collection.

An alley in San Francisco's Chinatown, c. 1880. Photograph by Isaiah Taber; Carl Mautz Collection.

certificate or vouch for him. "America's first internal passport system," it suspended the Bill of Rights for Chinese who failed to comply.[9]

Feeling that the Geary Act was unconstitutional, the Chinese Six Companies advised the Chinese in America not to sign the registration documents and asked each to contribute one dollar to challenge its constitutionality. Sixty thousand dollars were raised to assemble a team of top constitutional scholars to abolish the law.

In a decision that surprised almost everyone, the Supreme Court found the Geary Act to be constitutional, and thousands of law-abiding Chinese were subject to deportation. The Six Companies had lost their prestige

and moral strength and suffered humiliation. Exploiting this opportunity, the tongs seized control of San Francisco's Chinatown during the early 1920s.

San Francisco's Chinatown Boundaries

The Chinese in San Francisco usually lived in Chinatown, whose boundaries were Dupont (Grant Avenue), Pacific, Stockton and California streets. If a Chinese ventured outside those lines, young thugs took delight in attacking him. Only those working for White households or engaging in necessary business ever dared to leave Chinatown.

Sam Ahtye was one of the few who broke through this invisible boundary. When he first moved outside of Chinatown to a home in the wealthy Pacific Heights area, people threw garbage at his house. He had initially bought the property by placing his attorney's name, Harry C. Symonds, on the title. In 1925, the home was legally deeded to Ahtye.

Ahtye's appearance also allowed him to move in and out of the boundaries of Chinatown. He dressed like any American businessman in the early 1900s, wearing a business suit, a white shirt with a crisply starched collar, and a necktie. He always had shiny shoes and wore a derby hat.

Sam was secretary of the Suey Sing tong, founded by his father, Yee Ah Tye, for the purpose of protecting merchants from the Sze Yup (fourth dialect) area. In the 1920s, illegal means of making money, such as opium smuggling, gambling, and commercial sex, flourished. The six tongs—the Suey Sings, Bing Kongs, Suey Dons, Sen Suey Yings, Jung Yings, and Hip Sings—often engaged in combat when their territories collided. With the Chinese confined to such close quarters in the Chinatown area, the friction was compounded.

Laundry Supply Store

Sam Ahtye served as secretary of the powerful Yee family of San Francisco and of the Chinese Laundry Owner's Association of California. Most of the San Francisco laundries in the early 1900s were owned by the Yee family. Owners kept overhead low, because a laundry required little capital and only a few simple pieces of equipment. Since laundry was picked up and delivered, the business's location was also unimportant.

When Carl Jung (who was later to marry Beulah

Ah Tye) was fifteen years old, he often visited a laundry supply store on Grant Avenue, near Sacramento Street. Sam Ahtye visited this laundry supply store several times a week. He was friendly to Jung and spoke to him in both English and the Cantonese fourth dialect.

Jung remembered that the laundry supply store was small, about twenty feet wide and less than one hundred feet long. Sacks of soap, rolls of vanilla paper (similar to butcher paper), and soda were stored in back with smaller laundry supply items in front. A clerk sat at the counter to take orders, and a manager oversaw the business. Four or five Yee men usually congregated at the store to chat.

A Typical Chinese Laundry

Jung recalled that a typical Yee laundry had one big electric washing machine. The bigger laundries had large cylindrical dryers, while the smaller laundries hung their clothes outside to dry. Some old-fashioned laundrymen dampened their clothes to be ironed by taking a mouthful of water then blowing onto the garments. Some of the more modern laundries used a brass cylinder with a reservoir inside with a tube that led to the top. The laundryman blew on the tube to create a spray of water.

Everything was ironed by hand. Tall cast-iron stoves were constantly fueled by wood or gas to keep the irons hot. When an iron resting on a stove top became hot, the laundryman used it. When the iron became cool, the laundryman returned it to the stove then grabbed another iron next to it. As many as a dozen irons would be resting on a stove ready for use.

Jung remembered when the Yees had a disagreement with another family association, and the conflict was carried into the streets. Anyone who was a Yee, whether he was a member of the family association or not, could be killed. All of the Yees had to go into hiding. To earn a living, some Yee laundrymen had to continue to collect dirty laundry to take back to the store to wash. Such an innocent occupation could sometimes prove fatal.

Money Squandered

Regarded as one of the most cultured Chinese in California, Sam was well-read, had modern tastes, and often bought tickets to legitimate San Francisco plays. However, there was a more egotistical side to Sam.

Sam's sister, Charlotte, said that after Yee Ah Tye's death, Sam was supposed to take care of his sisters and brother, but instead squandered the money on gambling, opium, and women. Ah Tye's wife, Chan Shee, wasn't the type of mother to create trouble between her

sons. After her husband's death, she set aside some gold bricks that were worth five to six hundred dollars each and sold a brick as needed to cover expenses.

Sam's daughter-in-law, Summi Ahtye, remembered him as a regular playboy. Before getting married, Sam went to Hong Kong and was a "hell raiser." By the time he was to return, he had gotten into so many scrapes that the Hong Kong police escorted him to the ship to make sure he would leave. Even after he was married, other Chinese and Caucasian women boldly telephoned Sam at his home.

Court Interpreter

Summi Ahtye said that Sam was an interpreter for the tongs. If someone was arrested, an attorney was hired, and Sam always served as the interpreter. The court interpreter prepared the tong witnesses to see that they testified as instructed. During the trial the interpreter occupied a seat next to the tong's attorney. By a system of signals to the witness, the interpreter indicated whether a question posed by the attorney should be answered "yes" or "no."

Tong men rarely testified in English. Testifying in Chinese gave the witness more time to form an answer and watch the interpreter for signals. The interpreter also obtained alibi witnesses when necessary, and prepared them for testimony.

Carl Jung remembered that all of the Yees looked to Sam Ahtye for advice and aid. Sam was well-qualified to handle everyday problems, such as robberies and laundry citations, because his experience as a court interpreter had acquainted him with most of the policemen, attorneys, judges, and courthouse workers. The importance of an interpreter was reflected in the price placed on his head during a tong war. The price for the death of an interpreter could be as high as $8,000, compared to $6,000 for the president and $250 for a common tong member.

Sam's grandson, Stanley, remembered that Sam rode in a limousine with two bodyguards. The limousine had two fold-down seats in the back where rifles and pistols were concealed.

Tong Gunmen

It was rare for a tong gunman to be killed. In times of trouble, the gunmen traveled together as a threesome when they pursued a victim. After they had shot their victim, they usually left their guns at the scene of the killing and fled in different directions. No evidence would then be found on the gunmen in the event of their arrest.

Members of San Francisco's Chinatown Squad break up an opium den with axes, crowbars, and sledgehammers. *Standing:* Sgt. Harry Walsh, George Hipley; *kneeling:* Tommy Hyland. San Francisco Public Library.

Chinatown reached a peak. The six powerful tongs were in the throes of a bloody war, and merchants and residents in Chinatown were concerned about its violence and dwindling population. Detective Sergeant Jack Manion was named head of the Chinatown police squad.

During his first day on duty, two men were killed by tong warfare. Manion captured two men, and charged them with the murders. A strong case presented in court convicted them; one was hanged, and the other died in San Quentin. This example of Manion's swift justice put fear in the tong men.

Manion's tactics would not pass today's legal scrutiny, but they proved effective. Tong officials were forced to sign a peace pact that, to Manion, meant "no more killings," or the tong officials who had signed the pact would be deported to China.[10]

During Manion's tenure, there were no more slave girls, no more extortion of businessmen, and no more opium. Lottery tickets were still sold in Chinatown, but the actual drawings were held outside the city. Peace prevailed in San Francisco's Chinatown, and the Chinese community came to respect and admire Manion. Originally appointed to the Chinatown squad for three months, Manion retired as its head after twenty-five years in 1946.

If arrested, no Chinese would testify against a gunman, unless he was a member of the opposing tong. Gunmen always tried to kill when no White men were present. If the gunmen were arrested fleeing from the scene of the killing, they would say they had been terrified and wanted to get out of the danger zone. With no one to prove the contrary in court, charges were eventually dismissed. When gunmen reported the killing of a victim, their telephone or telegram message told how many fish were caught, meaning how many opposing tong men had been killed. Some Chinese laundries used acid vats to process their laundry, and tong gunmen put bodies in the vats to destroy all evidence.

Sergeant Manion

On March 28, 1921, the terrorism in San Francisco's

Chan Shee, Yee Ah Tye's Widow

Chan Shee is remembered by her family with great affection. Dilly's daughter, Beulah, said that her grandmother liked to live with her large family because she felt needed. Chan Shee helped change diapers and feed her grandchildren. She liked to putter around the garden and grow vegetables.

Chan Shee raised many chickens in their big back yard and waited for them to grow bigger so she could cook them with bitter melon. "We were so terrible," recalled Beulah. "We'd eat apricots, and there would be little kernels in them like almonds. We were feeding the chickens those almonds, and those poor chickens died because they couldn't digest them. My poor grandmother . . . but she never disciplined us. We got spankings, because my father and mother believed in disciplining us. Mostly the boys [got spankings] more than the girls. And we'd put our hands around the waist of Grandmother and run around and around her; all she'd do was sigh and say in Chinese, 'You shouldn't be so naughty.'" Beulah said, "I think it hurt her more than it hurt us."[11]

Raymond Ah Tye remembered his grandmother as a very, very lovable person. "She kept her eye on us like a mother hen. When we were on the street playing outside, she would keep an eye on us . . . very protective. She told us stories, and if we scratched her back, she'd have candy for us. . . . When my father gave candy out, she would stick her hand out, too. That was funny. . . . She always wanted us to be gentlemen. She didn't want us to be boisterous or rough."[12]

Chan Shee was very healthy until she suffered a stroke; the last six months of her life were very difficult. She lived with Sam's family in San Francisco, where Mo-Mo Ahtye cared for her. Sidney Jr. was just three years old, but remembered his great-grandmother as an invalid. When Chan Shee wanted something, she rang a bell. Sidney Jr. pushed her wheelchair up and down the hall and carried her bell.

In 1926, Chan Shee died of chronic inflammation of the heart muscle at age eighty-five. Her funeral services were held at the Chinese Presbyterian Church on Stockton Street.

Salinas Chinatown

Opium was introduced into Chinese culture by British traders. Although illegal in China, the drug was allowed in the United States until 1906. Sam's Ahtye's addiction began in La Porte, where many Chinese miners smoked opium to relax at the end of the day.

The substance was not used by Chinese alone. It was an integral part of many American drugs such as laudanum, widely used by American women of European descent. Cocaine, heroin, and laudanum are all opium derivatives. It was so common that an 1896 Sears catalogue advertised opium for sale.

Manion's strict ban against opium in San Francisco was probably the cause for Sam's move to Salinas, California around 1922. It was the county seat of Monterey County, and Sam was listed as a Republican merchant. Much of what is known about Sam's years in Salinas' Chinatown is based on the recollections of Salinas native, Hughes Chin.[13]

Salinas' Chinatown was on Soledad Street, the block between Lake and Market streets. Soledad Street was like the vertical line of a "T," and Lake Street, where the Japanese lived, was the horizontal line of the "T." By the mid-1920s, the Chinese Exclusion Act had reduced the

Middle row, second from left: Sam Ahtye. Mr. & Mrs. Wallace Ahtye Jr.

Chinese population in America to 62,000, the lowest point since the early 1870s. Salinas' Chinatown reflected this reduction with only three or four Chinese families remaining.

Chin remembers about fifty to sixty Chinese bachelors in Salinas, many of whom never went back to China. If a person got into an argument with one of those bachelors, one of the nastiest questions one could ask was, "How many times have you been back to China?" The bachelor's inability to go back to China, even once, was very embarrassing; it was like cutting out his heart.

Sam's Opium Den

Sam Ahtye owned Salinas Chinatown's opium den, where many people met to socialize or smoke opium. It was a popular hangout for gambling house dealers at the end of an evening's work.

Sam's wife, Ko Shee, ran the opium den, weighing the drug and selling it. Opium is like tar—sticky and brownish-black in color. To sell it, Ko Shee took portions out of a jar, weighed it, put the opium in the center of an old playing card, folded the ends to make a container, then handed it to the customer.

Smoking opium was a tedious process, because the substance first had to be cooked. The smoker went to a bed and lay down alongside an oil lamp. He'd heat the point of a six-to seven-inch needle then dip it into his playing card, scooping up enough opium to make one pill. Then he'd hold the opium over a hole above the lamp flame and cook it.

One could actually see the opium bubble harden as it cooked. The smoker worked the opium on the smooth face of the opium bowl, heated and worked it again until it was cooked into a little ball the size of a pea. He'd place the pill into the opening of the bowl, then withdraw the needle.

The pipe with the pill was then held over the flame. The heat burned the opium, creating fumes. The smoker inhaled the fumes, experiencing a sense of euphoria and relaxation. The preparation of each opium pipe took about two or three minutes, the smoking about thirty seconds. Once the opium smoker became addicted, he had to have it; otherwise his muscles would hurt, and he would suffer withdrawal pains.

"There were many Chinese addicted to opium in the old days," said Chin. Chinese viewed opium smoking as a habit or craving that could not be helped. Chin likened it to the American habit of drinking several beers to unwind at the end of a day. After a while the American has a craving which he has to satisfy, just like the opium smoker. According to Chin, Chinese had a more harsh attitude toward drunkards, and felt that people who wanted to drink should know their limits and not get drunk. If a person constantly got intoxicated, others looked down on him. They would say, "Look, his parents never taught him better." To a Chinese, blaming parents made it doubly disgraceful.

Salinas Gambling Houses

There were about a dozen houses in Salinas' Chinatown, and five or six were gambling houses. Sam Ahtye's son, Wallace, and Hughes Chin's father, Bow Chin, opened a gambling house on Lake Street around 1926.

Gambling in Salinas in the 1920s and 1930s was illegal. Sometimes the gambling house had an "understanding" with the police, but most of the time the house would open and close depending upon circumstances and the tolerance of the policemen. For example, when the district attorney went on vacation, the gambling house opened. When the district attorney cracked down on gambling, it closed. "It was a haphazard living, but that's the way it was," said Chin. One in four Chinese depended on gambling for a living. It did not carry the stigma among the Chinese that it did in White society—it was a way to earn a living without a lot of sweat and bone-aching work.

Chinese men in an opium den. An opium pipe, cooking lamps, and other paraphernalia are laid out on a tray. California State Library.

These Chinese lottery tickets were from seven lottery houses, where the drawings were held every hour or half-hour. The selected characters were punched out. "Night" refers to the Longevity Night drawing that took place on the 10th, 20th, and 30th day of each month. The calligraphy originally composed an eighty-character Chinese poem, but eventually evolved into numbers for non-Chinese players. The game is now known as keno. See Appendix B for translation. Philip P. Choy.

Chinese considered gambling as a *wahng toy* business.[14] *Wahng toy* is the fairly large sum of money one wins in a gambling game, money earned outside of legal business or normal labor. Chinese considered it non-legal, rather than illegal. Many Chinese owners of legal businesses dabbled in gambling businesses as a sideline.

Most, but not all, of the gambling dealers came from China. In the 1920s, even a Chinese American with a good education had a hard time finding a job, so he'd often go into the gambling business. Jobs in Caucasian factories, restaurants, grocery stores, and government offices were not open to the Chinese until the 1930s.

Gambling house dealers made five dollars a day. It was a Chinese tradition for a business to feed its workers; besides their wages, gambling house workers got three meals a day. A good gambling house cook was important to keep the workers satisfied.

Games were the Chinese version of dominoes, fan tan, blackjack, stud poker, craps (a dice game), keno, and sometimes chuck-a-luck.[15] The gambling hall had tables scattered around a very large room. There were round tables for Chinese dominoes, and a fan tan table that was usually longer than it was wide. Players usually stood to play the games, except they would sit to play blackjack.

The gambling house made money on its commission—about five percent. The average bet was about twenty-five cents. In Chinese games the odds were absolutely even. The house's advantage was its commission. For example, if a person won ten dollars, fifty cents went to the house.

Luck and Charisma

Much of gambling depended upon the luck and charisma of its owners. Wallace and Bow Chin were once down to their last $1,000. A popular American fellow who owned the cigar store on Main Street bought a ticket, got the eight spot, and won the $1,000 limit. After deducting a commission of eleven percent, he won $890, which was a lot of money. The cigar store owner happily told people about the gambling house's good luck, and many of his friends became patrons. This started a business reversal for Bow Chin and Wallace and their place became the most popular in town.

Tong Membership

The success of this business caused much envy. Chinese were inclined to pick on one another, and a person who did not belong to a tong was easy prey.

At first, Bow Chin did not belong to a tong, so other tong members would harass him and be very difficult. Some tong members would lose at his gambling house then say, "We won ... you pay me off."

By joining the Suey Sing tong—the merchant group founded by Yee Ah Tye—Bow Chin gained greater strength and protection. Instead of facing an individual, the troublemakers faced a whole tong, so they didn't dare pick on him.

There was an understanding that if the Suey Sing tong had four gambling houses, the Bing Kong tong would also have four. Suey Sing gambling houses were the most successful in Salinas. They had about twenty workers for each house, a total of around one hundred employees.

Gambling House Lookout

The agricultural field workers in Salinas in the late 1920s were mostly bachelor Filipinos, also regular gamblers. As a teen-ager, Hughes Chin was a lookout at the gambling house's heavy main door, which slammed loudly on closing to intimidate the few mischievous individuals who wanted to create trouble. When Chin recognized his regular customers, the Chinese and Filipino bachelors, he'd let them in. However, if Chin saw a police raiding party, he used an alarm device. A fly swatter hung on a nail in front of a little button that Chin pressed if the police were coming. The button sent an alarm, and he would pull out the nail so no one could find the buzzer.

Chin remembered mornings when nothing was going on in his father's gambling house, and the dealers talked among themselves. The two topics most commonly discussed were women and food, especially the latter. They reminisced about the food they had eaten when they lived in China—how it was cooked a certain way, if it were purchased locally or elsewhere. In those days, people didn't travel much, so Chin surmised that their knowledge of homeland food was acquired from reading or hearsay.

Legalistic Mind

Hughes Chin feels that if Sam Ahtye were alive today, he would be a very fine lawyer. But then, Sam didn't stand a Chinaman's chance of becoming one. Sam read a lot about law and had a very legalistic mind. "He even had the tall, lean, and incisive look of a good lawyer," said Chin.

When Hughes' father, Bow Chin, had trouble with a landlord, Sam told Bow what to tell his lawyer in order to win in court. The case involved a building that was located several blocks from Main Street. Bow Chin had helped to pay for remodeling the building, but the owner claimed sole ownership and wanted to evict him. The owner of Tynam Lumber Company appeared on the stand as a material witness for the defense. When the owner referred to notes in a little black book to refresh his memory, Bow Chin's lawyers reached over and took the book as material evidence. The owner's face turned several colors, because the book proved that he wasn't telling the truth. The black book provided evidence that Bow Chin was a partner in the remodeling costs, and he won the case.

Hughes Chin remembered another incident that demonstrated Sam's incisive mind. People in one gambling house would use the toilet and spit on the floor. Chin was in the process of writing a sign in English, "No spitting." Sam saw the sign and said, "That's not the way to say it. You should say, 'Don't expectorate.'" Hughes did as Sam suggested then thought later, "God, how many people know what 'expectorate' means?"

Suicide

Hughes Chin was a shoeshine boy in Chinatown when he saw Sam Ahtye, age fifty-eight, the day before his death, running around in his pajamas covered over by his coat. He was apparently settling all of his debts in the best of Chinese tradition before leaving this world.

The *Salinas Index Journal* reported that officials believed Sam had contemplated suicide for some time. The week before, Sam had deeded a lot at Soledad and Sausal streets to his son and daughter-in-law, Wallace and Lily, "in consideration of love and affection."[16] At the time of Sam's suicide, his wife, Ko Shee, had gone for a visit to San Francisco. No one heard the shot that ended his life.

Sam wrote a death note saying that his thirty-eight-year opium habit had been his dread, and that he had no one to blame but himself. Sam sent a bullet through his temple in his living quarters at 41 Soledad Street. His body, clad in underwear and lying on the floor near his bed, was found by his son, Wallace. His note expressed "love to my dear wife and all" and urged them "not to take it too hard."

Chin had heard a rumor that Sam had a disagreement with some Suey Sing tong members. Sam had been the perennial English secretary of the Suey Sing Association and was the foreign contact for all transactions that involved English. There was intense competition for the position, and one year someone else was

Ko Shee, Sam Ahtye's American-born wife, ran his opium den in Salinas Chinatown. Mr. & Mrs. Wallace Ahtye Jr.

elected. Feeling that he wasn't given proper consideration, Sam was shamed, slighted, and had lost face.

Surviving were his widow, Ko Shee; their three sons Sidney, Wallace, and Allen Ahtye; and daughter, Dr. Alice Ahtye.

Ko Shee—Sam's Wife

Hughes Chin remembered that "Ko Shee was kind of old Chinese, dignified." Although she worked in her husband's opium den, she observed a certain propriety.

In 1927, there was a carnival in Salinas. Ko Shee had never been to one and asked Chin to accompany her. Her feet had been bound, and she had difficulty walking. They bought hot dogs, and as they were about to munch on them, Ko Shee said in Chinese, "How are we going to eat them?" "It was kind of embarrassing and undignified for her to eat a hot dog wrapped in paper

while strolling amongst the strangers," thought Chin.

Although Sam had moved to Salinas, he kept his Pacific Heights home in San Francisco for his family. Sam's daughter-in-law, Summi, recalled that Ko Shee didn't want her children to mix with ordinary Chinese, so she sent them to Catholic schools. Her only daughter, Alice, was one of the earliest Chinese women dentists in San Francisco's Chinatown, with an office above the Chinese opera house (Mandarin Theater) on Grant Avenue.[17]

Always protective of Alice, Ko Shee sent Summi to accompany her when she had an evening appointment. Ko Shee was so protective that she didn't want Alice to marry. In her later years, Ko Shee lost all but one tooth, but refused to let Alice extract it and make dentures.[18]

Sidney Ahtye Jr. later recalled that all of the women in Sam's family lived in San Francisco, because Salinas was considered a frontier town. There were two flats on 2406 Washington Street. Ko Shee, Mo-Mo, and Alice lived in the upstairs flat, and Allen and Summi (Alice) Ahtye lived with their children, Conrad and Roberta, in the downstairs flat.

Sidney Jr. remembered the dinners cooked by his mother, Mo-Mo, and the eight or nine family members sitting around a large dining room table. Ko Shee sat at the head, with Sidney Jr. on her right. No one picked up chopsticks or ate anything until Ko Shee sat down. She placed food on Sidney Jr.'s plate, because he was the oldest grandson, then she took some for herself before the others could begin eating.

Ko Shee attended Chinese operas every chance she could. Sidney Jr. said, "We lived on the streetcar line on Washington Street, and everybody knew her so well that the streetcar stopped almost in the middle of the street to let her get on. She'd go downtown and walk to the Chinese theater." Ko Shee always had the same seats in the box section. There were only two seats in the back, and she bought the other seat so no one would sit next to her.

In 1939, Ko Shee died of a cerebral hemorrhage at age sixty-four. After she passed away, Sidney Jr. said that for a long time no one would buy the Chinese opera seats that had been hers.[19]

Portrait of Charlotte Ah Tye in her Chinese wedding gown. Ah Tye Family Collection.

Chapter Eleven
A CHINESE DIPLOMAT'S WIFE

On March 14, 1897, in San Francisco, Yee Ah Tye's third daughter, Charlotte (age twenty-two), married Hong Yen Chang (age thirty-seven) in a Christian ceremony.

Chinese Educational Mission

Charlotte's new husband came to the United States under a program called the Chinese Educational Mission. Its originator, Yung Wing, was the first Chinese to be educated at a major American university, graduating from Yale in 1854. This project fulfilled his life-long desire to help reform and regenerate China.[1] The plan was to educate 120 young Chinese boys in the United States for Chinese government service and the Imperial government paid all expenses. They would acquire technological knowledge of the West, and it was hoped this would help China resist foreign aggression in the future. It would also give China a growing body of trained engineers to build railroads, erect telegraph lines, construct warships, and manufacture guns and ammunition.

In the summer of 1872, the first group of thirty students started on their journey to the United States. Charlotte Ah Tye's future husband, thirteen-year-old Hong Yen Chang (Kang-jen Chang), was among them. His merchant father, Chang Shing Tung, had died when Hong Yen was only ten. His mother was Yee Shee. Hong Yen came from Yung Wing's district, Heungshan (Chungshan or Zhongshan), a district adjoining the Portuguese port of Macao.

Upon arriving in the United States, Chang lived with the Guy B. Day family in Bridgeport, Connecticut, to learn English and American customs more quickly. Once these skills were mastered, Chang and fellow classmate, Mun Yew Chung (Wenyao Zhong) attended the Hartford Public High School in Connecticut and boarded with William B. and Virginia (Thrall) Smith.[2]

At first the boys were required to wear the traditional long gowns of Chinese scholars and braided queues. But this attire gave rise to unmerciful teasing because they looked like girls. After many fights, the Chinese dresses gave way to American coats and pants. The boys either hid their queues under their coats or coiled them around their heads.

From 1878 to 1879, Hong Yen Chang was enrolled in a college preparatory program at the exclusive Phillips Academy in Andover, Massachusetts. He completed his studies in the classical department and graduated from Phillips in 1879.[3] Hong Yen showed unusual intelligence and gave an English oration at his 1879 commencement exercises.

Since the primary goal of the program was to educate Chinese students to return for government service, it was important that the students maintain their studies in Chinese language and Confucian classics. These courses were provided at the permanent headquarters in Hartford, Connecticut, in a large, double, three-story house spacious enough to accommodate Yung Wing and his co-commissioner, teachers, and seventy-five students. The facilities included a schoolroom where Chinese studies were taught exclusively, a dining room, a double kitchen, dormitories, and bathrooms. Pupils were divided into classes of twelve, and each class stayed at the Mission House for two weeks every three months. They rose at six a.m., retired at nine p.m., and between those hours, took Chinese instruction in reading, calligraphy, recitation, and composition.

Educational Mission's End

The last group of Chinese students arrived in the United States in 1875, and the program continued to go well for six more years. Arriving in America at the impressionable ages of twelve to sixteen, the Chinese boys quickly became Americanized. Indeed, it became increasingly difficult to keep them focused on their Chinese studies.

The first Chinese Educational Mission boys, photographed just after their arrival in America. *Left to right:* Yung-Kwang Kwong, Ting-lang Ho, Hong Yen Chang (Charlotte's future husband), Yu-Tchu Su, Kowh-On Tong, and King-hoon Kwong. Connecticut Historical Society.

Program of Phillips Academy commencement, June 17, 1879. Hong Yen Chang gave an English oration, "The Influence of Greece Beyond Greece." Phillips Academy.

Ἀπὸ Πείρας Πάντα.   En Rapport.

ORDER OF EXERCISES

AT

EXHIBITION:

PHILLIPS ACADEMY,

ANDOVER, MASS.

JUNE 17, 1879.

ANDOVER:

CLASS OF '79.

5

14. ENGLISH ORATION. — (of Salutatorian Rank). The Comparative Importance of English and Classical Studies.
    HENRY FAIRBANK, - - - - - *Ahmednugger, India.*

15. CLASS ORATION. — War and Arbitration.
    EDWARD STEVENS BEACH, - - - - - *Worcester.*

Music.

16. ENGLISH ORATION.† — American Interest in Archaeology.
    HENRY CORWITH ROSS,* - - - - - *Galena, Ill.*

17 ENGLISH ORATION.† — The Value of a Scientific Education to the Orator.
    HENRY WILLARD TAYLOR,* - - - *Portland, Me.*

18. ENGLISH ORATION.—(of Valedictorian Rank). Conditions of Success in Study.
    EDWARD WILDER BOUTWELL,* - - - - *Andover.*

19. ENGLISH ORATION. — The Influence of Greece beyond Greece.
    HONG YEN CHANG, - - - - - *Haing Shan, China.*

20. ENGLISH ORATION. — The Army Bill.
    HUGH REID BELKNAP,* - - - - - *Keokuk, Iowa.*

21. ENGLISH ORATION.—The Effect of the New England Factory System on New England Character.
    FRANCIS JOHNSON PHELPS, - - - - - *Andover.*

Students in the graduation class of 1879 wore garments of stiff brocaded satin, thick-soled and padded slippers, and round satin caps. Phillips Academy.

Yung Wing favored this complete break with Chinese culture because he felt it was the only way the youths would be able to overcome the difficulties of introducing Western technology and machinery into the hostile Chinese government environment. However, the increasing neglect of the students' Chinese education proved to be a major factor in the premature end of the Educational Mission. Attendance at Sunday school and church services, play, and athletic games produced Chinese boys far too Westernized for many conservative Chinese leaders.

Yung Wing's "ardent championing of westernization" on a personal level was also a factor in the mission's premature end.[4] He had converted to Christianity and in 1852 became an American citizen. In 1875, he took another step toward Americanization when he married Louise Kellogg, the daughter of one of Hartford's leading physicians. His marriage was personally very happy, but it furthered conservative Chinese statesmen's suspicions and opposition.

In the climate of growing anti-Chinese sentiment in Washington, D.C., the State Department refused to admit qualified Chinese Educational Mission students to the Military Academy at West Point and the Naval

Academy in Annapolis. This affront moved the Chinese conservatives to recall the government-sponsored students under the pretext of protecting them from being "contaminated" by American ideas.

The Chinese Educational Mission lasted from 1872 to 1881—five years short of its goal. The recall came at a disastrous time for the students, since they were only half prepared to carry out their goal. More than sixty students were enrolled in colleges and technical schools, but the majority of them were just beginning their technical training.

The students eventually proved themselves in the fields of science and technology, but only after years of discouragement and always under the handicap of insufficient training. Some became leaders in establishing modern Chinese communications through the development of railroads, telegraph lines, and coal mines, as hoped. Others became China's first modern-trained army and navy officers or consulars and diplomats.

Chang's Return to America

Hong Yen Chang was one of the few Chinese Educational Mission students who did not remain in China, returning instead to America on his own to complete his education. Chang had been studying at Yale College (now Yale University) since 1879, when the Chinese government recalled the Educational Mission students in 1881.

The *Hartford Daily Courant* reported that Chang was "very much disappointed and chagrined at not being able to complete his studies. He went, however, with the determination that he would return [to America] as soon as practicable to resume his course."[5]

Upon Chang's return to China, Chang was placed in the naval school at Tientsin (Tienjin). When the students first returned, their Western training and attitude was so markedly different from the old-style, Confucian-trained officials, they were treated with hostility and looked upon as only a little above coolies.

The *Hartford Daily Courant* reported that Chang soon grew tired of the monotony of the naval school and obtained a release. He visited his aging mother, but only to say farewell for a second time. With the help of friends and his small savings, he reached Shanghai, then in 1882, sailed for Honolulu where his brother was a merchant.[6] He read law in the office of A. S. Hartwell for a year, and "showed himself so apt a student that at the end of the year he was offered a salary of $1,200 to remain. He was anxious to become better educated in law, however, and so returned to the United States."[7] Chang went to New York in 1883, and managed to

NOT ELIGIBLE.

A Mongolian Refused Admission to the Bar.

Yesterday was Chinese day in the Supreme Court. There were but two decisions handed down and both affected the rights of Chinese.

In the case of Hong Yen Chang, the young Mongolian who applied for admission to the California bar, the court denied the application. The decision recites the facts of the case, quotes the naturalization laws, which limit the right of naturalization to aliens who are white persons and to aliens of African nativity and to persons of African descent, cites the cases of Ah Yup and of Look Tui Sing, both in the Federal courts and in both of which the right of a Mongolian to naturalization was denied, and then concludes:

Only those who are citizens of the United States, or who have bona fide declared their intention to become such in the manner provided by law (and we hold that they shall be persons eligible to become such as well as to have declared their intention), are entitled to be admitted to practice as attorneys and counselors of this court on presentation of license to practice in the highest court of a sister State. * * * Holding, as we do, that the applicant is not a citizen of the United States and is not eligible to become such, the motion must be denied.

It is understood that Hong Yen Chang will ap-

Newspapers documented the story of Hong Yen Chang's ordeal.
Right: Hong Yen Chan. c. 1890.

enter Columbia Law School without his Yale undergraduate degree. He obtained his law degree in 1886.

First Chinese Lawyer in America

A newspaper article reported that Hong Yen Chang was the first Chinese lawyer educated in America. Known also as Henry Chang, he received his diploma among 108 Americans at the 1886 Columbia Law School commencement. The article described Hong Yen as "taller than the majority of his race" and "unusually intelligent in his looks." His "abilities in legal investigation" were among the finest in his class, and he had excelled in special branches of the law.

Chang had been in America for sixteen years and was said to be extremely fond of it. During the rule of the foreign Ching (Qing or Manchu) Dynasty from 1644 to 1911, the queue was imposed upon Chinese men. It was the emblem of obedience and loyalty to the Manchu regime; those who refused to wear one were severely penalized. If a man wanted the option of visiting or returning to China, it was important to have a well-kept queue because of its significance socially and politically. After finishing law school in 1886, Hong Yen Chang cut off his queue.

Chinese Exclusion Act's Effects

The brutal effects of the 1882 Chinese Exclusion Act dashed Hong Yen's hopes of being admitted to the New York bar with the rest of his classmates. Citizenship was required, but was forbidden to the Chinese under the 1882 act.

A well-known judge became interested in Chang's plight and succeeded in passing a special bill in the New York legislature that removed the disability in Chang's case. Hong Yen drafted the bill and argued in support of it before New York Governor David Hill in April 1887.

The solution was to naturalize Chang as a United States citizen in the Court of Common Pleas in New York City on November 11, 1887, then admit him to practice law in the state of New York on May 17, 1888. On June 12, 1889, he obtained a certificate of passport describing him as an American citizen. The document was signed by Secretary of State James G. Blaine.

Chang then went West to California, where he planned to serve the large Chinese community of San Francisco as a lawyer. In 1890, he went before the California court and made a motion to practice law. He had to meet two conditions under California civil code: 1) he could present a license to practice law in the highest court of another state; and 2) he was a United States citizen or was eligible and intended to become a citizen.

Chang presented his New York license and his certificate of naturalization to the California court. However, the court refused to give him permission to practice law, despite the fact that he had met both criteria.

Naturalization of Chinese Forbidden

Under United States statutes, the naturalization of aliens was limited to free White people and those of African nativity and descent. In addition, a California act passed on May 18, 1882, expressly forbade the naturalization of a "Chinaman."[8] It was on the basis of this act that the court ruled that Chang's certificate of naturalization had been issued "without authority of the law" and was therefore invalid.[9]

Chang took his plea all the way to the California Supreme Court. His case was widely reported in the San Francisco newspapers. A headline in the May 18, 1890, edition of the San Francisco Examiner read: "Chinese Cannot Practice; Chang Not an Attorney, Though (Secretary of State) Blaine Says He Is a Citizen."[10]

The San Francisco Morning Call announced "A Mongolian Refused Admission to the Bar." It pointed out that in an earlier case, a lawyer who had been disbarred in New York applied for admission to the California Bar. When his California application was denied, he immediately went to Nevada, was admitted to that state's bar, then returned to California at once and reapplied for admission. In admitting him, the California court said it

had no power to inquire behind the genuine certificate of the highest court of a sister state. It reached a different result in Chang's case, however, where there had been no prior disbarment, but the applicant was Chinese.

Despite the devastating setback, Chang went on to a very successful and distinguished career in banking and diplomacy. He served as an adviser at the Chinese Consulate in San Francisco from 1888 to 1895.

By 1900, the United States census listed Chang as a banker for the Yokohama Species Bank of Japan in San Francisco.[11] Hong Yen and Charlotte were then renting a home on Stone Street, a tiny alley below Powell. Charlotte's widowed mother, younger sisters, and brother lived on nearby Washington Street.

Republic of China—1912

Hong Yen Chang quit his banking job in San Francisco in 1907, and returned to China at the end of the Ching (Qing or Manchu) dynasty. China was economically and politically unstable internally, and had suffered under foreign pressures from unequal treaties externally. Because of his past experience, Chang was appointed to deal with foreign interests in China.

In 1907, he became the accountant-general to the Shanghai branch treasury. Silver was the official medium of exchange at the time, and he received a monthly salary of 200 taels (ounces) in silver with an additional 100 taels for administrative and living expenses.[12]

Chang was appointed to a chair at Nanking Government University to lecture on international law and

Back row, second from left: Hong Yen Chang, wearing a bowler hat, was photographed with other high-ranking officials c. 1910 when he served as Accountant-General to the Shanghai branch treasury. It was unusual to see Chinese dressed in Western suits together with those in traditional attire. The official's imperial status was identified by an embroidered insignia badge displayed on the chest and back of a three-quarter-length dark coat called a pufu. Chang Family Collection.

banking in 1909 for a monthly salary of 100 taels of silver. His knowledge of English and his legal training qualified him to write and negotiate foreign contracts.

During his travels, Chang frequently sent postcards to his children Ora and Oliver. On board the S.S. *Korea*, he wrote:

About half way to Honolulu July 11, 1907
Am writing in my bunk. There's an electric bulb over my left shoulder. Am using the postal taken off a bill of fare as the writing pads are in the trunk and this cubby hole of a cabin is too small for the trunk. We've opened (illegible) to save the postals for Ora and Oliver. There will be many more cards to be had since at every meal a different menu card with postal (card) attached is provided. Every table has three or four (postal cards). If I am prompt at meal times, I can get one. I have not missed a meal so far because there has been no rough sea, though white caps can be seen on every side. The ship is so large that it is quite steady. The first night was a restless one for me. I took a cold sea water bath at six o'clock. The bath room is a short way's back on same deck. I had on my trousers and overcoat. I saw no one except the servants at the time.[13]

In 1908, Hong Yen Chang was transferred from the University of Nanking to the Chinese diplomatic corps in Washington, D.C. where he served until 1910. As a member of the Chinese legation, Chang wrote this picture postcard to his son:

12/20/08
Dear boy—
This is the picture of the White House where the President lives. In the spring during Easter, children from all over the city roll eggs on the lawn and frolic there to their hearts content. How would you like to do that? I don't think you would like to stay with papa in the Embassy because there are no young ones in it. Be good.

Love from Papa

Chang was the Chinese consul in Vancouver, British Columbia from 1910 to 1913, where one of his duties was to protect the Chinese commercial interests. While there, the Chinese government awarded him a third government degree, comparable to today's doctorate of law.

The Chinese in foreign countries were instrumental in founding the Chinese Republic by helping Sun Yat-sen overthrow the Ching (Qing or Manchu) emperors in 1911. In 1895, Sun took part in an unsuccessful rebellion and he was forced to flee China to avoid arrest. He spent the next sixteen years in Chinese communities in the United States, Japan, and Europe, gaining support for his plan for revolution.

During Sun Yat-sen's exile in Japan, Yee Ah Tye's eldest daugh-

Dr Chang Kang Jen and Party at PRINCE RUPERT. B.C

The above is translated from a cipher cable message received this day from Peking, which translated into English as follow:
You are promoted Consul General to Panama; Chang Hong Yen appointed Consul at Vancouver. Please urge Chang to take office as soon as possible in order that you might proceed to Panama. Lin. Jan.22.

Received at Vancouver, Jan.22, 1910.

A cipher cable message from Peking (Beijing), January 22, 1910, was translated into English announcing Hong Yen Chang's appointment as Consul at Vancouver, Canada. *Fourth from left, wearing cap:* Hong Yen Chang; *fourth from right:* Charlotte, with a party on board ship in Prince Rupert, British Columbia. Chang Family Collection.

ter, Emma, and her husband, Koa Cheong, like so many overseas Chinese, befriended him. It was hoped that Sun's cause would create a new, strong China that would improve the treatment of overseas Chinese. Sun Yat-sen and his wife became close friends, and the Cheongs named them godparents of their adopted daughter, Alice.

The Republic of China was founded in 1912, and Sun Yat-sen became its first president. Under the new government, Chang served as first secretary at the Chinese Legation in Washington, D.C. from March to November 1913. The 1914 *Washington Social Register* listed him under the Chinese Office of Legation as "First Secretary and Charge d'Affaires."[14] Now, thirty years after his first studies in America were cut short, Yale conferred an undergraduate degree upon Chang with enrollment in the class of 1883.

mats, in their brilliant state uniforms, excited the attention of another throng almost as large in size.[15]

The newspaper described the nation's dignitaries, envoys of foreign courts, jurists, legislators, warriors, and social leaders "bedecked with flashing jewels, gold lace

San Francisco's Chinatown printed two million dollars in special currency to finance the revolution and the establishment of the present Republic of China.

White House Wedding
On November 26, 1913, the *Washington Post*'s front-page headline read, "Nations of All the World Do Homage to White House Bride As She Takes Solemn Vows Amid Scenes of Unequaled Splendor."

The *Post* devoted seven out of twenty-two of its pages to the wedding that united President Woodrow Wilson's second daughter, Jessie, to lawyer Francis B. Sayre. When Jessie Wilson became the thirteenth bride at the White House, Hong Yen Chang, charge d'affaires of the Chinese legation, and his wife, Charlotte, were among the honored guests.

Diplomats Arrive
More than 5,000 people crowded near the White House to watch the guests arrive. The *Post* described the scene:

The crowd that gathered to witness some of the side-lights of the biggest social event of a half dozen years was somewhat cosmopolitan in its make-up. Handsomely dressed members of the fair sex, who predominated, gave the throng a distinguished tone. . . . Men, women, and children of all ages, and from every station of life, were represented in the groups that were banked on the sidewalks. The greater part of the crowd picked out vantage points directly in front of the east front of the mansion, and watched intently as the equipages rolled up one after another and their occupants alighted. At the southwestern gate, the diplo-

and shining swords," combining to make "a fairyland picture unequaled in White House Annals."

Charlotte Chang wore a black-velvet calling costume and a black-velvet hat trimmed with plumes. Hong Yen Chang found himself in a predicament when it was announced that diplomats must wear a uniform. As the *Post* explained:

The new (Chinese) republic has green and gold state uniforms, but the representative in this country (Chang) has not yet received his. So the Chinese legation, which, in former years at such affairs, was represented by an envoy clad in a brilliant, silk embroidered robe, was represented yesterday by Mr. Chang in an American frock coat and striped trousers, forming something of a contrast to the gold lace uniforms of the other diplomats.[16]

Charlotte Ah Tye Chang was born in La Porte in 1875 and grew up in a time when Chinese girls were allowed to attend Christian church schools only through grammar school. Her description of the wedding was printed on the second page of the *Post* with the heading "Gowns Worn at Ceremony as Seen by Oriental Eyes."[17]

From 1916 to 1917, Hong Yen Chang was the director of Chinese naval students in the United States at Berkeley, California. He retired, then, after an illness of two and a half years, died of a heart attack at age sixty-six on August 4, 1926.

Dragon parade during the Bok Kai Festival in Marysville, late 1800s.

Chapter Twelve
YOUNGEST DAUGHTERS

On March 3, 1897, Marysville's Chinatown was preparing its annual parade and Bomb Day festivities. The *Marysville Daily Appeal* reported that the dragon parade would take place on the principal streets in the afternoon, and the shooting of bombs for prizes would be at four p.m. near the city pound. The Chinese considered it lucky to win a prize, believing it would keep sickness from their doors and bring good fortune.

Many were disappointed by the announcement that there would be no fireworks in the evening. Unable to get new varieties, the Chinese organizers were not satisfied with repeating the types and order of their fireworks from the previous year. The local newspaper reported, "With the exception of sky rockets and firecrackers, no entertainment will be furnished 'Melican man' in the evening."

The Ah Tye family arrived in Marysville from La Porte via stagecoach. The roads had been constructed with picks, shovels, and wheelbarrows, and travel was dusty, rocky, and hot. The journey from La Porte to Marysville took about twelve hours, and the horses were changed at several stops.[1]

A Very Americanized Family
A newspaper article on the Ah Tye family showed how uniquely Americanized they had become. Chan Shee, along with her daughters Charlotte, Alice, and Bessie and son, Dilly, arrived from La Porte in the evening of March third and planned to transfer to a train bound for San Francisco the next morning. They stayed overnight at the New Western Hotel, which advertised its first-class accommodations at rates from one to two dollars per day. The hotel was remodeled and newly furnished, with large, elegant "sample rooms," where merchandise was displayed for sale. Free transportation was provided to and from all trains.

The same Marysville newspaper that described the Bomb Day festivities also found the Ah Tye family's overnight stay a notable item:

THE AH TYE GIRLS—They Entertained Several Visitors at the Western Hotel Misses Alice, Bessie and Charlotte Ah Tye, the daughters of the rich Chinese merchant who died about a year ago in La Porte, arrived in this city this evening accompanied by their mother and brother Dilly, en route for San Francisco. The girls are highly accomplished. They were for several years pupils of Miss Mussey, daughter of Dr. Mussey, of La Porte. . . . Alice . . . is not only a vocalist, but plays exceptionally well on the piano. Charlotte . . . has a sweet, well cultivated voice and has educated her youngest brother, who speaks English fluently. The girls were found seated in the parlors of the Western Hotel last evening and with a little pressing consented to sing for some ladies present. The selection they chose was "An Evening Prayer to the Virgin." It was faultlessly rendered.[2]

As was the Chinese custom, Chan Shee, and her eldest daughters, Emma and Annie, stayed sheltered at home during most of their early years in La Porte. However, by the 1890s, the Ah Tyes had become such an integral part of La Porte that the younger children, Alice, Bessie, and Dilly, had many American friends. Like their Caucasian counterparts, they were all second-generation Americans.

Caucasian Friends
Claire Cayot O'Rourke remembered that as young girls, she and Bessie Ah Tye would often visit each other. At Bessie's home, Claire was led through the Hop Sing store to the Ah Tye family living quarters. She recalled Yee Ah Tye as a tall Chinese man with a queue wrapped around his head. He usually stood behind the Hop Sing store's counter to the right of the entrance.

Series of photographs of Alice Ah Tye is signed, *For Mrs. Mussey With love from Alice.* Chang Family Collection.

Along the sides of the dimly lit store Chinese men socialized—sitting, talking and eating. A hallway led to little rooms furnished with cots for opium smokers. Further down the hallway were the family's living room and sleeping quarters.

Mary Schwegler often rode a stage from Howland Flat to La Porte to visit her sister, Annie, who cared for store owner Jimmy Jones' children. "The Ah Tyes were good friends of the Jones family" and went to the Jones' house for dinner, remembered Mrs. Schwegler.[3] The Ah Tye girls were also frequent visitors of Dr. and Mrs. Mussey's home, and the Mussey's eldest daughter, Alice, was their piano teacher.

Alice's Early Death

By 1900, the United States Census listed Yee Ah Tye's widow, Chan Shee (age sixty), as a resident of San Francisco's Chinatown living with her youngest children, Alice (age twenty-one), Bessie (age seventeen) and Dilly (age sixteen).

In the summer of 1900, the *San Francisco Evening Post* reported the death of Yee Ah Tye's fifth child, Alice. Her death cut "short the promising career of one of the most prominent young Chinese women" in San Francisco. The newspaper article explained that the fortune "Old" Ah Tye had made "enabled him to afford his children every opportunity for securing an English education." It was his ambition to place his children on an intellectual footing with the American children they had grown up with in La Porte.

After she graduated from the public schools of Plumas County, Alice's family moved to San Francisco "in order that she might perfect herself in the higher branches of study."[4] Having done this, she graduated from Heald Business College, then turned her attention

Alice and Bessie's photograph was taken in their La Porte home by Plumas County surveyor, Charles W. Hendel, c. 1900. Their living room shows an interesting blend of Chinese and American furniture and decor. California State Library.

to music. At the time of her death, Alice was a pupil of Professor Fleissner, a well-known organist.

The article explained that heart failure was hereditary in the family, and Alice's sudden death was no surprise to her immediate relatives. Mo-Mo Ahtye remembered that Yee Ah Tye knew of Alice's weak heart and predicted that she would die young.

East is East . . .

Perhaps a broken heart also hastened Alice's early demise. According to LeRoy Post, Alice and Bessie were good friends with Dolly Trescott, the daughter of a mining cook in La Porte. Dolly moved from La Porte to San Francisco just before her marriage to a Chinese man.

LeRoy said that in the early 1900s, it was unusual for a Caucasian to marry a Chinese.

According to oral history, Alice had met a Caucasian in school, and they had fallen in love. Alice traveled from San Francisco to La Porte to seek approval for her marriage from her eldest brother, Sam. But Sam totally disapproved of her marrying a Caucasian, believing that "East is east and West is west, and never shall the two meet."[5]

Funeral services for Alice were held at the Ah Tye home. She had been prominently identified with Chinese mission work at the First Presbyterian Church, and a large number of Christian women attended, along with friends who knew Alice socially. Reverend Dr. MacKenzie officiated at the funeral, and the church choir provided the music.

Youngest Daughter, Bessie

Bessie, the youngest of Yee Ah Tye's daughters, was born in La Porte in 1882. The local newspaper reported that at age seven Bessie attended the La Porte school and was studying music. After her father's death, she moved with her family to San Francisco, graduated from a young ladies' finishing school, then turned to music. Bessie was also a pupil of Professor Fleissner and became a talented pianist. For several years she lived in Oakland with the Ng P. Chew family.[6]

Bessie met her future husband, Chee Soo Lowe, when he was a student at the University of California at Berkeley. He graduated with a bachelor of science degree in mining in 1906, known as "The Earthquake Class."[7]

San Francisco Earthquake—1906

The San Francisco earthquake struck on April 18, 1906, when Chee Soo Lowe was a senior. The earthquake lasted only two minutes, but the fires that raged for three days left San Francisco devastated. During the fire, Chee spent several weeks as captain of a company of university cadets that were detailed to help guard San Francisco.

Carl Jung (who later married Beulah Ah Tye) was six-and-a-half years old and lived in Chinatown when the earthquake struck. Jung's father had died, leaving his mother with five children. His mother was a hairdresser who catered to the prostitutes in Chinatown. Jung remembers that his mother did such a good job on the prostitutes' hair that they always called for her and paid her well.

Jung's family lived in an apartment on the top floor at Dupont (Grant Avenue) and Jackson streets. Shops and stores were housed on the street level. The Chinese red-light district occupied an entire alley just east of Dupont. Sometimes when Jung and his playmates didn't have a yard to play in, they played in the alley. Unable to afford toys, they rolled a newspaper into a make-believe ball and played catch. Jung remembers that all the houses in the red-light district had little windows and the prostitutes occasionally threw money to the children.

Jung was at home when the earthquake struck, and it seemed that the whole town went down in an instant and everything was on fire. Chinatown burned with the rest of San Francisco. Jung recalled that the fire started on the waterfront and the firefighters ran out of water. They dynamited buildings one at a time, trying to stop the fire, but to no avail. The Chinatown homes were built of wood and they all burned to the ground. Everything was lost.

Firemen dynamited the Kong Chow building to check one course of the spreading fire. However before this was done, the temple keeper carefully carried the statue of Kuan Ti to safety.

Jung's mother rented a wagon with a driver, and she and her five children fled to a train station. When they boarded the train, everything was burning. At every train station en route to San Jose the Red Cross provided Jung's family with food—doughnuts, sandwiches, and coffee. Jung remembered asking his mother why they had so much food. "We oughta have this every day," Jung remarked. "It's a picnic."

Chinese and Caucasians in Portsmouth Square watch the fires that destroyed Chinatown, 1906. Chang Family Collection.

The 1906 San Francisco earthquake lasted only two minutes, but the fires raged for three days and left San Francisco devastated.
Chang Family Collection

A New Chinatown

After the fire, city officials proposed to relocate the Chinese quarter away from the sixteen-square-block area that included some of the choicest San Francisco real estate. Their plan was to establish a new and sanitary "Oriental City" at Hunter's Point.

While seemingly a gentle and tractable people, the Chinese were obstinate on this issue and firm in their desire to return to their old location. A delegation from the Chinese legation to the United States expressed the Empress Dowager's displeasure with the San Francisco authorities and the relocation plan. The proposal was also turned down because Hunter's Point was just on the county line. San Francisco didn't want to risk losing poll taxes to neighboring San Mateo County; it needed the revenue now more than ever.

Chinatown was eventually rebuilt in its former location on the side of Nob Hill. After a very short time, Jung's family moved from San Jose to Oakland, then back to a newly built home in San Francisco.

Paper Sons

The 1906 earthquake and fire were disastrous, but they yielded one positive benefit to the Chinese. They destroyed almost all of the official birth records. This allowed many Chinese to claim citizenship by saying they had been born in San Francisco but the earthquake had destroyed the records. They were thus free to send for their children in China because all children of United States citizens were given automatic citizenship, regardless of their birthplace.

Chinese immigrants often reported sons in China who would request entry as offspring of United States citizens. These "slots" were often given or sold to extended family or villagers and sometimes sold through brokers. These immigrants were called "paper fathers and sons."

A Voice From the Tomb

When the earthquake struck, Hong Yen and Charlotte Chang and their daughter, Ora, and son, Oliver, fled their home with virtually nothing. Ora insisted on wearing her new patent-leather Mary Jane shoes, even though the leather was so tough they hurt her feet and she could barely walk. The family survived the catastrophe and moved to Berkeley.

Hong Yen received the following letter from Oliver C. Smith, M.D., son of Chang's guardians during his Chinese Educational Mission days in Hartford, Connecticut:

May 5, 1906
My dear Hong Yen:

Your letter which reached me three days ago, came like a voice from the tomb.

I had given you up as lost and gone forever, and if not lost, I was sure you had entirely forgotten me. I cannot tell you how happy it made me to hear from you again, and to be assured that you had passed through the terrible catastrophe unharmed bodily, although you suffered severely from financial distress and discomfort, I am sure. I am delighted too, to learn that you are happily married, and have two fine children, and I assure you I am more than proud to know that one of them bears my name.

I am enclosing a small cheque, dear Hong, which I would like you to divide equally between the children,

as a little token of the esteem and affection of their father's old-time friend....

You probably have learned of the death of my father and mother. Father (William B. Smith) died in 1896; mother (Virginia Thrall Smith) died three years ago last January. Both of them frequently spoke of you, and always had a warm spot in their hearts for you....

I trust that you will be soon settled in another home, and that your sufferings from the great disaster will soon be relieved.

I remain as always,
Very affectionately yours,
Oliver C. Smith[8]

Ladies Home Journal Wedding

Eight months after the earthquake, on December 27, 1906, Bessie Ahtye married Chee Soo Lowe. The *San Francisco Call* reported that Bessie and Chee were "born in California, and since childhood have known only the customs and speech of the country of their birth." Unlike traditional Chinese-style weddings of their day, Bessie and Chee's wedding was "carried out in the manner approved by the *Ladies Home Journal.*"

The First Presbyterian Church was decorated with

Second row, far left: Ora Chang is pictured with her classmates at McKinley School on Haste Street, c. 1909. Chang Family Collection.

Chee and Bessie's first child, Bola, was born in the Lowe family home on Benvenue Avenue in Berkeley, 1907. Lowe Family Collection.

Bessie's 1906 *Ladies Home Journal* wedding, *San Francisco Call*, December 28, 1906.

pink and white carnations, smilax, palms, and ferns. A star of tiny electric lights gleamed over the altar. Three hundred guests gathered for the wedding. Reverend J. H. Laughlin, pastor of the Chinese Presbyterian Mission of California, performed the ceremony, and his daughter, Isabelle, was maid of honor. The officiating clergyman was assisted by Reverend Soo Hoo Ham Art, superintendent of the Chinese Presbyterian Mission of San Francisco.

The wedding party marched along a flower-strewn path. Louisa Yee, Clara Chan, Mary Chu, and Rachel Lee were the bridesmaids. Wearing a gown of white silk and a beautiful veil, Bessie was given away by her brother, Sam. Bessie Carolyn Chew, daughter of the Chinese editor, lecturer and clergyman, Ng Poon Chew, was the flower girl, and Oliver Chang was the ringbearer. The bridegroom, son of a rich importer, wore the conventional black of the "up-to-date wedding." Toy Lowe was his brother's best man, and Luther Jee, Pond Moar, Dr. Charles Lee, and Yit Owyang were ushers.

Soon after the ceremony, Chee and Bessie departed on their honeymoon. They planned to spend two years

in the mining camps of California and Nevada, then move to China.[9]

Homesick For America

In 1907, after the American birth of his first son, Bola, Chee moved to China. He worked as a government engineer in Szechuan province from 1907 to 1909; as a general manager of the Kwangtung Government Cement Works from 1911 to 1913; then as chief engineer of the Liang Kwang Coal Mines Company[10] Four more children, Lyman, Lona, Grace, and Milton, were born to Bessie and Chee while they were in Canton.

Bessie's daughter, Lona, remembered that her mother was homesick for America and often said how much she missed the *Ladies Home Journal.* Bessie taught music in China.

Chee and Bessie were active in the Young Men's Christian Association. In 1915, Chee was president of the Canton Y.M.C.A. when it laid the cornerstone of a building to honor Dr. Robert Morrison, a pioneer missionary to China. The structure was to be the finest building on the Bund in Canton, and "nearly the entire body of missionaries and native ministers" were among the eight hundred people in attendance.[11]

Lona said her parents talked about the dance parties that were held in a large dining room with its big mirror. Passersby would look through the window and see the dancers reflected in the mirror.

Bessie and Chee's Return to America

Chinese college graduates around the turn of the century, like Chee Soo Lowe, often pondered whether their future was in China or America. Chinese in America seldom found jobs outside of Chinatowns. Even university graduates were reduced to taking jobs as waiters, dishwashers, janitors, or Chinatown store clerks for a few dollars a week.

As a mining engineer for the Chinese government, Chee had traveled all over China and spent months in Tibet and other parts of Asia. In 1923, his eldest son, Bola, caught malaria in Canton and was sent back to Berkeley to live with his grandmother. Even though Chee had little chance of finding a job in America, he did not want his family to be separated. He returned with his family to America to join Bola and tend to his father who was severely ill.

For many years Chee lived off of the money he had made in China. While living with her in-laws, Bessie helped to supplement the family income by teaching English to adults.

From about 1932 to 1937, Chee tried his hand at gold mining in Yreka in northern California. Bola, who had suffered severe burns in an accident, decided to help with his father's mining company rather than return to his university studies.[12]

Chee used the process of dredging with a system of steam shovels and dredge lines. A bucket scooped the gold-bearing gravel from the river bed, transported it by a high line to a hopper, then processed it by sluicing.

"We mined up at the Klamath River and struggled for three or four years and got nothing out of it," remembered Bola. "But right after we moved out, another mining outfit moved on the same river bar and made quite a lot." Chee had worked on one end of a pond, and the group that followed him worked on the other end. "That's the way with gold mining," commented Bola. "You hit it right; you hit it right."[13]

In 1940, Chee became the executive secretary of the San Francisco Chinese Chamber of Commerce.[14] After thirty years as a mining engineer in some of the world's loneliest spots, including Tibet, Mongolia, Hainan, and Wyoming, he was happy to settle into a quiet job with a regular routine of duties. Chee's travel background and knowledge of key trading areas in the Far East enabled him to help American traders who wanted to bargain and buy goods.[15] Chee worked for Kaiser Permanente Hospital during his later years. In 1944, he died of a heart attack at age sixty-two.

From 1935 to 1948, Bessie was a teacher at Lincoln School in Oakland's Chinatown, part of the Oakland Public School District. She taught English to foreign-born adults in the evenings.

After living in Oakland for fifty-eight years, Bessie moved to Salinas and spent her last five years under the care of her son, Lyman, and his family. She died in her sleep at age ninety-nine in 1982.

Dilly Ah Tye is listed on a stagecoach ledger sheet as "Young Ah tye," traveling from Marysville to La Porte for $7, April 29, 1899. Cayot Family Collection.

Chapter Thirteen
YOUNGEST SON

Dilly Ah Tye was the baby of his family. He was born in La Porte on August 6, 1885, at a time when anti-Chinese sentiments were escalating nationwide. In December 1885, the antagonism reached its peak in La Porte and Chan Shee set sail for Hong Kong with her youngest daughters and four-month-old Dilly. In 1888, when danger to the La Porte Chinese had subsided, Chan Shee and her children returned home.

Dilly was about three years old when he returned to his La Porte birthplace. Chan Shee was very refined and raised her sons to be gentlemen. Always neat and clean herself, Chan Shee dressed her young son in white shoes and white clothes. She forbade Dilly to do many things because of her fear that he might get hurt. For example, he was not allowed to use a hammer.

When Dilly was only twelve years old, his father died. He moved with his mother and younger sisters to San Francisco where he completed high school and took some business courses at Heald Business College. When his brother-in-law, Hong Yen Chang, resigned from the Yokohama Specie Bank's San Francisco branch in 1907, Dilly started to work there.

Although Dilly was thirteen years younger than his brother, Sam, they could be mistaken for one another. Their features were identical, except Sam's face and body were thinner and his opium addiction had given him a pale, yellow complexion. Both stood about five feet, ten inches in height—tall for a Chinese at that time. Sam and Dilly liked to wear derby hats and had a similar gait.

As one of the main leaders in the Yee family association and Suey Sing tong, Sam was sometimes in danger of assassination. When Dilly leisurely walked through San Francisco's Chinatown, people often warned, "You'd better not walk around so nonchalantly, because from the back you look like your brother and they'll kill you."

Dilly's Future Wife, Rose Wong
Rose Wong was born on July 22, 1887, in Red Bluff, California. Her father, Wong Jim Sing, came to America during the forty-niner gold mining period. Rose's affidavit of birth listed her father as a laborer for the Sierra Lumber Company in Red Bluff. Rose recalled that her father knew a little English and later became a lumber foreman with four hundred laborers under him.

Rose's mother, Chin Shee, came from Canton, and her father came from Hong Kong. Her father was forty years old, and her mother was only sixteen when they married in Red Bluff. Their matched marriage produced three boys and three girls, Alice, Rose, Albert, Loy Duck, Gum Duck, and Marian.

From experience, Rose knew she had two things going against her: first, she was Chinese, and second, she was a girl. Her oldest sister, Alice, received the Chinese name *Choy Tie*, which means "get a younger brother." When the Wongs' second child, Rose, was yet another girl, they named her *Woon Tie*, meaning "next child change to a brother."

Rose's mother was a very strict and traditional Chinese. Like most Chinese fathers, Wong Jim Sing did not believe in educating his daughters. Rose never received a formal education, but when her brothers were tutored, she tried to listen while helping around the house.

When she was four, Rose and her family moved from Red Bluff to San Francisco. After being uprooted by the 1906 earthquake, Rose's family moved to Oakland, where she later met Dilly.

No Matched Marriage
When Rose reached the age of twenty, her parents became deeply concerned about her marriage and future. They took her aside and asked if she would be willing to be matched to an older Chinese merchant. Rose was adamant; she wasn't going to be matched in marriage the old Chinese way; she would marry for love.

Rose Wong is seated in the middle flanked by her girlfriends. Chang Family Collection.

Rose and Dilly met while playing the card game, casino, at a friend's house. When Dilly returned home he told his mother, "I'm going to marry Miss Rose Wong." His family wanted him to marry someone with more education, but he said that if he couldn't marry Miss Wong, he wouldn't marry at all. They saw each other three times before marrying.

Traditional Chinese Engagement

While Dilly and Rose's courtship reflected their Americanization, their engagement and marriage were traditional Chinese. They believed that one's whole life depended upon their horoscope. When it came to marriage, the groom's side held a special interest in the bride's horoscope, because it provided a portent of the couple's future.[1]

Rose Wong's engagement papers were written on formal red paper embossed with gold designs. Her horoscope showed that her family came from Hoiping (Kaiping) district, Canton (Guangdong) Province. It listed the names of her great-grandparents, grandparents, father, and mother and her birth date, the year 1887, sixth month, third day at noon (July 23).

For the formal engagement, the future bride and groom remained with their individual families to celebrate. Engagement gifts were exchanged between both families, and were recorded in Chinese calligraphy on red paper in a certain form.

A red-paper invitation with Dilly's Chinese name written on the front said that the gifts came with his greetings. Chinese gave many things in pairs or in even numbers for good luck.

Gifts given to Rose's family were:

Dilly's horoscope—a document that included the four pairs of cyclical characters, indicating the hour, day, month, and year of birth. This was sent as a formal proposal of marriage; the sending of the bride's horoscope in return constituted a formal betrothal.

A set of decorated candles—to be used by the young married couple as their initial ritual of honor and respect to the ancestors of the bridegroom's family. It was also used to thank Heaven and Earth for their blessings.

One box of betel nuts—these were always found at a traditional Chinese engagement.

1,500 wedding cakes—150 were moon cakes, and the others were a variety of less expensive cakes.

Four roast pigs and forty-nine live chickens—hens and roosters symbolizing fecundity.

Six boxes of seafood—dried oysters, dried shark's fin, and dried scallops.

Also given were a box of tea, $30 to buy cakes, six cases of liquor, one box of cane sugar, one box of peanuts, one box of dried fruit, two boxes of fresh fruit, one box of lychee fruit, and one box of longan ("loong ngon") fruit.

Dilly's family also sent $495 as a symbolic appreciation to Rose's family for their effort and devotion in raising the bride to marriageable age. Some of the money had to be in a variety of denominations, such as dollars, half-

A gold design decorated Rose Wong's list of engagement gifts given to her bridegroom's family. Ah Tye Family Collection.

dollars, quarters, dimes, and nickels. This represented the concept of "big and small," connoting a large family of all ages in their future together.

In exchange, the bride's family sent gifts to Dilly's family:

Rose's horoscope—southern Chinese were especially wary against leprosy, tuberculosis, and mental illness in one's lineage.

A pair of dragon-decorated candles—representing male, strength, goodness, and the spirit of change or life itself. The groom's family reciprocated with a pair of phoenix-decorated candles, representing female, peace, harmony (in the family), and fertility.

Two boxes of jin duey—fried glutinous rice balls, desserts that symbolized wholeness.

Two boxes of fat go tay—cakes that rise up and split on top when steamed, symbolizing expansion and great wealth.

One box of deep-fried, coin-shaped desserts—cooked in various ways according to the practices of the locality.

Four live chickens and a portion of fresh pork—symbolizing abundance.

One case of lettuce—symbolizing riches and wealth.

Also given by the bride's family were a pair of pans, one pair of silk pantaloons, two paper fans, a pair of handkerchiefs, and a pair of embroidered bags.

The foods were eaten at engagement parties held in each family's home. Some food was also distributed to friends and relatives, with each family returning home to pay respect to their ancestors at the family altar.

Traditional Chinese Wedding

In a traditional Chinese wedding the bride and groom are considered legally married when they perform homage to their ancestors before family and relatives. Dilly's sister, Charlotte, remembered that Rose was carried in a traditional bridal sedan chair. They married in Oakland on an auspicious date selected by their parents —May 21, 1908.

On the wedding day many of the bride's girl friends came to her house to congratulate her. They ate and had fun together before the bride left for the bridegroom's house. The bride paid respects to her ancestors at the family altar and bowed to her father and mother at the doorway before getting into the sedan chair.

The groom met the procession at his parents' home. After the bride entered her new home she paid respects to the groom's ancestors and to Heaven (bai

Dilly Ah Tye at age twenty, c. 1905, and postcard he wrote to Rose. Ah Tye Family Collection.

tin). A woman escort, generally a relative of the bride, would lead her in performing the wedding traditions.

The bride knelt on a cloth or cushion to offer tea as an act of submission and respect to her new in-laws. The bride knelt down once and bowed deeply three times to her new in-laws. After that, she rose and knelt again, then bowed three times to the floor in respect to the Earth. This ritual of kneeling and kowtows were acts of foremost courtesy.

Rose Wong wore this traditional Chinese embroidered jacket and skirt as Dilly's bride, May 21, 1908. Ah Tye Family Collection.

Rose's feet were not bound. She wore these embroidered wedding shoes, which show some wear because her daughters used them for play. Ah Tye Family Collection.

The bride served tea to all the relatives and guests. Traditionally, people who accepted the tea and the bride's kowtow gave gifts in return. When the bride had served tea to all the elders, uncles, aunts, and relatives it was an act of her acceptance into the groom's family. This act of serving and accepting tea is the legal foundation of a traditional Chinese marriage.

The bride's return to her home on the third day after the wedding was another tradition. After a month, the bride and her husband visited her home again. Thereafter, the bride became a member of her husband's family, and her allegiance was to them.

According to custom, a banquet followed Dilly and Rose's wedding. Several of their Sunwui (Xinhui) relatives toasted the bride and groom with hopes that they would bear many sons, because their home village in China was known to have an overabundance of girls.

From the Bay Area to the San Joaquin Valley

In Dilly's notebook of "Things to Remember" he listed in cursive hand the details of his children's birth. Beulah was born on March 25, 1909, at half past six o'clock in the evening. In the spring of 1910, Dorothy was born, and on June 19, 1911, their first set of twins were born. Dilly Jr. was born at five minutes to two o'clock in the afternoon, and Rose Jr. was born five minutes later. They were the first twins on either side of the family, and their maternal grandmother elatedly bought silk clothes for the newborn babies.

Rose remembered arranging a chair for each child in the kitchen. At day's end, each child undressed by a designated chair, went to bed and, upon waking the next morning, returned to his or her chair and dressed for school.

Dilly Sr. had contracted pneumonia because of the cold weather in San Francisco, and his doctor suggested a trial stay in Oakland. The family lived with Rose's eldest sister, Alice, for one year. Dilly Sr.'s health improved, so the family moved to Oakland permanently. Howard, Edward, Raymond, and Janice were born there, making a total of eight children.

Rose recalled that every time she gave birth, Dilly Sr. had her stay in bed for ten days to rest, and he would do the cooking. He was a good cook. Later, when they had more children, he hired an American nurse to help her for two weeks after each birth. She would give Rose a sponge bath, cook, and care for the children for only seven dollars a day. Chan Shee would also help.

Dilly Sr. worked for the Yokohama Specie Bank's San Francisco branch from 1907 to 1917, then friction between Japan and China caused the bank to lay him off.

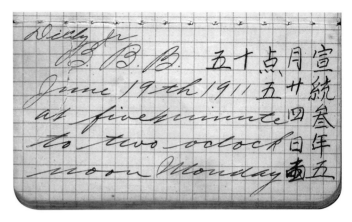

In his "Things to Remember" notebook, Dilly wrote in English and Chinese the details of his fifteen children's births. Ah Tye Family Collection.

Dilly Sr.'s letter of recommendation stated that for ten years he had "performed his duties very faithfully and diligently." The bank found him "to be honest and trustworthy and courteous and agreeable to everybody." He left the bank simply because of business conditions.[2]

A job with the Bank of Italy, forerunner of the Bank of America, was offered to Dilly Sr. in Stockton, ninety miles from San Francisco. Stockton had been a bustling supply base for the Mother Lode mines during the Gold Rush. Its rich delta land and inland port soon made it the commercial center of the San Joaquin Valley.

On December 4, 1918, just as World War I had ended in a victory for the Allies and a defeat for Germany, a ninth child was born to Dilly Sr. and Rose. The whole country celebrated and was thankful for victory. Equally thankful, the Ah Tye family chose to name their new son "Victor" for the victory and peace that had come to the free world.

The sixth child, Edward, remembered the Stockton apartment his family moved into on West Market Street as "more or less in a slum area." Next to the apartment was a big, three-story hotel, and across the street was a house of prostitution. Next door was an Italian boarding house with a barber shop and poolroom down below. Ed remembered listening to piano music coming from the poolroom, as well as the noise of fights and shootings.

Ed remembered that his mother, Rose, did most of the children's disciplining. She used a Chinese feather duster to whip the children when they misbehaved. Made of bamboo, the whip stung because it was flexible yet tough. Beulah didn't remember her mother using the feather duster to discipline the girls, but Ed remembered how much the whip hurt, raising welts on his legs. Dilly and Rose prohibited their children from going to Chinatown where the gambling houses were located. "They were kind of strict with us when we were kids," Ed reflected. "Since there were so many of us, guess it was a job to see that we didn't run around the streets and be wild. That's why the Chinese community always respected Mother. In spite of the fact that she had fifteen children, none of us ever got in trouble with the law or committed any crime that would bring disgrace to the family."

Stockton Banker

At the Bank of Italy, Dilly Sr. had the title—"manager Oriental Department," working at the bank window selling Hong Kong exchanges.

A close work friend, Charles Bloch Sr., remembered the bankers using Monroe calculators with carriages that moved back and forth. "You could multiply, subtract, and divide, and everything," recalled Bloch. "Dilly did it faster than we could with his 'Chinese bookkeeping machine,' an abacus. He could really use the abacus fast."

Bloch observed, "He did a lot of business with Chinese people. We had a big Chinatown in Stockton in those days, and they used to come to see Dilly. He smoked cigarettes in an ivory cigarette holder. Dilly and I got to be good friends, and we used to go to Chinatown and have good Chinese dinners there."

Like his brother, Sam, Dilly dressed immaculately. The eighth child, Janice, remembers her father as "a gentleman of the old school." "He was very courtly in his manners and his ways. He didn't talk rough, and people who met him were often impressed."

Dilly wore silk shirts, detachable collars, cufflinks, a necktie, and sometimes a little handkerchief matching the tie in his breast pocket. The thirteenth child, Barbara, remembered that he didn't allow his children to swear. "He didn't even like us to chew gum, because he said it was unladylike."

At the end of a work day, Dilly's youngest children ran out of the house to greet him. The children fought to get onto a stool to help their father remove his coat, because the one who helped him would get a nickel.

On Saturdays in the 1920s, Dilly worked half a day at the bank. When the older children became old enough to baby-sit the younger ones, Rose met her husband at two-thirty in the afternoon. They had lunch together and sometimes saw Nelson Eddy and Jeannette MacDonald musicals or Laurel and Hardy movies. Beulah remembers that her parents loved music; sometimes they'd stop at a record store to buy records for their Victrola.

Each time Rose and Dilly Sr. had a new baby, his boss gave him a raise. After the birth of yet another child, the boss took Dilly aside and said he couldn't give him another raise because he'd be making more than himself—the bank president.

Literate in both English and Chinese, Dilly "knew how to write quickly and fancy," recalled Rose. Stockton farmers who didn't know how to read their leases would ask for Dilly's help. Chinese also asked him to write letters for them, and he was often paid for these favors.

Dilly Sr. helped translate in the courtroom like his older brother, Sam. Beulah remembered that her father was approached many times by gamblers from Oakland who wanted him to set them up in gambling in Stockton. Dilly knew many Stockton judges and attorneys, which would have enabled him to make contacts for the gamblers and make payoffs. Beulah recalled that her parents decided to have nothing to do with gambling. They felt that many people gambled their paychecks away, leaving their families practically starving.

Sam Ahtye, the eldest son, never shared any of the family's inheritance, but Dilly Sr. did not hold a grudge. Edward surmised that his father might have been determined to make it on his own. Although generous and good-hearted, Dilly wasn't a very good businessman. For example, he invested in gas and electric stocks, but wasn't able to keep them long enough to make a profit. He also co-signed on a bad loan, and he was left liable.

After living on Market Street for seven years, the Ah Tye family had saved enough to make a down payment on a newly built home on East Anderson Street. A second set of twins, Barbara and Beverly, were born the day after the family moved into the new home on April 12, 1925.

At first the family couldn't tell the identical twins apart, and the same baby would be fed twice. A solution was found: one baby was given a bracelet for her left hand and the other for her right hand. In the winter of 1926, the twins contracted pneumonia; Beverly died of whooping cough and bronchial pneumonia at age one year and seven months.

Chinese Methodist Episcopal Mission

A converted store on the fringe of Stockton's Chinatown became the first meeting place for the Chinese Methodist Episcopal Mission. Minister Hon Fun Chan lived in an apartment above the Ah Tyes. He brought the Ah Tye children to Sunday school when Rose was too busy to attend church. Later, however, Rose accompanied her children to church and was baptized in 1921. Every Sunday Rose gave each of her children a penny to put in the Sunday school offering.

On one occasion, the district superintendent said the Chinese Methodist Mission had to be closed because its membership and support had declined. When the superintendent met with the leaders of the church,

Dorothy and Jansing Pond's wedding party, 1929. *Standing, left to right:* Frank Yee, Ella Low, Bola Lowe, Rose Ah Tye Jr., Jansing Pond (bridegroom), Beulah (Ah Tye) Jung, Harold Kim Lew; *seated:* Dorothy Ah Tye (bride). All were killed but Frank Yee, Bola Lowe, and Beulah Ah Tye Jung. Ah Tye Family Collection.

Rose brought her entire family of more than a dozen with her. She told the superintendent in no uncertain terms that he could stop sending the subsidy if he had to, but he wasn't going to close the church: She and her family would keep the doors open. The superintendent agreed to postpone the final decision.

In the meantime, Rose called on the business people of Chinatown (many of whom were owners of gambling houses) and received enough contributions to pay for six months' rent. This so impressed the superintendent that he recommended that the subsidy be continued.

In 1925, the mission moved to the newly constructed Chinese Benevolent Association Building on Lafayette Street. With the aid of lay workers and benefactors, student pastors from the College of the Pacific brought the mission new life.[3] From 1936 to 1949, Dr. George H. Colliver, a professor of Bible and Religious Education at the College of Pacific, was the pastor of the Chinese Methodist Episcopal Mission. In 1941, it was renamed the Chinese Christian Center, the heart of a Chinese youth movement within the community.

The center remained in the Chinatown area until it consolidated with the Clay Street Methodist Church in 1954. In 1956, St. Mark's Methodist Church was the official name chosen for the combined church.

Wedding Tragedy

The second daughter, Dorothy, married the boy who lived upstairs above the Ah Tyes' apartment on West Market Street. Jansing Pond ran the San Diego Toggery. Every Christmas Jansing showered gifts on the Ah Tye family and he continued his visits even after they had moved to their new home on Anderson Street. Beulah felt that Dorothy agreed to marry Jansing because she wanted to please her mother. Jansing was a quiet person, very reserved, neat, and clean. Rose approved of him very much.

Of the three oldest Ah Tye sisters, Beulah felt that Dorothy had the best personality. She was peppy,

The front page of the *Stockton Record*, August 12, 1929.

extroverted, and modern; she was a good dancer and could dance the Charleston. Her high school major was Latin, and she was very good at public speaking. Teenaged Rose Jr. was quietly sweet but very intelligent. She had just graduated from Stockton High School with a gold seal on her diploma for continued high scholarship. Rose Jr. became the first Chinese and the first girl to serve as editor of her high school weekly publication, *The Guard and Tackle*. Her work won the silver trophy cup for the best school newspaper in the state at the University of California journalistic convention in 1929.

At church Rose Jr. met Harold Kim Lew, a University of California medical student in San Francisco. He had already won three scholarships during his college career and been elected to the Phi Beta Kappa national honor society on the basis of an unusually high scholastic record. Rose Jr. wore Harold's fraternity pin, a step toward formal engagement.

Dorothy and Jansing were married at the Central Methodist Church on August 11, 1929, at six p.m. The Lincoln Hotel, a five-story hotel built by the Wong brothers in 1920, hosted the reception. Its full dining room, spacious lobby, damask-upholstered furniture, and basement parking equaled other first-class hotels in Stockton, and made it the pride of Chinatown. Wedding guests were served dinner and danced to an orchestra. The *Stockton Record* on the following day described the wedding as "one of the social events of the year in the Chinese colony."

Several hours after the festivities, the bride and groom, accompanied by three other couples, piled into a Chevrolet sedan. The wedding party was accompanying the newlyweds to the Senator Hotel in Sacramento.

Near Elk Grove, a car coming from the opposite side of the highway collided with the bridal car, hitting its rear hubcap. At that time, hubcaps were an extension of the rear axle. The sedan tipped over and caught fire. Six of the eight occupants burned to death.

Among the dead were the bride and groom, Dorothy and Jansing Pond. Rose Jr., age eighteen, died along with her twenty-four-year-old fiancé, Harold Lew. Ella Low, a bridesmaid and a graduate of the University of California, and Hong Yen and Charlotte Chang's daughter, Ora, also died.[4]

The driver of the bridal car was Bessie and Chee Soo Lowe's eldest son, Bola. He was critically burned on his face and hands. Jethro Yip (an entomologist with the nickname "Bugs") was Ora Chang's fiancé. He was the only person in the bridal car to escape with slight injuries—burns to his hands. Yip and Lowe, despite their injuries, were able to crawl from the car and were attempting to free their companions when the gas tank burst into flames. Other rescuers were beaten back by the heat of the fire. The August 12, 1929, issue of the *Stockton Record* explained that the gasoline tank on the overturned car had exploded, spewing the gas over everything.

The driver of the other car, Harry A. Kreutzer, a Stockton salesman, received only slight cuts and bruises. He had started home from Fallon, Nevada, at about three o'clock Saturday afternoon. The *Sacramento Bee* stated that the charges by the Chinese that Kreutzer was intoxicated at the time of the accident were later denied by the Deputy District Attorney Chris Johnson, who arrived at the scene of the accident to conduct an investigation.

"I found Kreutzer in a highly nervous condition, as one would expect following such a tragedy, but there was no evidence of intoxication," stated Johnson.

The next day wedding guests came to the Ah Tye home to offer their condolences. Mrs. Humbert, a neighborhood seamstress with whom the Ah Tyes had developed a special bond, lent them her car. "The wedding was a very happy moment, and then the next day it was the worst moment in our family's life. That much of a contrast in that fast a time," said the seventh child, Raymond. Student pastor Frank Fung knew the Ah Tye family well and was there to help. "We were really flattened," remembered Ray.

Coroner's Jury

Two days after the crash, a hushed audience and a coroner's jury of eight men and two women listened for two hours while the accident was described by witnesses. Oakland cannery workers Walter Harting and Lewis Willis came upon the death scene within a few moments of the accident. They stated emphatically that Kreutzer had the odor of whiskey on his breath. But Constable J. C. Cann of Elk Grove, who had "handled many drunken persons," was equally certain that Kreutzer was not intoxicated and that his breath gave no indication that he had been drinking.

Harting and Willis testified that shortly after the crash Kreutzer was still rummaging in his battered car, while the vehicle containing the six Chinese burned fiercely. The salesman then hailed a passing car, suitcase in hand, but the driver refused to pick him up.

"I intended to seek the aid of authorities; I had no intention of fleeing," Kreutzer told the jury. He could not explain how the accident happened and said he was completely unnerved by it.

Constable Cann, describing Kreutzer's actions after his arrest, said "the man seemed dazed." Taken to the Elk Grove jail, the salesman "flopped on a bed" and fell asleep within ten minutes. In response to a question from attorney E. G. Harvey Jr. of Stockton, who represented the two surviving Chinese, the constable admitted that Kreutzer's conduct appeared "most unusual."

Arthur Storms, a Stockton printer who also arrived at the scene shortly after the collision, told of taking what he thought was the dying statement of driver Bola Lowe. "I'm dying, don't bother with me; get that other driver; he went all over the road, and I didn't know where he was going next," Lowe said, according to Storms. Lowe was in critical condition at the Sacramento hospital during the inquest.

Jethro Yip also testified that Kreutzer's breath smelled of liquor. "We were going about forty-three miles an hour," Yip related. "I could see the salesman's car approaching, and it seemed to be weaving all over the road."

Dorothy and Rose Jr.'s brother, Edward, was age fifteen when he went with others to identify the bodies. "It was impossible to identify them because they were burnt and their bodies just shriveled up."

Ed remembered that, during the coroner's inquest, the constable stated that Kreutzer was so drunk that he could hardly stand up. But Ed recalled that the constable had a different story on the following day. He never said that the man was drunk. Instead, he said the bridal car was overloaded with four persons sitting in the front, a violation of the state motor vehicle code.

Deputy District Attorney Johnson declared that the evidence was insufficient to hold Kreutzer on a manslaughter charge, and a coroner's jury held that the accident was unavoidable. Harry Kreutzer was set free.[5]

Some Chinese believed the wedding tragedy was pre-determined fate, *jing ding*. Some time afterwards, other Chinese speculated that the Ah Tyes had picked a bad date for the wedding. According to the Chinese horoscope it was a day of fairies going to heaven.

Depression—1929-1939

Several people felt Dilly Sr. was never the same after the wedding tragedy. For him, the tragedy was compounded by the Great Depression, ill health, and the eventual loss of his job. During the Depression, the Ah Tye family found work wherever they could. The older daughters did housework and worked at the National Dollar Store during Christmas vacations.[6]

Rose sold hosiery. Ed surmised that "a lot of people bought from her, because they sympathized with her having so many children." Rose did quite well selling to these friends.

"It's a matter of the brothers and sisters, wherever we could find work, we'd turn the money over to Mother," Ed remembered. "We never kept any of it for ourselves. I had one new sweater in the four years that I went to high school. I remember Mother would say that almost every week my father would have to buy a new pair of shoes for someone in the family. So I guess if it wasn't for everyone working and pitching in, we would really have had a hard time."

Cheaper By the Dozen

When they were young teen-agers, the eldest sons Dilly Jr., Howard, and Edward, waited on tables in a Chinese restaurant. As older teens, the boys spent their summer vacations picking pears at a ranch owned by Chinese. They worked among older bachelor Chinese men who knew little English. When Howard mentioned that his grandfather was Yee Ah Tye, old-timers replied in Chinese, "Yes, he's the one that donated the land for the Kong Chow temple."

All the fruit pickers slept in the same bunkhouse and it had a communal kitchen. About ten workers sat around each table. "You had to learn to eat fast, because they'd place the food in the center of the table and if you didn't eat fast, you wouldn't get too much food to go with your rice," Ed remembered. "Usually, we had a group of four to five second-generation Chinese boys who would hang around together."

Ed recalled, "We were sort of 'prejudiced against' because we were of the Sze Yup (fourth) dialect, and the others were of the Heungshan (Chungshan or Zhongshan) dialect. People in the Walnut Grove area were mostly Heungshan and they let their people work by contract—they picked fruit according to the weight or boxes. If they worked faster and picked more fruit, they got paid more money. Whereas, we were only allowed to work by the hour; so we didn't get a chance to make money like they did."

"For the season," recalled Howard, "we'd bring home about $130. During that era, $130 went a long way. We gave practically all the money back to Mother. We only kept enough money to buy ourselves a pair of slacks and a pair of shoes to go back to school."

Family friends also helped. A cousin named Arthur Wong, a rancher, brought five-gallon cans of milk to the family. Another uncle, Wong Si Sek, who worked as a ranch cook, brought pies, eggs, fruit, and meat.

Richard, the twelfth child, felt that although his family was big, they always had enough to eat. "I had a lot of older brothers, and, of course, I had a lot of hand-me-downs. We weren't poor, but we survived, and I guess you would say things were cheaper by the dozen." In the 1930s, "welfare did not exist, only county assistance, and Rose would not accept one penny of charity."[7]

Rose's Helping Hand
The fifth child, Howard, remembered that many Chinese women who were beaten and abused by their husbands, approached his mother for help and guidance. In more severe cases, Rose appealed to Donaldina Cameron, head of the Presbyterian Home for Girls in San Francisco.

During the 1930s, Rose sympathized with the plight of many elderly Chinese men, some of whom were blind. They were lonely because their families had remained in China, they were poor because they were too old to work, and they were helpless because they did not speak English. Rose contacted the public-assistance department and, for many years, helped in the monthly distribution of rice, salt pork, and canned goods to the needy men. In addition, they also received a pair of denim overalls or a warm union suit, sometimes both, once a year.[8]

Liberty Park
One of the main reasons the Ah Tyes had built their new home on East Anderson Street was because of the park across the street. Liberty Park was bounded by Anderson, Grant, Jefferson, and Stanislaus streets. It became a meeting place for neighborhood children of different ethnic backgrounds—Mexican, Irish, French, Italian, Greek, and African-American. There was always a playmate to be found in the park, and it was the site of football games, running races, and evening games such as "dare base" and tag.

Raymond, Thomas, and Richard remembered Liberty Park fondly. "Everybody was close," reminisced Tom. "The neighbors and all of us knew each other, and in the evenings we played in the park a lot. It was a good, young upbringing for us."

Growing up in the 1930s, Tom recalled that the people of the neighborhood were mostly middle-class. Some fathers worked with the railroad, and a few had their own businesses. Neighbor June Flowers was the society editor of the *Stockton Record*. The Kenyan family's father was a judge.

The Mormon Slough was about two blocks from the park, providing a natural playground for neighborhood boys. A slow current ran through the slough, with water four to five feet deep and even deeper in places. The Ah Tye boys and their neighborhood friends built rafts of redwood railroad ties. Although crudely made, the rafts held three or four boys and floated well. Willows grew along the water's edge, and carp, catfish, and frogs were abundant. Traffic bridges made of wooden slats spanned the slough. Bats lived in the gaps between the slats, and when the bats came out at night, boys often shot them with their BB guns.

Rose spoke Chinese in their home, and most of her children would reply in Chinese. Tom, the eleventh child, wished he had learned more Chinese. Tom explained, "Mother would speak to me in Chinese, and I would understand her, but I'd always answer in English. She sort of sensed what I was saying, just like I sensed what she was saying in Chinese. My father spoke both Chinese and English. He'd speak to me in English all the time."

Equality
Saturday morning was house-cleaning day, inside and out. All the children had chores, down to the youngest, Perry. Janice remembered Perry's job was to sweep the kitchen floor every day.

"We had wooden stools, which we'd push under the table. Perry had to move them out and sweep under them. When we washed windows, everybody joined in, five or six of us would get all the windows washed in no time."

Janice recalled, "Some Chinese families were so old-fashioned that the girls did the household chores, and the boys would sit around and be served by them. But Mother didn't believe in that. She felt everyone had to pitch in and do his share." Chores lasted until noon, then the family would enjoy reading the Sunday newspaper, which was delivered on Saturday.

Sino-Japanese War

In 1937, Japanese forces invaded north China, and the Sino-Japanese war began. Chinese in every major Chinatown across the United States supported the campaign to raise money for the China War Relief Fund. Rice Bowl parties, monthly donations, cultural performances, warm-clothing roundups, and other events raised money for food for the needy during the Sino-Japanese War, and, later, World War II.

The campaign spanned the years 1937 to 1946, and in those nine years more than five million dollars were raised. This was a remarkable feat, because the donations were collected during the Depression when Chinese Americans feared for their own economic security. The Stockton community alone contributed over $411,000, a reflection of their patriotism and dedication to the Nationalist Chinese cause.

Dilly Sr.'s Death

Dilly Jr. remembered that his father had a reputation for being able to hold his liquor. "He would drink his liquor like we drink water out of a glass . . . straight . . . no chasers of any kind." According to Rose, Dilly Sr.'s social drinking began as a little boy in La Porte when Yee Ah Tye and his friends would prod him to take a drink from the large barrels of liquor in the merchandise store. Dilly became accustomed to liquor and his mother did not discourage his habit.

Dilly Sr. always had one big glass of rice whiskey with his dinner at home. Many of his children remember confrontations between their mother and father over his drinking. Once Rose poured liquor into a dish, put a match to it, and said, "See? This is what you're doing to your stomach."

The seventh son, Richard, said his father sometimes went out for drinks after work. "I used to hear a telephone call to come to get him. One of the older sons would have to go and drive him home."

In 1939, Dilly Sr. died at age fifty-five of cirrhosis of the liver, heart trouble, and inflammation of the kidneys. He was cremated and given an Americanized funeral at the B. C. Wallace Funeral Home in Stockton. Dilly Sr.'s eight sons were his pallbearers.

A jade exhibit was held at the Haggin Museum in 1939 to raise funds for war-torn China. Rose Ah Tye wore a sign around her neck, "give til it hurts," and carried a donation basket. Ah Tye Family Collection.

Right: Dilly Ah Tye Jr., founder of the Ah Tye Brothers Shell Service Station, nicknamed the "doctor of mechanics" because of his expertise in fixing cars. *Left:* Raymond became the mainstay of the family business during World War II. Mr. & Mrs. Dilly Ah Tye Jr.

Chapter Fourteen
CHANGE OF FORTUNE

Eldest Daughter Rose Ah Tye told the story of Yee Ah Tye's eldest daughter, Emma, as a lesson in life: a wealthy person can meet with misfortune then adapt to a life of hard work. Brought up as the daughter of a well-to-do Chinese merchant, Emma continued her charmed existence by marrying Koa, a steamship executive. His early death changed Emma's status from a lady who was waited on by Japanese servants to a widow who worked almost like a servant herself. Emma's husband and their adopted daughter, Alice, both died in Japan. In the 1910s, no government benefits existed for widows, so Emma returned to America with the responsibility of supporting herself and her adopted son, Chew.

One of Emma's jobs was as a helper to new mothers. For a month or so, Emma helped a recuperating mother with her baby and the household chores. In 1918, Emma's high school-aged son, Chew, held a part-time job. One stormy summer evening he was making a store delivery on his bicycle. Rain poured down so hard that he put his head down so it wouldn't splash on his face. Chew rammed his bicycle into a car and suffered internal injuries. He died in the county infirmary one week short of his seventeenth birthday.

Emma tried living with her sister, Charlotte, in Charlotte's spacious Berkeley home from 1937 to 1938. But the sisters' terrible tempers made them incompatible. Emma began living alone in an Oakland apartment, and as she grew older and was unable to work, she sold her Chinese jewelry—beautiful jades and pearls—one piece at a time, until all of it was gone.

Emma often visited relatives. She'd take the ferry from Oakland to visit the Ahtyes in San Francisco. Sidney Jr. recalled that his Great-Aunt Emma seemed to appear from nowhere. She never gave advance notice. She'd just ring the doorbell, enter the house, read both the English and Chinese newspapers, occasionally partake in a meal, then walk out.

An energetic woman, seventy-year-old Emma walked across the Golden Gate Bridge on its opening day in 1937. She said to her nephew, Allen, and his wife, Summi, "Why don't you go?" They replied, "You already did the walking; we don't have to."[1]

Her visits to the Stockton home of her brother, Dilly Sr., usually lasted for a week or two. She was always considered a helpful hand in caring for Dilly's growing family and delighted the little ones with gifts such as hand towels and toothbrushes. One day Emma visited her teen-age nephew, Dilly Jr., at the garage where he worked part time for a Japanese man. Aunt Emma surprised Dilly's boss by carrying on a conversation with him in fluent Japanese.

In 1946, Emma died of cancer in Oakland at age seventy-eight.

Service Station
Dilly Jr. learned to work on cars at Stockton High School during four years of auto shop classes. It was Rose's idea to open a service station in 1931 because Dilly Jr. exhibited natural mechanical skills.

The youngest of the fifteen children, Perry, started work at the service station at age twelve. "I wanted to work at the station because everyone else did. Ray thought I could keep the oil bottles wiped, but Tommy thought I was just a pest, kinda in the way. It's like a lot of Chinese families in business, where everyone kind of pitched in and helped."[2]

World War II
After the Japanese bombed Pearl Harbor on December 7, 1941, the United States entered World War II against Japan and its allies, Germany, and Italy. Known as "the good war," it was a struggle for empire and power—democracy versus fascism—a war that America and its allies won.

The Sino-Japanese War had unified the Chinese American community. Now World War II gave

Chinese Americans opportunities to become a part of American society in its hour of need. The six sons of Rose and the late Dilly Sr. were among the 15,000 to 20,000 Chinese Americans who served in the armed forces during World War II.

Dilly Jr.—Mechanic

Gasoline was rationed throughout the United States during the war and could only be purchased with stamps issued by the Office of Price Administration. Gasoline rationing slowed the service station business, so Dilly Jr. decided that he could make more money by working at the government motor pool in Stockton.

"I enlisted before they drafted me," Dilly Jr. said. "Actually, when I was working for the government motor pool my boss, who was an ex-Army man, wouldn't defer me. I beat him to it: I enlisted."

In 1943, Dilly Jr. worked in motor pools at Camp Livingston in Louisiana, Fort Knox in Kentucky, and Camp Roberts in California. He worked on government trucks that came from overseas—four-by-fours, six-by-sixes, Jeeps, and command cars.

Howard—Navy Man

The second son, Howard, passed a test that qualified him to be a radar yeoman. Recruiters asked him what he had done before the service, and he replied that he was in the grocery business. When asked, "Do you know how to cut meat?" Howard replied yes, so he was assigned to attend Cook and Baking School because of his experience in handling food. Howard was furious, but the lieutenant curtly informed him, "Either attend school or go to the brig for the duration of the war!"[3]

Howard was stationed at San Francisco's Treasure Island, working in a galley that fed between 12,000 and 15,000 men each meal. There were constant activities on Treasure Island: troop movements, arrivals of hardened veterans from overseas, and sailors and marines leaving to be assigned. On departing from Treasure Island, Howard remembered many soldiers saying, "Gee, I'm sure going to miss this Navy chow!"

Unlike Army cooking, which was always done on the move, the Navy was able to prepare food in a short time for thousands of soldiers with its special cooking equipment. The galley was equipped with a huge, revolving oven that could cook fifty turkeys in a three-hour period; thirty-gallon, stainless-steel, vat-like containers lined with jackets for quick heating; and rows of grills designed to accommodate one hundred pork chops.

After Treasure Island, Howard was assigned to the USS *Salamaua*, an escort aircraft carrier (CVE), also called a "baby flat-top." "The worst enemies were the typhoons in the South Pacific," Howard remembered. One time Howard's ship sailed in the midst of a typhoon for two-and-a-half hours. The only thing the crew could do was hang on to anything solidly bolted to the deck. The typhoon swept away a gun mount, taking the sailor on duty along in its fury. Even though the planes were tied up, many were smashed against each other. When the typhoon was over, the flight deck had curled upward at least five degrees.

"We had to limp in to Okinawa for repairs. A destroyer escort was sunk in the same typhoon," recalled Howard.[4]

The captain ordered the sailors not to sleep on the flight deck because of the danger. But one night in the South Pacific it got so hot that Howard disobeyed orders. That evening a patrol search plane (PBM) returned to the ship with its five hundred pound bombs and landed so low that one of its wheels fell off, missing Howard by just two or three feet. The bomb attached to the belly of the plane could have also detonated.

"After that," Howard said, "I slept back in the quarters, hot or no hot."

Edward—Engineer Top-Turret Gunner

The third son, Edward, was actually the first in the Ah Tye family to enter military service. He enlisted on September 30, 1943, and his first flying mission was as an engineer top-turret gunner on June 21, 1944. His B-17 plane's target was Berlin, a very dangerous site because it was surrounded and defended by more anti-aircraft guns and fighters than any other city. German fighters hit the group of planes ahead of, and behind Ed's bomber. Twice when Ed was on leave, fighters hit his squadron, eliminating four out of the twelve planes. Another time, Ed's crew was on liberty, and six out of twelve planes were lost.

B-17 bombers could also be shot by anti-aircraft guns on the ground. Many bombers were hit by flak from below, but usually by the time Ed's plane passed that area, the flak was lighter. Ed surmised that it was all a matter of luck.

"When I was overseas and near the end of my missions, they called me 'Lucky.' They said, 'Oh, Ah Tye is going on this mission, you don't have to bring your guns.' I never encountered any fighters, which were really the most dangerous. I never had to shoot except for one time, and one burst."

At an orientation meeting in England, Ed was given rules such as these:

Crew of the *Wild Hare. Front row, left to right:* 1st Lieutenant Andrew Caswell, Michigan, navigator; Technical Sergeant Edward Robjohns, New Jersey, radio operator; Staff Sergeant Everett Webster, Iowa, ball gunner; 1st Lieutenant Earl Thomason, Texas, bombardier. *Back Row:* 1st Lieutenant Kenneth S. Smith, New Jersey, co-pilot; Technical Sergeant Edward Ah Tye, California, engineer/gunner top turret; Staff Sergeant Neal Smith, Oklahoma, waist gunner; Staff Sergeant Archie Moldrem, Nebraska, tail gunner; Captain Phillip Collins, Iowa, pilot & captain. Missing from photo: Luther Carico, Virginia, waist gunner, killed in action August 15, 1944 over Cologne, Germany. The men's ages ranged from 19 (co-pilot Smith), to 26 (Ah Tye). Smith retired from the Air Force as a full colonel.

1) *Always be watchful and ready when in the air.*

2) *On a mission, even when returning across the English Channel, don't relax or strip your guns until your plane touches the ground.*

3) *If you are shot down, give only your name, rank, and serial number.*

4) *If you are shot down over France, mix with the civilians and wait to be picked up by patriots, who will try to smuggle you back to England. Also, act mute so your speech won't give you away.*

As the only Asian gunner on base, Ed asked the orientation officer, "Since I'm Chinese American, what should I do if I'm shot down and won't blend in with the Frenchmen?" Everyone laughed. The officer shook his head and answered, "Don't get shot down."[5]

Ed flew a total of thirty-five missions—fifteen in France and twenty in Germany. He received the United States Air Medal with three oak clusters and the Distinguished Flying Cross.

Raymond—On the Home Front

Sixteen million Americans joined the armed forces while 123 million others helped on the home front. The only son who didn't qualify for the service was the fourth son, Raymond, due to his asthma and hay fever. "Ray was the mainstay (of the service station) at that time," said Dilly Jr.

As American men entered military service, many women took their places in the factories. Likewise, Marie (Dilly Jr.'s wife) and Audrey (Ray's wife) assisted Ray in running the business while the Ah Tye brothers were in the service.

In addition to filling gas tanks, wiping windshields, and checking the oil, Dilly Jr.'s wife, Marie (Lee), made sure the station's gasoline ration stamps corresponded with its allotted gallonage. Mr. & Mrs. Dilly Ah Tye Jr.

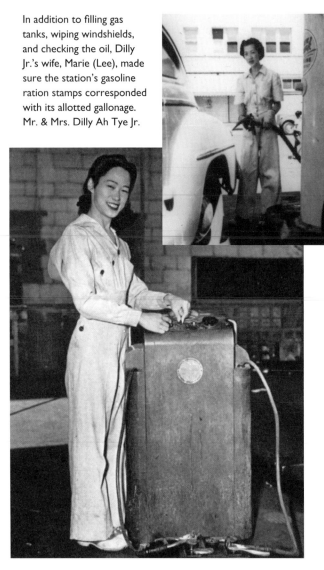

Raymond's wife, Audrey (Fong), designed a coverall to wear while working at the service station, attaching a hood inside the collar to protect her hair in the lubrication room. *Shell Progress,* November 1943.

Marie and Audrey filled gas tanks, wiped windshields, and checked the oil. Audrey recalled, "I did get under the cars once in a while to grease them. . . . Got more on myself than the cars." Another time Audrey lifted the hood of a heavy Cadillac. When the hood went up, ninety-pound Audrey went right up with it.

Chinese and Filipinos were the service station's best customers. Perry remembered that Filipinos believed that Shell Oil was a good product. They also trusted Chinese people as merchants because they didn't feel that they were looked down upon by them. "We never cheated the Filipinos," said Ray. "They came to our place, and we treated them well." The Filipinos left their cars to be greased and filled with gas while they patronized Chinese restaurants and gambling houses in Stockton's Chinatown.

Ray remembered that before World War II the Ah Tye service station pumped the most gasoline in Stockton and sold more gas than the city of Lodi. Despite the service station's high gallonage, teen-age Perry found it very frustrating work when practically all of his brothers were gone. "I'd have to go to work. It was just kind of drudgery after a while. I felt that we ought to sell the business."

His mother, Rose, however, said she'd go down and work at the service station herself to hang onto the business. Perry knew that his mother was a very forceful person and smart, even though her educational opportunities had been few.

Rose—Entertaining the Soldiers

Rose also helped in the war effort by folding bandages for the Red Cross. She felt sorry for Chinese soldiers stationed in the Stockton area, because they were away from home like her own sons.

Thinking that the servicemen must surely miss Chinese food, Rose would invite them for home-cooked dinners on Sundays. She was an excellent cook with a special patience for cutting, slicing, and dicing food with great exactness. Rose prepared from eight to ten dishes for dinner to make sure there was enough food.

The fourth daughter, Janice, remembered that in a small town like Stockton, people didn't leave home for entertainment. After Sunday dinner the Ah Tyes and their guests sang or played cards and mah jong. Rose loved to play mah jong, but didn't like to play for money: "I'm a Christian; playing for money is gambling."

Many servicemen left the Stockton area with a vest knitted by Rose. Janice remembered her mother knitting at least thirty-five vests to give to the soldiers. The vests were sleeveless and khaki color, so they could be worn under uniforms.

In the midst of the war, Howard remembered several servicemen walking by the Ah Tye home on Anderson Street and feeling compelled to visit the home. The reason for the attraction was the six blue stars in the window that represented Rose's six sons in the armed forces. The beautiful piano music emanating from the home also increased their curiosity; it was the music of Blossom, an accomplished pianist. The servicemen stayed an hour for cookies and coffee and said as they departed, "Enjoyed it immensely—as good as some USOs."[6]

Blossom—War Bonds

The fifth daughter, Blossom, had married Mark Kai-Kee, a liaison officer of the United States Army attached to a unit of the Chinese Army operating in the jungles of Assam, and later in the countryside of China.

Blossom worked as a receptionist for the United States Employment Service and ran the telephone switchboard for the office, while living with her family in Stockton. War bonds were heavily promoted. Blossom's vivacious personality helped her to meet or exceed her monthly quotas as chairwoman of the war bond drives in her office.

Barbara—Ration Board

During World War II there were critical shortages of automobiles, refrigerators, radios, stoves, and hardware. Automobile tires were the first commodity rationed.

The youngest daughter, Barbara, worked for the Stockton ration board's tire department. People applied for new tires or first- or third-grade tires, and a board of four men reviewed their applications. If people lived close to the streetcar in Stockton, the board refused their request, saying that they could walk the two or three blocks to the streetcar to get to work.

Barbara remembered that her boss, Mr. Clements, hesitated to hire her because he didn't know whether people would take "no" from an Asian. "Mr. Clements hired me anyway," said Barbara, "and I got many compliments. They said I was an asset to the place. I had to go back home and ask somebody, 'What does an asset mean?'"[7]

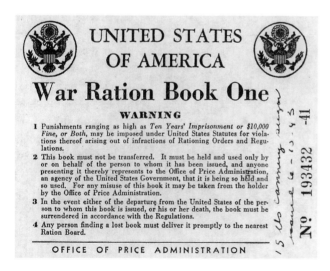

For four years, Americans endured the frugality of rationing, from butter (four ounces a week) to shoes (three pairs a year), and gasoline (three gallons a week).

Victor—Navy Machinist

After Pearl Harbor, the fifth son, Victor, began work at the Mare Island Naval Yard in Vallejo, California. He was employed there until June 1944, when he was inducted into the Naval training camp at Farragut, Idaho. In August, he transferred to the Service School Command in Great Lakes, Illinois, where he completed basic engineering training. From his duty station at the Naval Air Station in Pensacola, Florida, Victor advanced from third to second class as a machinist mate specialist.

As a machinist, Victor made steel products, parts, and tools on lathes. He worked on firing pins for Navy torpedoes and pressure valves, which could be dangerous if the valves blew up.

Victor's eldest son, Terry, remembered hearing about the incident that left his father with a jagged scar on his left wrist. During Victor's training period in the machine shops, his company officer sent him to the dispensary to have a cut sutured. Anesthetics were in short supply, so Victor elected to have his cut sutured without them.[8]

Thomas—"Draft Me"

After seeing many of his brothers, friends, and acquaintances enter the armed forces, the sixth son, Tom, wanted to do his part for his country by joining up, too. But Tom knew that his mother, Rose, would object.

Tom secretly went to the draft office and told them to sign him up. Two weeks later, he was drafted, and his mother felt there was nothing she could do but accept it. Little did she know that Tom had asked to be drafted.

Tom went to Sacramento with the regular Army and was given a battery of tests that showed he had an aptitude for the Air Force. He went to Tonopah, Nevada, for a year and did administrative paperwork. Desiring to see more of the world, Tom volunteered for flight training as a tail gunner on a B-17 flying fortress, the same type of plane his brother, Ed, was flying.

Gunnery training for Tom was in Las Vegas, Nevada, followed by flight training in Lincoln, Nebraska, and Rapid City, South Dakota. Accustomed to mild West Coast winters, Tom experienced the coldest weather of his life in South Dakota—forty degrees below zero. Sometimes the wind blew snow at an angle, making conditions even more difficult.

Tom mixed well with his fellow crew members from Oregon, New York, Philadelphia, Montana, and Chicago. The group arrived in England about one month before the war ended in Europe and did not see any action. After eight months in England, Tom was scheduled to return to the United States to train on the more advanced B-29 for combat in Japan. But the surrender

Rose Ah Tye and her six sons who served in the armed forces. *Clockwise from top right:* Dilly Jr. (Army), Howard (Navy), Edward (Air Force), Victor (Navy), Thomas (Air Force), and Richard (Air Force). Collage by Gordon Ah Tye.

of Japan one month after Victory in Europe (V-E) Day hastened Tom's return to civilian life.

Richard—Armament Man and Ball Gunner

The seventh son, Richard, or Dick, as he was known, graduated from high school and worked at the Coleburg Shipyard in Stockton for about eight months before trying to enlist. Dick was barely eighteen years old.

Rose was very upset at the thought of another son going into the service and tried to stop him. However, Dick was told that he was going to be drafted, so instead of enlisting he waited until he was drafted shortly thereafter.

When Dick was in gunnery school in Texas, an actor named Sabu was also attending the school. Sabu had a role in the 1942 movie, *Jungle Book*, based on the classic story by Rudyard Kipling about a young boy reared by wolves in the jungles of India.

One day Dick and some soldier friends went into town. They entered a restaurant, and a young girl asked Dick if he was Sabu. Dick got a big kick out of it, and his buddies got an even bigger laugh ribbing him about it.

Dick encountered segregated restrooms for the first time at a bus depot in one of the Southern states. When he saw one restroom for Whites and another for Blacks, he walked into the White men's restroom.

"Some fellows were watching me," Dick said, "but they didn't do anything about it. They were wondering what I was going to do, I guess."

Dick was the only Asian in his crew and got along well with fellow crewmen from Michigan, Massachusetts, Texas, and Oregon. Since the enemy was the Japanese, intelligence officers told Dick he should sew American flags on his flying jacket.

The 72nd Bomb Squadron, 5th Bomb Group, 13th Air Force was Dick's assignment in the South Pacific from 1944 until the end of the war. The B-24 had a twin tail that was unable to withstand as much stress as the B-17, but it held more of a bomb load. More gasoline could also be added to its bomb bay, allowing the B-24 to fly longer missions.

Luck flew with Dick's B-24 crew. By the end of World War II, the United States Navy had shot down most of the Japanese fighter planes. As an armament man and ball gunner, Dick was in charge of all of the plane's turrets and helped to load bombs into the bay. His position underneath the plane gave him an excellent vantage point. He could see the bomb bay doors open and follow the bombs all the way down to the ground and see their impact. The main danger to Dick's plane was enemy fire from the ground, and during these attacks he could smell the bursting bombs of ascending flak.

Dick's crew completed forty-four missions in the South Pacific. He participated in the bombing of Corregidor, an island in the northern part of the Philippines. He also took part in the invasion that recaptured the Philippines, flying on the support staff. While Dick's crew was resting in Manila waiting to fly home for reassignment, all planes were mysteriously held up. Then on September 1, 1945, they heard the announcement that the Japanese had surrendered as a result of the atomic bomb.

Instead of flying back home, Dick and his buddies returned on a small luxury liner that usually sailed from New York to San Francisco. The liner, which normally held three hundred passengers, was converted into a transport ship that carried over seven thousand servicemen. Its two swimming pools were cleaned and used to hold water for drinking and cooking. Hammocks were stacked five or six deep throughout the ship. Due to the overcrowding, the servicemen had to stand up to eat. Meals were served twice a day, rather than three times. The trip from Manila to America took twenty-six days.

World War II's End

Barbara never heard Rose express concern for her sons' safety, but she often saw her praying. Toward the end of the war, Rose broke out in eczema on her arms and legs, indicating that she was indeed worried. Despite having medicinal calamine lotion covering her body, Rose continued to solicit money for the church. People gladly opened their doors to donate to her. Rose enjoyed seeing the name and amount of each donor's contribution added to a little book. In answer to Rose's prayers, her six sons returned home healthy and whole when the war ended.

Several of the Ah Tye brothers had developed warm friendships with their wartime buddies from all parts of the United States. Many of those friendships endured throughout a lifetime.

For Chinese Americans, World War II marked a breakthrough in their acceptance and progress as an ethnic minority in America. Unprecedented cooperation between China and the United States brought about the repeal of the Chinese Exclusion Act.

Chinese immigration was set at a quota of 105 persons per year, a token gesture when compared to the annual quota of 65,721 White emigrants from Great Britain. More importantly, however, Chinese aliens in the United States were now able to apply for citizenship.

In 1945, the War Brides and Fianceés Act contributed to the increase of the number of Chinese women in the United States. In 1948, the Supreme Court ruled that restrictive covenants that had limited Chinese, African-American, and other minorities from buying property and living in certain neighborhoods could not be enforced by the courts. Another important change was that many companies, particularly in the white collar and professional fields, began to hire Chinese and other minorities. This improved their social and economic status. California also repealed its law banning interracial marriage in 1948. However, other states' laws prohibiting intermarriage between Whites and Asians stood until 1967.

Rose's Passing

Rose Ah Tye was twice named Stockton's "Chinese Woman Community Leader of the Year," in 1963 and 1970. She died at age eighty-seven in 1975. A letter written by Rose's former pastor, Bishop Wilbur W. Y. Choy, was read at her funeral, "She was widowed when many of her children were very young. But she instilled in them a sense of familyhood, mutual respect, and responsibility, love and concern, integrity and character, and joy in living."[9] All twelve of Rose's grandsons were her pallbearers.[10]

Architectural details of the Kong Chow building. Nanying Stella Wong.

Chapter Fifteen
THE KONG CHOW TEMPLE DISPUTE

Three years after the San Francisco earthquake had destroyed the Kong Chow Temple, a new one was built on the same site.[1] A Chinese man designed the new structure—a three-story, red-brick building. The ground floor housed the Kong Chow school, and the second floor held the organization's council chamber. Custom called for places of worship to be placed as near to heaven as possible, so the third and topmost floor housed the Temple.

A unique feature of the Kong Chow building was its large courtyard. It reflected the imperial Manchu days when the mandarins and nobility needed ground space for their horsemen, sedan chairs, and procession of retainers and servants.

The statue of Kuan Ti, the god of war and peace, was the main artifact dating back to the temple's beginnings. Other gods and goddesses in the temple represented a cross-section of the popular deities worshiped by the common people in China, especially those from southern China.

Some of the gods originated in native mythology and the Buddhist religion, while others were deifications of historical figures. The wood carvings in the temple were all made by hand in Canton, an art form now being replaced by machine work.

A notable visitor to the Kong Chow Temple was Bess Truman. In late October 1948, just a few weeks before the presidential elections, Harry and Bess Truman stopped in San Francisco for a short visit. Albert Chow, the unofficial mayor of Chinatown, was a strong Truman supporter despite predictions that Thomas Dewey would win overwhelmingly. Chow brought Mrs. Truman to the Kong Chow Temple, where she was urged to shake a canister of thin bamboo sticks until one fell out. The temple keeper then read the characters on the stick and consulted the temple's oracle book for the fortune's answer. It predicted a victory by Truman over Dewey and proved correct.

Charlotte Chang at Ninety-six

In 1968, Charlotte Ah Tye Chang was ninety-six years old and had lived in Berkeley for forty years at the same address: 2413 Fulton Street. She was one of the first Chinese social workers in the Bay area and had helped found the Chinese Young Women's Christian Association. Every Tuesday she could still be found rolling bandages for Oak Knoll Naval Hospital, despite her advanced age.

Natural foods, such as fresh vegetables and fruits, were abundant in Charlotte's diet. Her daughter-in-law, Lillian, said she ate like the "good old-fashioned days." She had eggs and bacon every day. Charlotte "hated all the new-fangled things," and drank fresh-perked coffee every day and would have nothing to do with instant coffee. She ate butter, not margarine, daily. A teapot full of water on the pilot light of her stove gave her easy access to warm drinking water throughout the day.[2]

Chinese Plymouth Rock

When Charlotte learned that there were plans to sell the Kong Chow Temple and build a new structure, she began a one-woman protest. She said her father, Yee Ah Tye, had given land to the Kong Chow Association for a temple and haven for Chinese immigrants with the stipulation that the land should not be sold. She claimed the land had been given to her father by the federal government in return for his services as an interpreter in the San Francisco courts.

In a *Chinese World* article written by Charlotte's nephew, Howard Ah-Tye, the Kong Chow Association secretary, Robert Yick, stated that the temple was in poor condition and would cost approximately $50,000 to restore to conformity with building codes. The Kong Chow Benevolent Association had already purchased other property on the corner of Stockton and Clay streets for $200,000 and intended to move the temple there. Payments on this new property and the upkeep of the old temple were quite a burden to the association.

San Francisco Examiner and Chronicle documented the battle waged by Charlotte (Ah Tye) Chang to save one of the oldest Joss houses in the nation. "California Living," February 23, 1969.

CAN THE LITTLE TEMPLE BE SAVED?

Bitter division over proposed sale splits Kong Chow Society

SAN FRANCISCO'S venerable Kong Chow Friendly Society may be developing into an unFriendly society before our very eyes.

New Year's prayers sent heavenward on wings of smoke at the society's 520 Pine St. temple probably shocked the gods who've presided there for more than 100 years.

The reason — there's a bitter division in the society over whether the temple, oldest Chinese joss house in the nation, should be sold.

In favor of the move, which would include relocation on Stockton Street, are elders of the Kong Chow Benevolent Association, their supporters, and American President Lines. APL has purchased other property in the area and wants to assemble a highrise package.

Asking price is $700,000 on the temple real estate which the assessor appraises at $200,000.

Opposition in the society and outside it centers around a matriarch, Mrs. Charlotte Chang, 96, and her vocal grandniece, Stella Wong. Mrs. Chang claims her father, Yee Ah Tye, donated the temple land with the stipulation that it never be sold at any price. She wants the temple restored and designated a historical landmark.

The elders claim the temple site was swapped with Yee for farm land in China, cancelling all obligations to his heirs. Neither side has proof.

As usual, the caretaker beat the massive gong at the altar to welcome this year of the Rooster and awaken Buddha to the pleas of the faithful. But worshippers on the temple balcony this year exchanged cold stares in addition to watching their prayers wing heavenward on incense smoke.

Now — the supplicants await an answer. □

The 22-story International Building towers over Kong Chow Temple, oldest Chinese joss house in the nation. To Mrs. Charlotte Chang, right, the temple is a flower growing out of the rock.

Manchester Fu (a nom de plume of Ken Wong) in his *East/West* newspaper column found it remarkable that at age ninety-six, temple defender Charlotte stood "erect as a redwood" and could "climb a flight of stairs as the one at the Clay Street YWCA without puffing like a calliope." In giving his support, Fu stated that the Kong Chow Temple provided "a living monument" as one of the first Chinese temples in America, where the early Chinese immigrants spent their first night. "It is almost like Plymouth Rock," wrote Fu.[3]

Charlotte Chang emphasized her father's wish that the temple gods not be disturbed and suggested that the temple be preserved and restored and its rooms converted for use as education and recreation facilities for Chinatown youth. She led a protest in front of the Kong Chow Temple complete with signs, television cam-

eras, and a mimeographed, epic poem in blank verse written and distributed by Nanying Stella Wong. Still, letters and telephone calls to the Kong Chow Association went unanswered.

Finally, Charlotte appealed for the help of the Intercollegiate Students for Social Action at the University of California at Berkeley. The group's president, Mason Wong, began agitating to save the temple, and Charlotte soon got results. The editors of two Chinatown newspapers and a young Chinatown lawyer, Gordon Lau (who later became a supervisor of San Francisco) joined her cause.

On behalf of Charlotte Chang, Lau filed a suit to prevent the Kong Chow Benevolent Association from selling the Pine Street property and moving the temple to the new location.

The suit was based on two legal grounds. First, could the association sell the property in light of Yee Ah Tye's stipulation in 1852 that the land never be sold? Second, Lau attempted to have the historic temple declared a city landmark and thus be saved.

The documents pertaining to the Kong Chow land transaction were thought to have been lost in the 1906 earthquake and fire. However, in an old wooden crate handed down from one Kong Chow president to another, the original 1866 Kong Chow deed was found. This key document contained no limitation on the sale of the land. Kong Chow Association records also showed that "in appreciation" for Ah Tye's generosity to the Kong Chow Association and "to reward him," Ah Tye had received funds to buy more than twenty mus of rice paddies in his native village.[4] This effectively cancelled all obligations to Ah Tye's heirs.

Although the temple was one of the oldest of its kind in the United States, the 1968 landmark commission failed to recognize its historical significance.

"I knew it was going to be a loser the minute we filed it," said Lau.[5] "If the community had acted sooner, the temple may have been saved. If it had happened in 1984, with today's landmark commission, we probably could have [saved it]."

Kong Chow Temple Demolition

In 1969, the Kong Chow board made the final decision to sell the Pine Street land to Ralph K. Davies, chairman of the board of American President Lines, for $630,000. This price did not reflect the value of the temple building proper, but the value of the property for commercial purposes when joined with other parcels at the corner of Kearny and Pine streets. Davies planned to raze the temple and other surrounding structures that he owned. In their place would rise a modern office building.

Before the temple's demolition, Kong Chow director Charles Young told the *Chronicle*, "We are being very, very careful. All this, all the altars, the plaques over the doors, the tables, everything, has been packed in sawdust and nailed into crates. Some of those crates weigh 900 pounds."[6]

New Kong Chow Temple

In 1977, a new Kong Chow Temple was dedicated at Stockton and Clay streets. Donald Young, president of the Kong Chow Benevolent Association, said, "We're certain that our ancestors are appeased and pleased by this new landmark. We're in a more central Chinatown location now. And all the treasures of the old temple have been preserved in our new building."

Workers move one of the large urns during the dismantling of the temple. Thomas W. Chinn Collection.

A four-story building with a curved roof of golden yellow tiles was built in the commercial center of Chinatown. Over its entry is the original carved marble plaque with the Chinese calligraphy, "Kong Chow Temple." The street-level floor is rented by the United States Post Office, and the other floors are rented or used for association purposes. The fourth and top floor houses the temple.

In an *Asian Week* article Howard Ah-Tye wrote, "True, the temple in its present location is quite attractive, with new additions and improvements, but somehow it seems hollow; something's missing."[7]

From a business point of view, the decision to sell the Kong Chow Temple land seemed pragmatic, but a price tag could not be placed upon one aspect—*feng shui*, or "wind-water." The Pine Street land had been chosen because its location brought harmony and prosperity. No amount of money could replace the loss of good *feng shui* or the displacement of the gods who had been worshiped on that land for over a century.

Although the original 1866 Kong Chow deed showed no restrictions on the sale of the Pine Street

Oliver Chang with one of his intricately hand-crafted kites. Chang Family Collection.

The doctor asked her, "When were you in the hospital last?" Charlotte replied, "I've never been in a hospital. I hate hospitals!"[8] Perhaps, like the Chinese placer miners in the La Porte of her childhood, Charlotte believed hospitals were places where people went to die. After the hospital stay, Charlotte entered a convalescent hospital but soon returned home where she felt she would recover faster.

Lillian saw her mother-in-law's decline as more mental than physical. Charlotte began to forget and couldn't recognize people. In 1970, Oliver and Lillian went on a trip to the Orient, and their godson, Alan, took care of Charlotte. Upon Oliver and Lillian's return, Charlotte greeted them with a "Hello," and told Alan, "You may seat the guests now."

"She still went back to her glory days," explained Lillian, "when she had everything."

As the daughter of a well-to-do merchant and the wife of a lawyer and diplomat, Charlotte was accustomed to wealth. Lillian remembered Bessie had said that Charlotte gave away and sold possessions, thinking that her wealth would never end.

When her husband, Hong Yen, died in 1926, there were no widow's pensions or Social Security. Charlotte worked as a social worker for the International Institute branch of the YWCA from 1928 through the early 1930s. Lillian said when Hong Yen's money ran out, it was quite a shock to Charlotte. Oliver supported his mother for the remaining forty-six years of her long life.

No Chang Descendants
Charlotte died in 1972, at age ninety-eight, and her son, Oliver died about two years later at age seventy-three. There were no heirs to Charlotte and Hong Yen Chang's branch of the family. Their daughter, Ora, died in the Ah Tye wedding crash, and Oliver married late in life and had no children.

Oliver graduated from the University of California at Berkeley in 1927 with a degree in agriculture. He had planned to be a farmer, but, as an undergraduate, he enjoyed working with youngsters at Berkeley's Chinese Athletic Club so he accepted a job as director of the Chinese Playground. He was San Francisco's first playground director of Chinese descent. He is best remembered for his contributions to both the community and the Chinese people as a master kite-maker and as a tennis advocate.

In 1980, a playground and recreation building on Sacramento and Waverly streets in San Francisco's Chinatown was dedicated in honor of Oliver C. Chang. Then-Mayor Dianne Feinstein praised the architectural

land, it is possible that Ah Tye had a verbal agreement in an era when "a man's word was as good as gold." Ironically, the Kong Chow deed also proved to be important to the Ah Tye family history. Ah Tye signed the deed in both his Chinese name "Yee Dy" and his Americanized name "G. Athei." Based on these two signatures, his descendants claim that he was the same "Athei" who was a leader in the early days of California.

Charlotte's Decline
At ninety-six, Charlotte enjoyed walking to the neighborhood grocery store, located only half a block from her home. She loved to shop and monitor the price of groceries. On one of these walks, robbers grabbed Charlotte's purse and knocked her down. She didn't tell her son, Oliver, or daughter-in-law, Lillian, what had happened, but several days later Lillian noticed that Charlotte's arm was swollen. It was only then that Charlotte told about the assault and was taken to the hospital.

design, planning, and construction of the project and complimented its original aim: maximum use of minimum space.

Oliver's widow, Lillian, unveiled a dedication plaque that read in part: "Oliver possessed a special reverence for all living things. Trained in the science of farming, it was our fortune that he directed his great talent to a far richer crop: two generations of outstanding citizens."

Oliver C. Chang Recreation Center in San Francisco Chinatown. Photograph by Doreen Ah Tye.

Front of village homes. Photograph by Dr. Edmond Chong.

Chapter Sixteen
CHINA: VILLAGE ROOTS

In October 1984, Yee Ah Tye's grandson, Edward, and his wife, Blanche, visited the Chinese district (or county) of Sunwui (Xinhui). They made a special trip to Chang-wan village, the birthplace of Ah Tye.

The taxi ride from Canton started at seven-thirty in the morning, and it took more than four hours to reach Chang-wan. The main roads were in good condition, and trees lined the sections that had two lanes.

Along the route, they passed the cities of Fat-shan (Foshan City), Shekwan (Shiwan), Sah Ping (Shaping), and Gong Moon (Jiangmen). New roads, homes, and apartments were going up everywhere, adding to the hustle and bustle of city life. The taxi driver was quick and skillful, able to scoot in and out of traffic, pass cars, and really "fly." But Ed explained, "The taxis can 'fly' because most of the vehicles they pass are trucks. There are lots of trucks and buses on the highway. Tractors and human-drawn carts are also frequently seen."

Lush, green rice fields lined the roads in the countryside. Dried rice stalks were stacked one on top of another in cones, a method of storing fuel for cooking in rural communities. They passed many outhouses for men, lean-tos made of straw mats. These weren't built very high, so passersby could see a man's head as he used the outhouse. Halfway to the village, the Ah Tyes asked to use a restroom. Their driver told them, "Wait until we come to a nicer one." They rode until they came to a restroom built of mud bricks; one side was designated for men and the other for women.

"It was really primitive," said Blanche, "a squat Eastern toilet—Eastern meaning just a narrow rectangular opening in the ground. The toilet was made of cement with no running water, so everything was left in the open."

Around eleven a.m. Ed told the taxi driver to stop at a restaurant for lunch. They entered a medium-sized hotel restaurant filled with many local patrons. The driver ordered lunch that included steamed fish, sauteed Chinese chard, fried chicken, and white rice. After the meal the driver paid the bill with his Chinese money, and Ed reimbursed him later with Foreign Exchange Certificates.[1] The taxi driver explained that if the Ah Tyes had ordered and paid for the meal, they would have been charged at least twice as much because they were tourists.

Ferry Ride
In earlier days, travelers in China had to take several ferry rides to get to Chang-wan village. By 1984, the travel route was reduced to only one five-minute ferry ride across the Gow Gong (Jiu Jiang) River. When the taxi was about fifty feet away from the river, the driver told the Ah Tyes to get out. A law required passengers to disembark from vehicles before boarding the ferry. A local bus and the taxi were the last vehicles to scoot onto the vessel. Ed, Blanche and the bus riders ran frantically and barely got on board just as the ferry left the shore.

No Direct Descendants
After asking several people for directions, the taxi driver found Chang-wan village beyond a grove of bamboo trees. Upon entering the village, Ed and Blanche saw a courtyard with houses and alleys built around it; the roads were all dirt. The courtyard contained a pond with stagnant water, a sty sheltering two pigs weighing seventy to eighty pounds each, and chickens and ducklings running about freely. The village looked like snapshots of Chinese villages, homes, and alleyways Ed and Blanche remembered seeing while growing up in the 1920s and 1930s.

Through the family oral history in America, the Ah Tyes knew that no direct descendants of Yee Ah Tye now lived in the village. A letter to a friend's relative, Seh Kil Yee, had been sent a month in advance of their visit, so the villagers were expecting them. Many were surprised that Ed and Blanche, both third-generation Chinese Americans, still

Chang-wan villagers and children. Photograph by Dr. Edmond Chong.

spoke fluent Cantonese, and their own dialect. They were able to communicate with ease. The villagers said Ed and Blanche were the first overseas Chinese to return to the village of their ancestors in more than one hundred years.

Rural villages in China are made up of clans; this one numbered about two hundred people, all of whom have the last name "Yee" (Yu). Seh Kil Yee apparently was the main Mr. Yee (Yu) of the village. He took the Ah Tyes to visit seven houses, the homes of his brothers and cousins. Crowds of village people followed Ed and Blanche as they walked to each home. Someone went out to the rice fields to tell the men of their arrival, and they all returned home to see the Ah Tyes, too, since it was nearly time for their afternoon break.

Chinese Village Homes

The village homes were neat but very plain, and were furnished with simple wooden furniture. Flies were everywhere. There was electricity but no running water or indoor plumbing.

Each home had an altar for ancestor worship. Incense sticks, cut-out pictures, and good-luck sayings written in calligraphy decorated the altars. Framed pictures of overseas relatives in formal poses were displayed on some living-room walls.

According to the Yee family tree, Edward was of a higher generation than that of the villagers, so he was called *Dai Gung*. Blanche was called *Dai Pau*, forms of address that show respect for elders. Each host served their guests tea, showing good Chinese hospitality. One cousin came in from the fields just before the Ah Tyes arrived at her home. She served them tea, even though her feet were still a little wet and soiled from field work.

A Chinese woman who had escorted Blanche around the village took the Ah Tyes to her home. This house appeared to be the best in the village, because it had a recently built stairway that led from the living room to new bedrooms upstairs. The woman said, "Most families in this village have girls, but I have two sons and two daughters. My older son is on road construction, driving a three-wheeler that can haul, pull, and push. My younger son stays at home, because we have no money to send him on to continue his education."

Nothing is wasted in China; even rice stalks are used for cooking. Blanche asked, "When you cook rice with these stalks, aren't you afraid of burning your rice?" The woman replied, "No, as soon as the rice starts drying up in the pot, we take it away from the fire. We never burn our rice."

The Ah Tyes had brought two bags of gifts for Mr. Yee's relatives. The women and children received cookies, ballpoint pens, tablets of paper, bar soap, and candy. The men were given packs of cigarettes; Marlboros were a favorite brand. When the sacks were emptied of gifts, one of the women put a coin wrapped in red paper into each one. It is a Chinese custom that one does not leave with an empty bag.

Sunwui Economy

The main source of income in Yee Ah Tye's home village was rice farming. The Chinese men expressed happiness over their government's new system which encourages greater capitalism. The farmers explained that when everything went to the government, they weren't so industrious. People didn't work very hard because whether they produced a large or small crop, they all got the same, fixed amount from the Communist government.

With the new system, farmers can sell a certain amount to the government, then market the surplus and keep those funds for themselves. Like capitalists, these farmers have a chance to make more money and hard workers are rewarded.

While the Ah Tyes saw little modernization in the homes, the village economy was improved by two businesses, both involving local women. The sewing factory produced clothes for a business in Canton (Guangzhou). When Ed and Blanche walked past the factory, all the women workers charged out to look at them. The older women wore black tops and pants; the younger girls wore colorful blouses and pants and some had modern hairstyles.

In the second enterprise, women, young and old, wove baskets in their own homes. The expertly made baskets of different sizes and shapes were then sent to another area, where the clasp, handle, and decorative paint were added.

Dried mandarin orange peels were also a specialty of the area. Villagers peeled the oranges, dried the rinds, then sent them to market. The dried peels were known for their fragrance and were used to flavor soups and other foods.

Chinese Oral History

In 1984, only two elderly men, ages seventy-nine and eighty, remembered Yee Ah Tye's original name, Yee Dy. The men were too young to have known him personally, but they recalled the village oral history that Yee Ah Tye was twelve or thirteen years old when he left Chang-wan (Zhangwan) village for Hong Kong.

The Chinese land given by the Kong Chow Association to Ah Tye in exchange for the Kong Chow Temple land in San Francisco was left to his closest relative in the village. This relative did not spend much time working on the land because, shortly after receiving the land, he moved to Hong Kong and never returned. The house built on Ah Tye's land was found neglected and in disrepair.

On the way out of the village courtyard, Blanche and Ed met Mr. Yee, who had lived in Canada and spoke a little English. He looked more Westernized than the other village men, and wore a light-blue, striped, Western-style shirt.

Mr. Yee had earned money overseas and had returned to Chang-wan village in the late 1960s when he was eighty years old. At this meeting with the Ah Tyes, he was ninety-six years old and healthy, except for a hearing loss. Even now, Mr. Yee thought like the overseas sojourners who had lived nearly a century before him: He had returned to his China homeland to live out his days.

Sunwui—1996

In the spring of 1996, Zhen-Ya (Grace) Wu and Si-Jing (Ann) Zeng participated in a sister-city program between Stockton and Foshan City, China. They visited Stockton to experience life in America and to improve

Entrance to Chang-wan village, 1988. Photograph by Dr. Edmond Chong.

their skills as secondary-school English teachers.

Grace Wu worked near Yee Ah Tye's village of Sunwui and noted that, since the Ah Tyes' visit in 1984, the standard of living had improved for most of the villagers. The Chinese government had divided the land among the farmers who can also raise fish to sell in the city at good prices.

Ferries like the one the Ah Tyes rode are no longer necessary because bridges connect all the roads from Kwangtung (Guangzhou) to Sunwui. Roads have been rebuilt and widened, making it easier for farmers to transport their crops to market.

Most of the young people are leaving the village to work in the city. They send some of their earnings to their parents, many of whom have built beautiful, new brick homes. During harvest time, the young people often take a ten-day leave from work to help their parents. While some of the young people return to their village, most do not, because city life is more exciting.

"Their thinking is different than their father and mother's," observed Grace Wu.[2] "They're not willing to live in the village their whole lives."

Most Chinese in China retained records of their family trees, even when the Japanese invaded China during World War II. However, many of these documents were destroyed during the Communists' Great Cultural Revolution that lasted from 1966 to 1976, when Chairman Mao Tse-tung sought to annihilate the old culture.

Ann Zeng said, "In China, there is a saying: We, as Chinese people, all have the same origin," meaning that everyone is a descendant of the first emperor.

But Grace Wu commented, "In China, we say the skin is yellow, the hair is black, the eyes are brown, and sometimes we don't know if they're real (Chinese) or not." The Yee family tree is a unique and rare treasure, written proof that the Ah Tyes are ancestors of the king's many sons.

Ah Pok, the last Chinese miner in La Porte. Jann Garvis Collection.

Chapter Seventeen
AMERICA: LA PORTE REVISITED

The Last Chinese in La Porte: In 1905, after yet another fire nearly destroyed La Porte, the only Chinese structure rebuilt on China Alley was the Hop Sing store. Bud Adams from Clipper Mills recalled that the small store sold groceries, Chinese rice, and tea. Ah See worked at the store and delivered groceries to miners on a beautiful mule. Ah Wye, a well-dressed, educated Chinese doctor, lived with Ah See in the store.

William Miguel remembers the way Dr. Wye walked, talked, and held his head high, reflecting an aristocratic bearing. Miguel visited the Hop Sing building often, and recalled the large front room with a counter and a wood-burning stove where the Chinese would congregate to talk or read. Down the hall were separate little rooms on both sides. The furnishings were sparse, just a place to sleep, a table, and a chair.

Miguel vaguely remembered seeing Dr. Wye and Ah See smoking long pipes in the little rooms, presumably opium. The kitchen was large; a huge chopping block stood in the middle near another wood stove. Beyond the Hop Sing woodshed was a garden, and Miguel fondly remembered the fresh peas Ah See gave him. Pigs, ducks, and chickens were also raised in the back yard.

Miguel peddled meat on horseback to a dam construction site near the North Star Mine. Although he often arrived after the lunch hour, he said a Chinese cook always fed him good things, such as pie.

The Hop Sing building burned again in 1918. In 1919, Miguel, who had moved to San Francisco, heard that Ah See and Dr. Wye were staying in a little hotel in San Francisco's Chinatown on Kearney Street. Miguel delighted them with a visit before they boarded a ship to return to China. "They were well in their seventies," he said. "They didn't think they had too many years left and felt they had to go back to their homeland."[1]

Ah Pok
Many long-time La Porte residents vividly remembered the last two Chinese who lived and died in La Porte in the 1930s, Ah Pok and "Polly Wog" (Goon Yang).

Ah Pok was a reserved man whom people liked and respected. The 1880 United States census listed Ah Pok as a thirty-five-year-old miner and boarder in the Hop Sing lodging house in La Porte's Chinatown.

Later, in 1908, he and LeRoy Post worked together at the North America hydraulic mine in nearby Gibsonville. The two men provided the power for a hand derrick, a hoisting device used to lift heavy materials. LeRoy remembered that Ah Pok was a good worker, even in his later years. Ah Pok would go down to the creek to prospect for gold, and, from time to time, find a few flakes.

Richard Kingdon, a third-generation native of La Porte, remembered that "Polly Wog" and Ah Pok lived their later years in the Hop Sing building on a bluff on the edge of the diggings. As they got older, they'd get groceries at Maxwell and Son's store and say, "Mark book." It was recorded in a ledger, but they never paid any money. The grocery owners and charitable La Porte residents paid the bill. County welfare and the continued generosity of others gave the elderly men sustenance.

Ah Pok did his last mining at age seventy-three. When he was eighty-seven, he suffered a stroke and was taken to the county hospital in Quincy. Post recalled that, one autumn day in 1939, Ah Pok saw a road going down from the hospital between Quincy and Greenville and decided to walk home. In the early afternoon, Ah Pok left the hospital, walked about a mile down the road, then lay down for the night, where he died of fatigue and exposure. Searchers found him the next morning, close to the road. Ah Pok had lived and worked in California for seven decades as a miner, and fifty-five of those years were spent in La Porte.

Ah Pok and his snowshoes, outside the La Porte Post Office. A simple leather strap held each foot in place, and one pole was used to propel or retard the skier's speed. Jann Garvis Collection.

Goon Yang, "Polly Wog"

Fragments of information reflect Goon Yang's fifty-eight years in California as a miner. The 1870 United States census shows that Goon Yang arrived in La Porte at age twenty, and lived with four other Chinese placer miners. The census of 1880 listed him as a miner with others on the English Bar. According to a Cayot mining ledger entry made on February 28, 1890, Goon Yang worked five and a half days at $1.75 each day, a total of $9.62.

The origin of Goon Yang's nickname, "Polly Wog," is unknown, but the accident that left him crippled was recalled by Post. One day Polly Wog was mining on a creek about a mile from La Porte, a place called Clark's Ravine. A rock rolled onto Polly Wog's legs and broke both of them. He was taken to the hospital where the bones were set, but he kept taking off the bandages and splints. Hospital workers tried hanging his queue over

the head of his bed and then nailing it to the floor so he couldn't get at the splints, but even that didn't work. Polly Wog's legs healed poorly, leaving one crooked and shorter than the other.

Even though Polly Wog walked with a hobble, he was a jovial man who liked to joke and have fun. When Polly Wog first joined the Chinese community in La Porte, he spoke only Chinese. But as more and more of his countrymen left town, he was forced to learn English, developing a picturesque style of speech made up of a pidgin English vocabulary from the Chinese, and with phrasing learned from the Whites.

Polly Wog had many friends. Ah Bing was a bulky Mongolian miner from nearby Scales, who protected his smaller countrymen. When Whites teased Polly Wog, they had to deal with Bing.

Terry Riley, a stagecoach driver to La Porte, also

developed a close relationship with Polly Wog. Terry liked to torment Polly Wog, often getting him so incensed that he'd cuss Terry out in Chinese. But they always made friends again, and Riley would often take Polly Wog into the store and buy him clothes or food. Polly Wog also had a good relationship with a young, outgoing neighbor named Rita McFadgen. He'd tease her by calling her "Sally Yang."

Post remembered talking to Polly Wog a few hours before he died of lobar pneumonia in 1931. Polly Wog was in the lobby of the Hop Sing store, huddled close to the woodstove and looking very poorly. When Post asked how he was feeling, Polly Wog answered, "Going on mission, going on mission." In all the years before that day, he always answered, "Fine, maybe live twenty more years."[2]

Goon Yang had spent most of his adult life in La Porte. Appropriately, his funeral services were conducted by his friends in La Porte.

La Porte Chinese Cemetery
Polly Wog's grave is one of the three graves remaining in the La Porte Chinese Cemetery. The cemetery looks like any wooded area, except for numerous depressions in the ground, indicating areas where the bones of the deceased have been exhumed. Dry grass and pine needles cover the depressions.

Polly Wog probably wished to have his bones returned to China. But with the disruption caused by the Japanese invasion of China in 1937, and the establishment of the People's Republic of China in 1949, the shipment of bones back to China was discouraged.

Chinese cemeteries in outlying towns at lower elevations were generally laid out in more formal, orderly rows. The La Porte burials were more scattered, with no specific plan to its general layout. Jann Garvis, a fourth-generation resident and historian of the La Porte area, said archaeologist Donna Day viewed the La Porte Chinese Cemetery and claimed that it was one of the largest she had seen in the area. The size reflects the large Chinese population that had lived in La Porte throughout the years.

Feeding the Dead
A careful searcher might find a piece of pottery lying on top of the ground in the cemetery. Post said these shards came from rice bowls used in the Chinese custom of "feeding the dead." Foods are used as a way to communicate with gods, ghosts, and ancestors.

An American takes flowers to a grave. A Chinese might take a piece of pork and an entire chicken with its head and feet intact (symbolizing wholeness) to offer to the deceased. For the American and the Chinese, the essence of paying homage to ancestors is the same, but the offering is different.

There is an old joke about an American and a Chinese who meet at a cemetery. The American observed the Chinese paying homage to his ancestors with food, then asked, "When are your ancestors coming to eat the food?" The Chinese replied, "The same time your ancestor comes to smell the flowers."[3]

La Porte 1996
Coyotes have made rabbits scarce in the town that was originally named Rabbit Creek. The La Porte of 1996 has a winter population of only thirty to thirty-five people. The surrounding mountains, woodlands, and barren mountainsides still show the ravages of hydraulic mining.

Along La Porte's Main Street are Reilly's Cafe and Saloon, La Porte General Store, La Porte Snowmobile Service, Gold Country Restaurant and Cafe, and Union Hotel Restaurant and Bar. These businesses serve the residents and the vacationers who occupy 120 summer homes, enjoying fishing and aquatic sports around the Little Grass Valley Reservoir.

As third-generation La Porte native Richard O'Rourke explained, "People come here primarily to get away from the concrete jungle."[4] The Plumas National Forest is one of the last virgin forests in California, attracting those who love the outdoors and come to camp and trek in the backcountry. During the winter, they come for cross-country skiing and snowmobiling.

Most of these vacationers are probably unaware of the country's illustrious past. But every year when the snow melts, the changes in the land are uncovered, exposing a treasure of relics. An observant hiker might see old, hand-blown bottles, shards of Chinese pottery, remnants of hand saws, old coins, or iron snowshoes worn by horses and oxen.

The Union Hotel was built in 1855 as the Hotel de France. The three-story structure now boasts twenty-four rooms and a full restaurant and bar. The hotel is a local landmark. Its foyer leads through a steel-lined vault originally lined with brick. Tales of Black Bart's stagecoach robberies are still retold around the bar. In the 1970s, the hotel was extensively remodeled with private baths and a full sprinkler system in case of fire. Thus far, no televisions, telephones, or fax machines have been installed, to the relief of visitors seeking solitude. One visitor said it best when she explained that the Union Hotel afforded her the opportunity "to revive the lost art of conversation."[5]

Richard O'Rourke remembered that Sam Ahtye's

Nothing remains in La Porte's China Alley except these wooden cabins, built c. 1940. Photograph by Aileen Ah-Tye Davidson, May 1988.

water system piped drinking water to the Chinese colony in La Porte. When the Ahtyes moved, O'Rourke's father, Cleveland (Cleve) O'Rourke, his grandfather, Louis Hillman, and George McMann, gained full interest in the system. The mile-and-a-half pipeline still supplies water to the O'Rourke, Hillman, and Post homes.

China Alley is still there, one block east of Main Street, but all that remains of Chinatown is the basement of the Hop Sing and Company general merchandise store. The Hop Sing building had burned at least six times, and each time it was rebuilt smaller. After the fire in 1918, it was built for the Chinese under the leadership of two carpenters, Pike and Stewart. Shorty Whiteside was the last man to live in the Hop Sing building, after he had either bought it from Pike or paid its taxes. In 1945, the Hop Sing building was in such a dilapidated condition that it was torn down. There is a row of one-room wooden cabins on La Porte's China Alley now. These four cabins, built in 1946 to house workers for a sawmill, are now uninhabited.

When you walk the narrow back roads of La Porte today, the times of gold, wealth, and power seem far away. The thousands of people that once crowded the streets are gone. Some of the Chinese lived here without the comfort of families, coping with a multitude of hardships with dignity, hope, and good humor, and some died far away from their homeland. Others found it was a pathway that led to education, service, and accomplishments in distant places. Those who sought their dreams in La Porte left more than stories and memories—they played a vital role in developing California and left to us a heritage of grace and perseverance, an example for our own lives.

These temple ruins are the only reminder that the Lincoln Municipal Park Golf Course was once the Lone Mountain Cemetery, a gift of Ah Tye. The Chinese inscription means "Temporary resting place for Kong Chow sojourners," referring to the tradition of returning bones to China. Photograph by Doreen Ah Tye.

Chapter Eighteen
REMNANTS OF AH TYE

There is a saying that the measure of a man's character is not what he gets from his ancestors, but what he leaves his descendants.

Yee Ah Tye's *San Francisco Chronicle* obituary stated that he had secured a piece of land from the United States government near Point Lobos and given it to the Kong Chow Association for a cemetery. It was here that he was buried.

A *San Francisco Daily Alta California* article described the temple built on the cemetery site:

> *Chinese Temple at Lone Mountain*
>
> *The six leading Chinese companies of San Francisco are just finishing a new and odd-looking piece of grave-yard furniture, in the shape of a roofless temple or place of prayer on the highest point of the western edge of the hill at Lone Mountain Cemetery, where there is a fine view of the Pacific Ocean, and they can look as they kneel at their devotions out towards the "Central Flowery Empire."*
>
> *It is a queer structure resembling a gigantic French bedstead (the frame supporting a bed), with a high, arched headboard, at the eastern, and a lower footboard at the western end. . . . At the eastern end is a marble tablet bearing an inscription in Chinese.*[1]

In 1900, the Chinese cemetery at Lone Mountain was one of many entire cemeteries whose remains were exhumed and moved from San Francisco to Colma when the city needed land for expansion. Remnants of the cemetery's temple bedstead are on what is now the Lincoln Park Municipal Golf Course, a little south and west of the California Palace of the Legion of Honor.[2]

The temple fragments blend gracefully with a small grove of trees on the first hole of the golf course. However, one must be careful; an observer's tranquility can be quickly disrupted by a whizzing golf ball.

According to Mo-Mo Ahtye, Yee Ah Tye was originally buried in the cemetery's courtyard. After several decades, the Kong Chow Association officers asked his family to remove his bones for reburial in a new site. Since some members of his family had been buried in another cemetery, the decision was made to move his remains to that location.

But true to his deathbed wish, Yee Ah Tye is still buried for all times in the land where he had lived. His bones, along with the remains of his wife, Chan Shee, and daughter, Alice, are buried in the Chinese Presbyterian Mission section of the Mountain View Cemetery in Oakland. His eldest daughter, Emma, and her son are buried nearby. Not far from the cemetery is the Chapel of the Chimes, where niches contain the remains of Ah Tye's daughters Charlotte and Bessie and their spouses.[3]

Spreading Like Melon Vines

Glimpses of Yee Ah Tye's life in America can be seen in deeds, mining claims, tax assessments, newspaper articles, directory listings, temple remains, and land that he once owned. His legacy, however, is in his descendants.

Just as the history of a country is like a mirror that reflects its successes, failures, and lessons to be learned, a family can learn from its lineage. A genealogy identifies the origins of ones' ancestors so that descendants can understand their inheritance and determine who is a distant or close relative. Ancestors can also serve as examples and inspiration for greater self-knowledge and enlightenment.

Many Chinese with common last names like Chan, Lee, Fong, and Wong may have no relationship to one another. However, descendants of Yee Ah Tye have continued with this unique last name and varied its spelling to Ahtye, Ah Tye, and Ah-Tye. The Yee family genealogy states that the saying, "a tree can-

Grave offerings are designed to keep gods, ghosts, and ancestors content and in good humor. Photograph by Louis J. Stellman; California State Library.

not grow without roots," refers to ensuring that the branches and descendants are strong and flourishing.[4] Yee Ah Tye and Chan Shee's marriage produced more than 180 descendants through six generations, "spreading like melon vines, increasing continuously."

The Ah Tye clan now includes businessmen, doctors, dentists, health care workers, educators, government officials and employees, lawyers, homemakers, technicians, and artists.[5] Moreover, it includes a whole generation of veterans who did the best they could to bring peace and victory to the land of their grandfather and their own country—America.

ENDNOTES

Chapter One

1. *San Francisco Call,* June 14, 1896; *San Francisco Chronicle,* June 14, 1896.

   The *San Francisco Call* said Yee Ah Tye died at age seventy-eight, but the *San Francisco Chronicle* said he was seventy-six. Figures from the 1870 and 1880 United States censuses indicate Ah Tye was nearly seventy-three years old at his death. When a Chinese dies, three years are generally added to his age: one year for heaven; one year for Earth; one year for Man (as mediator between heaven and Earth). The *San Francisco Chronicle's* estimate of Ah Tye's death probably reflects this way of figuring.

2. *San Francisco Chronicle,* June 14, 1896.

3. Ibid.

4. One version of the Ah Tye family's oral history says that the town of Lodi, California, was named after Yee Lo Dy. Erwin Gudde, in *California Place Names,* p. 180, says the origin of the town's name is Lodi, Italy, the scene of Napoleon's first spectacular victory in 1796.

5. Because most of the people described in this book trace their ancestries to southern China, the Cantonese spelling of names is given first. The Mandarin spellings are in parentheses.

6. Based on translated testimony of the leading merchants of the four district association houses in San Francisco, a California Assembly committee reported that in 1853, most of the twenty-two thousand Chinese emigrants were from Kwangtung Province.

7. This Yee genealogy is based on L. Eve Armentrout Ma, "Genealogy and History: The Yu of Yi-mei and Chang-wan in Kwangtung's Xin-hui xian," *Asian Folklore Studies,* Volumes 43–1 (1984): pp. 109–131.

8. In the 1930s, Rose Ah Tye asked a relative returning to Yee Ah Tye's Chinese village of Sunwui to get a copy of their Yee family tree. For over forty years the document lay unread on a closet shelf in Rose's home. When Rose died and her home was emptied, Blanche Ah Tye saved it from being destroyed.

   The Yee family tree is written in an ancient, classical style that has no punctuation. Those who are familiar with modern Chinese writing can get a general understanding of it; however, because of its ancient phrases and words, some parts are difficult to comprehend.

9. Armentrout Ma, *Asian Folklore Studies,* p. 120.

10. Ibid., p. 119.

Chapter Two

1. *Daily Alta California,* October 31, 1850, morning edition.

2. Mo-Mo (Mrs. Sidney Sr.) Ahtye, interview by author, Salinas, California, July 12, 1981.

   Descendants of Yee Ah Tye vary the spelling of their last name. Eldest son Sam's branch generally write it as one word: Ahtye. Youngest son Dilly Sr.'s branch usually use two separate words or hyphenated: Ah Tye or Ah-Tye.

3. In tracing the activities of Yee Ah Tye in San Francisco, a key document is the record of a civil suit between his daughter, Charlotte Chang, and the Kong Chow Benevolent Association of San Francisco. Part of the record is an 1866 deed signed by Ah Tye in both English and Chinese. His Chinese name was written in calligraphy as "Yee Dy" and his American name as "George Athei." This record provides the documentation that Yee Ah Tye is to be identified as "George Athei," one of the agents or heads of the Sze Yup Association in San Francisco from 1853 to 1854.

4. Barth, *Bitter Strength,* p. 97, explains that the use of the term "Chinese Six Companies" obscures the fact that there were six district companies in the association only in the years 1862 through 1882. In later decades, eight companies formed the association and, after 1909, seven companies.

5. *Journals of the California Legislature,* Assembly Journal 1853, p. 9. Victor G. and Brett de Bary Nee, *Longtime Californ',* pp. 272 and 273.

6. *Journals of the California Legislature,* Assembly Journal 1853, p. 9.

7. *San Francisco Daily Herald and Mirror,* December 20, 1853.

8. *Daily Alta California,* May 31, 1853.

9. *San Francisco Herald,* May 29, 1853.

10. *Daily Alta California,* August 13, 1852.

11. Ibid., August 15, 1852.

12. *San Francisco Daily Herald,* March 8, 1851.

13. Daily Alta California, August 15, 1852.

14. Three years later, the *Sacramento Union* ("Sale of Female Celestials," March 22, 1855) stated that "the notorious Ah Toy, who has been the keeper of a house of ill-fame in San Francisco for the last three years, has lately left for China. She brought to this country a year ago, on her return from a visit, six or eight women, whom she had purchased at $40 each. Their passage cost them $80 each. She has from time to time sold out her stock at the rate of $1,000 to $1,500 each, to Chinese merchants and gamblers. On leaving for China, she disposed of the lot remaining at $800 each . . . these women dare not resist in these transactions, so much are they in

dread of their tyrannical countrymen."

Judy Yung, in *Unbound Feet*, p. 34, says that Miss Atoy announced to journalists in 1857 that she was retiring to China with no intention of returning. However, in 1859, she was reportedly arrested in San Francisco for keeping a "disorderly house." Ah Toy reportedly lived with her husband in Santa Clara County, California after 1868. She died in 1928, three months short of her one hundredth birthday.

15. *Daily Alta California*, May 27, 1853.
16. *San Francisco Daily Herald*, July 4, 1853.
17. *1856 San Francisco City Directory.*
18. *San Francisco Daily Herald*, July 25, 1853.
19. Ibid., July 4, 1853.
20. Ibid.

Chapter Three

1. William Hoy, *Kong Chow Temple*, pp. 3-4.
2. Him Mark Lai explained that the Kong Chow Association later inherited the land, building, and temple of the Sze Yup Association, and this gave rise to the widely held misconception that it was the first huiguan.

    For further information, see Henry J. Labatt, counselor at law, *Reports of Cases Determined in the District Courts of the State of California*, Volume 1, pp. 158–159, and "Historical Development of the Chinese Consolidated Benevolent Association/Huiguan System," *Chinese America: History and Perspectives 1987*, pp. 17–18.
3. *Daily Alta California*, July 10, 1853.
4. William Speer, *The Oldest and the Newest Empire*, pp. 564–565.
5. Ibid., p. 565.
6. *Daily Alta California*, July 15, 1853.
7. Ibid., July 19, 1853.
8. *San Francisco Daily Herald*, July 21, 1853.
9. Speer, *The Oldest and the Newest Empire*, p. 565.
10. Hoy, *Kong Chow Temple*, p. 4.
11. *Daily Alta California*, April 5, 1856.
12. *San Francisco Daily Herald and Mirror*, April 4, 1856.
13. *Daily Alta California*, April 5, 1856.
14. Kip, "Idol-Worship in San Francisco," *Colonial Church Chronicle*, October 1856, p. 140.
15. Ibid.
16. Ibid.
17. *Daily Alta California*, April 5, 1856.
18. *San Francisco Daily Herald and Mirror*, April 5, 1856.

Chapter Four

1. Miners bound for one of the southern Mother Lode towns, such as Angels Camp, Columbia, Coulterville, Chinese Camp, Sonora, or Hornitos, traveled to Stockton. Those traveling to the Northern Mines and towns such as La Porte, Auburn, Placerville, Oroville, Nevada City, or Grass Valley, journeyed to Sacramento then to Marysville.
2. Samuel Colville, *City Directory of Sacramento For the Year 1854–5*, p. 80.
3. *Sacramento Union*, July 14, 1854.
4. Ibid., July 19 and August 31, 1855.
5. *Shasta Courier*, July 29, 1854.
6. Ibid., May 20, 1854.
7. Ibid., August 12, 1854.
8. Ibid., July 29, 1854.
9. *Sacramento Union*, December 25, 1854.
10. Ibid., November 17, 1854.
11. Ibid., March 29, 1855.
12. Ibid., February 17, 1855.
13. Ibid., January 24 and 26, 1857.
14. Ibid., February 17, 1855.
15. Ibid., June 28, 1855.
16. *Sacramento Daily Bee*, March 17, 1858, and *Sacramento Union*, March 18, 1858.
17. *Daily Alta California*, September 10, 1854.
18. *Shasta Courier*, May 20, 1854.
19. *Daily Alta California*, September 10, 1854.
20. *Sacramento Union*, November 8, 1856.
21. Nothing more is known about the daughter born to Ah Tye's first wife. However, Mo-Mo Ahtye, interviewed by the author in Salinas, California, July 12, 1981, remembered that the Ah Tyes sent money back to the village from generation to generation.
22. *Sacramento Daily Bee*, December 7, 1861.
23. The Praetzellis, *Archaeological and Historical Studies of the IJ56 Block, Sacramento, California: An Early Chinese Community*, p. 164.

Chapter Five

1. J. D. Borthwick, *Three Years in California*, pp. 117–118.
2. Brown's Valley Mining District or Empire Hill and Yuba River, 1854–1864, Volume 1, Yuba County, Marysville County Clerk, Marysville, California.

    Yee Ah Tye's mining claims appear on pages listing other Chinese claim owners such as Ar Coey, Ar Chung, Ar King, Ar Kee, and Ar Jim and Co. The recorder used "Ar" before each Chinese name instead of the usual "Ah."
3. Borthwick, *Three Years in California*, p. 215.
4. *The Messenger*, March 14, 1863.
5. Ibid., October 31, 1863.
6. Ibid., December 19, 1863.
7. Ibid., March 12, 1864.
8. The claim was filed as "J. A. Denson to G. Athie and Co.," Sierra County book of deeds, Book 1, August 19, 1864, La Porte, California, Sierra County Courthouse, Downieville, California.
9. James Sinnott, author of History of Sierra County, was interviewed in Downieville, California, June 23, 1986. When asked if he thought Ah Tye used the arrastra technique in his mining, he answered, "Certainly, if there was a cabin on the land."
10. *The Messenger*, July 25, 1863.
11. Ibid., October 1, 1864.
12. Ibid., November 28, 1863.
13. Ibid., September 24, 1864.
14. Ibid., June 20, 1868.
15. Ibid.
16. March 19, 1864 was the date of the last issue of *The Messenger* printed in La Porte. An immediate demand for a pro-Union printing establishment in the county seat of Sierra County prompted the newspaper's move to

Downieville.

17. *Mountain Messenger,* June 18, 1864.
18. Ibid., April 22, 1865.
19. *Daily Alta California,* April 17, 1865.
20. Ibid., April 21, 1865.
21. The *Mountain Messenger,* June 14, 1873, reported that Chinese companies would telegraph when there was no more need for Chinese workers in the La Porte area.
22. *Mountain Messenger,* November 10, 1866.
23. Ibid., December 15, 1866.
24. Ibid.
25. "Reminiscences of Samuel H. Auerbach," pp. 34, 39, 40 and 41.
26. *La Porte Union,* March 6, 1869.
27. Ibid., March 27, 1869.
28. "Reminiscences of Samuel H. Auerbach," p. 57.
29. Gould, *La Porte Scrapbook,* p. 161.
30. A suit titled "Eldridge vs. See Yup Company" involved Ah Tye (named "George Athaie" in the case) as defendant over the Pine Street land that he gave to the Sze Yup Company. The case involved some complicated aspects of real property including deeds and trusts. See Labatt, *Reports of Cases Determined in the District Courts of the State of California,* pp. 158–159.
31. Asian-American historians estimate that for every ten Chinese entering California in the nineteenth century, seven were Sze Yup people. (For the original composition of the Sze Yup Association, see Chapter Two.)

   In 1853, the Sunning people, except members of the Yee (Yu) clan, broke away from the Sze Yup Association. In 1862, members of Sunning's Yee clan and emigrants from Hoiping and Yanping formed a new district association called the Hop Wo Association (Hehe Huiguan).

   All that was left of the Sze Yup Association were Sunwui people, the only remainder of the four founding groups. The Sunwui people, together with people from the neighboring county of Hoshan (Heshan), reorganized as the Kong Chow Association. Yee Ah Tye was a member of the Yee clan from Sunwui, a small minority group that remained with the Sze Yup Association. When the Yee clan broke away from the Sze Yup Association, Yee Ah Tye did not join them, because his roots were from a district different from most of the other Yees, who were from Sunning.
32. Eng Ying Gong and Bruce Grant, *Tong War,* p. 32.
33. According to the *Chinese Times,* August 4, 1973, the Suey Sing Tong celebrated its 107th anniversary in 1973. It was organized around 1866.

Chapter Six

1. *La Porte Union,* May 1, 1869. The collection of the foreign miners' tax ended in 1870 after the civil-rights bill was passed by Congress.
2. Auerbach Collection, Box 1, Folder number 93/13C, The Bancroft Library, University of California, Berkeley.
3. *Mountain Messenger,* January 8, 1870.
4. Fong, *Overland Monthly,* p. 524. Fong based his article on interviews with the president of the Ning Yung Company (one of the Chinese Six Companies), the president of

the "Meeting Hall of the Middle Kingdom," and some pioneer Chinese, who had been in the United States soon after the discovery of gold in California.

5. *Mountain Messenger,* August 27, 1872.
6. Ibid., July 18, 1874.
7. Ibid., August 5, 1876.
8. Mark and Chih, *A Place Called Chinese America,* p. 34.
9. *Plumas National,* June 7, 1873.
10. Ibid., October 4, 1873.
11. Ibid., June 7, 1873.
12. Ibid., August 19, 1876.
13. *Mountain Messenger,* May 10, 1879.
14. *Plumas National,* May 24, 1879.
15. Ibid., August 2, 1879.
16. Ibid., August 12, 1879.
17. *Mountain Messenger,* April 7, 1877.
18. Charles W. Hendel, "Report on the Plumas Consolidated Gravel Mining Company," p. 23.
19. *Plumas National,* August 17, 1878.
20. Ibid., June 14, 1879.
21. Ibid., September 20, 1879. Sierra County assessment rolls also show that "Ah Ty" paid taxes on mining ground in Eureka Creek, northwest of Downieville, from 1878 to 1880.
22. LeRoy Post, interview by author, La Porte, California, July 19, 1985.
23. The letters quoted below are from La Porte Bank copybook 1876-1880, letters number 65, 57, and 261, courtesy of Jann Garvis.
24. Howland Flat ledger books, courtesy of Jann Garvis.
25. *Plumas National,* April 22, 1876.
26. Ibid., April 14, 1877.
27. Ibid., June 9, 1877.

Chapter Seven

1. Jerry Brady, interview by author, Nevada City, California, October 28, 1984. Jerry's father, Thomas Bernard Brady (1874-1964), was in his thirties when he knew Sam Ahtye in You Bet, California.
2. Robert J. and Grace Slyter, "Historical Notes of the Early Washington, Nevada County California Mining District," p. 1, Searls Library, Nevada City, California.
3. Nevada County index to deeds, 1856-1880, Book 55, p. 501, Nevada County Courthouse, Nevada City, California.
4. H. P. Davis, *Other Times, Other Manners: Another Commentary on Early Revisions of the Ordinances of the City of Nevada.*
5. 1880 United States census, Goodwin Township, Plumas County, California, La Porte China Town [sic], California State Library, Sacramento.
6. *Mountain Messenger,* October 30, 1880. Research was complicated by the fact that La Porte was part of Plumas County, while most of the outlying mining communities lay within Sierra County.
7. Deeds Book "U," p. 307, "George W. Hughes to Ah Tye et al.," November 18, 1880, Sierra County Courthouse, Downieville, California.

   Sierra County assessment rolls for 1882, 1884 and 1885 also show that "Ah Ty" owned a house and lot at Morristown formerly owned by T. Debuque, bounded on the north by Main Street.

8. Company partnership names were compared to names in the 1870 United States census, La Porte Post Office.

9. The Chinese Exclusion Act was extended an additional ten years by the Geary Act of May 5, 1892. Then on April 27, 1904, the exclusion of Chinese laborers from the United States was extended indefinitely.

10. California's miscegenation law was ruled unconstitutional in 1948.

11. Mo-Mo Ahtye, interview by author, Salinas, California, July 12, 1981.

12. Lists of Chinese passengers arriving at San Francisco, 1882-1914, Roll 1, August 9, 1882, *Grenada* to May 22, 1885, *San Pablo*, National Archives of the United States, San Bruno, California.

13. Lillian (Mrs. Oliver) Chang, interview by author, Foster City, California, July 11, 1985.

14. *Mountain Messenger,* September 12, 1885.

15. Ibid., February 20, 1886.

16. Ibid.

17. Ibid.

18. Ibid., February 27, 1886.

19. Ibid., March 6, 1886.

20. Ibid., April 17, 1886.

21. Ibid., March 13, 1886.

22. Ibid., May 8, 1886.

23. *Plumas National,* May 8, 1886.

24. Claire Cayot O'Rourke, interview by author, Quincy, California, July 23, 1987.

25. *Mountain Messenger,* September 16, 1882.

26. Ibid., March 13, 1886.

27. Claire Cayot O'Rourke, interview by author, Quincy, California, July 23, 1987.

28. 1867–1905 Plumas County assessment rolls, Plumas County Museum, Quincy, California.
    The 1885 and 1886 Plumas County assessment rolls show that during these anti-Chinese league years Hop Sing and Company and Hop Kee and Company had the same amount of goods and paid the same amount of taxes.

29. "Ah Tie" was listed in some of Cayot's ledgers from 1885–1886, pp. 34 and 35. Used by permission of the Cayot family.

30. Sierra County Book of Deeds, Book V, "Ah Tie, et al. to Gibsonville U.W. Co., et al.," November 14, 1881, Sierra County Courthouse, Downieville, California.
    Names of members of the 1881 Hop Sing and Company and Pike and Company deed were compared to the statistics from the 1880 United States census, La Porte, California.

31. 1886, 1887, 1888, and 1891 Sierra County assessment rolls, Sierra County Courthouse, Downieville, California.
    The 1886–1890 Plumas County assessment rolls also show that Hop Sing and Company had another placer mine on a branch of the south fork of the Feather River, known as the Hop Sing Claim.

32. *Plumas National,* August 7, 1886.

Chapter Eight

1. John and LeRoy Post, letter to author, January 1986.

2. Jann Garvis, in an interview by author, Stockton, California, March 22, 1987, explained that even in the 1990s, one is required to build a house in La Porte with a certain degree pitch to the roof so the snow will slide off.

3. *Mountain Messenger,* May 20, 1882.

4. Ibid., November 5, 1892.

5. Ibid., November 26, 1892.

6. The corporation may have defaulted on a contract for supplies that Ah Tye had provided, or for goods he had paid for but never received. Sierra County minutes of the Superior Court, Book 3, p. 458, May 17, 1892, Ah Ty [sic] vs. Union Consolidated Drift Mines, Limited, a Corporation. Register of Actions, District Court, Sierra County, 1892, Number 647, p. 694. Sierra County Courthouse, Downieville, California.

7. *Mountain Messenger,* March 14, 1896.

8. Ibid., April 4, 1896.

9. *Daily Appeal,* June 16, 1896; and *San Francisco Call,* June 16, 1896.

10. Beulah Jung, interview by author, Stockton, California, February 19, 1985.

11. *Mountain Messenger,* August 2, 1890; and *San Francisco Call,* June 14, 1896.

Chapter Nine

1. LeRoy Post's remembrances are derived from interviews by Jann Garvis from 1977 to 1987, and interviews by author from 1985 to 1987.

2. Fan tan is a Chinese betting game in which the players lay wagers on the number of counters that will remain in a pile after it has been divided into four.

Chapter Ten

1. Durrant was found guilty of murder and hanged at San Quentin State Prison on January 7, 1898.

2. LeRoy Post, interview by Jerry Brady, Yuba City, California, April 19, 1984.

3. Charles William Hendel, 1853–1918, also owned a large interest in the Alturas tailing mine on Slate Creek and nearly all claims on Porte Wine Ridge, known as the Lucky Gold Hill Mine, nearly eight hundred acres.

4. According to the "Proof of Annual Labor and Improvements upon the 'Hop Sing Placer Mining Claim' for the years ending December 31, 1897 and December 31, 1898," 150 days of labor were performed on the Hop Sing placer mine. Index to Miscellaneous Records, Plumas County 1873–1937, "A" Listing, Volume 3, pp. 427–429, Plumas County Courthouse, Quincy, California.

5. *Mountain Messenger,* June 10, 1905. Extensive research has not uncovered any other records of AhTye's case; it apparently never went to trial. The arrest may have been made as a warning to Ahtye and other potential hydraulickers in the region to adhere to the proscribed regulations, with charges dismissed after the point had been made. Ahtye may have been a scapegoat, and his weaker legal position because of his race, prevented any retribution against his persecutors.

6. Thomas W. Brady, interview by author, San Bruno, California, April 29, 1987.

7. Although drift mining was used as early as the 1850s, no record has been found to indicate that the Ah Tyes utilized the technique before Sam's time.

8. The Riffle claim with "Sam Ah Tye" as owner is listed in "Mining in California," California State Mining Bureau, October 1924. The front ground on the Slate Creek side was hydraulicked. There was also a bedrock tunnel two thousand feet long to tap the back, or Port Wine channel, but the amount of breasting was unknown.

9. Charles J. McClain, *In Search of Equality—The Chinese Struggle Against Discrimination in Nineteenth-Century America,* p. 202.

10. *Police and Peace Officers' Journal,* July 1926, p. 15.

11. Beulah Jung, interview by author, Stockton, California, February 15, 1985.

12. Raymond Ah Tye, interview by author, Sacramento, California, May 29, 1985.

13. Hughes Chin is the author's maternal uncle, and Bow Chin is the author's maternal grandfather. Sandy Lydon, author of *Chinese Gold: The Chinese in the Monterey Bay Region,* asked Chin in 1986 why Salinas still had a Chinatown or a large, fairly cohesive Chinese group, when Chinatowns in San Jose, Gilroy, Watsonville, and Monterey had more or less disappeared. Hughes replied that one reason for Salinas' success was because it has a Chinese cemetery that has very good *feng shui* or "windwater." As a result of good *feng shui* all goes well for the descendants. The burial of Chinese in Caucasian cemeteries was not permitted in the old days.

14. The term *wahng* means horizontal, sideway, crosswise, and lateral. It differs from *jing,* which means proper, straightforward, honest, and virtuous. *Jing* is used to describe legal business or work.

15. Chinese lottery, now called keno, was a very common game in the San Francisco Bay area. The only difference was that in the early days it was played using eighty words written in calligraphy. Later, when more non-Chinese began playing keno, it was changed to numbers. Chuck-a-luck is a gambling game in which players bet on the possible combinations of three thrown dice.

16. *Salinas Index Journal,* June 2, 1930.

17. Alice graduated with two other women as a doctor of dental surgery, University of California, May 1927.

18. After Ko Shee died, Alice Ahtye married Hank Mar (1942), moved to Salinas, and retired from dentistry.

19. During World War II, Sidney was awarded the Silver Star for gallantry in action in connection with military operations against an armed enemy as a member of Headquarters Company, First Battalion, 355th Infantry, on March 27, 1945.

Chapter Eleven

1. The program was organized in memory of the 1870 Tientsin (Tienjin) Massacre, during which French Roman Catholic missionaries were murdered by a Chinese mob.

2. Mun Yew Chung graduated from Hartford High School in 1879, then attended Yale for two years where he was coxswain of the varsity crew. Chung rose high in the diplomatic service of China. Virginia (Thrall) Smith was a city missionary of Hartford and founder of the Home for Incurables in Newington.

3. Chang was one of eleven students from the Chinese Educational Mission who attended Phillips Academy.

4. La Fargue, *China's First Hundred,* pp. 41, 42.

5. *Hartford Daily Courant,* May 21, 1887.

6. While Chang was saving for his trip, a friend who had also been a student in the program asked for help to reach his home at a distant place in China. Chang willingly loaned him the entire amount, then set out for the second time to save his money to complete his education.

7. *1927 Yale Obituary Record,* pp. 109, 110.

8. The law pertaining to the naturalization of aliens was amended February 18, 1875 and limited the status to free Whites and those of African descent. It was amended by another act on May 18, 1882, which specifically forbade the naturalization of Chinese persons.

9. C. P. Pomeroy, *Reports of Cases Determined in the Supreme Court of the State of California,* Volume 84, pp. 163–165.

10. *San Francisco Examiner,* May 18, 1890. The *San Francisco Chronicle* also reported the same day that it was "probable the Chang will appeal to the United States Supreme Court." However, research done by Rachelle B. Chong seems to indicate that Chang did not appeal the California decision.

11. Hong Yen Chang worked with the San Francisco branch of the Yokohama Specie Bank from 1895 to 1907.

12. Hong Yen Chang's documents written in Chinese calligraphy were translated and interpreted by Florence (Mrs. S. L.) Fong and Harry L. Chin.

13. Postcards from the Chang Family Collection.

14. *Social Register, Washington, 1914,* pp. 25 and 164, Chang Family Collection. Hong Yen Chang served as charge d'affaires from December 1913 until March 1914.

15. *Washington Post,* November 26, 1913.

16. Ibid. A frock coat is a knee-length coat, fitting close at the waist and flared out at the hem.

17. Ibid.

Chapter Twelve

1. Claire Cayot O'Rourke described the stagecoach trip in detail. She lived in Quincy and died at the age of 111 in 1996.

2. *Marysville Daily Appeal,* March 3, 1897; *Mountain Messenger,* March 13, 1897.

3. Mary Schwegler, telephone conversation with author, December 15, 1988.

4. *San Francisco Evening Post,* August 23, 1900.

5. Mo-Mo Ahtye, interview by author, Cameron Park, California, June 19, 1989; Mary Schwegler, telephone conversation with author, December 15, 1988.

6. In the early 1900s, Ng Poon Chew brought about better mutual understanding between Chinese and American people as a Presbyterian minister, lecturer, journalist, and editor of the first Chinese daily newspaper in America, *Chung Sai Yat Po.*

7. *Senior Record Book of the University of California, 1906,* The Bancroft Library, University of California, Berkeley.

8. Oliver C. Smith, M.D., letter to Hong Yen Chang, May 5, 1906, Chang Family Collection.

9. *San Francisco Call,* December 28, 1906.
10. *California Alumni in China,* China Alumni Association of the University of California, Peking, 1916.
11. Newspaper clipping titled, "At Canton," written for the *China Mail,* 1915, Lowe Family Collection.
12. Bola went on to contribute much in radio communications during World War II, the Korean War, and the Vietnam War. During World War II, he received the War Department's Civilian Service Overseas Award for designing signal equipment in the Hawaiian and Canton islands.
13. Bola Lowe, interview by author, Kaneohe, Hawaii, March 25, 1985.
14. The San Francisco Chinese Chamber of Commerce was the first Chinese body of its kind in the world. The chamber has a history from 1890, when Chinese elders started the Chinese Merchants' Association. When the 1906 earthquake and fire destroyed Chinatown, the merchants' association was reorganized, taking the title of the Chinese Chamber of Commerce. It was incorporated in 1910.
15. Chee left this job because the 1937-1945 Sino-Japanese War hampered trade and reduced business potential.

Chapter Thirteen

1. The traditions described in this section are drawn both from family records and interviews with Florence (Mrs. S. L.) Fong and Mr. Harry L. Chin.
2. Letter of recommendation, The Yokohama Specie Bank, Ltd., San Francisco, California, February 24, 1917, Ah Tye Family Collection.
3. The University of the Pacific was chartered in San Jose, California, on July 10, 1851, and moved to Stockton in 1924. The University changed its name to the College of the Pacific in 1911 and changed its name back to the University of the Pacific in 1961.
4. In Stockton, Ora had been appointed as the only female police court interpreter in America in 1921.
5. *Sacramento Bee,* August 12 and 15, 1929; *Sacramento Union,* August 12 and 15, 1929; and *Stockton Record,* August 12 and 15, 1929.
6. The National Dollar Stores, Inc., was founded by the Shoong family. Originally started as a small store in San Francisco in 1907, it had become a chain with over fifty branches by 1928.
7. Howard Ah-Tye, "The Ah Tye Family—Growing Up in Stockton," *East/West,* September 27, 1978.
8. A union suit is a one-piece undergarment with long sleeves and legs, similar to thermal underwear.

Chapter Fourteen

1. Summi Ahtye, interview by author, San Francisco, California, October 20, 1984.
2. Perry went on to serve as a staff surgeon in the Vietnam War on the U.S.S. *Coral Sea* (1961–1962); a staff surgeon and postgraduate preceptor at the U.S. Naval Hospital in Newport, Rhode Island (1962–1966); chief of surgery and postgraduate preceptor, U.S. Naval Hospital, Yokosuka, Japan (1968–1971); and assistant chief of cardiothoracic surgery and postgraduate preceptor, U.S.

Naval Hospital, San Diego, California (1971–1976). He retired as a captain in the United States Navy Medical Corps in 1976. Perry was a thoracic surgeon on the staff of the Kaiser Permanente Hospital in San Diego, California, 1976–992.
3. Howard Ah-Tye, "A Chinese American in WW II," *Asian Week* commentary, May 6, 1982.
4. Howard Ah-Tye, "Chinese Americans in World War II," *Asian Week,* June 3, 1982.
5. Edward Ah Tye, a speech entitled "They Call Me Lucky," presented to the Stockton Cathay Club, June, 1987.
6. Howard Ah-Tye, "The Ah Tye Family—Growing up in Stockton," *East/West,* September 27, 1978.
7. Barbara's future husband, Dr. Edmond Chong, was an Air Force pilot stationed in Tampa, Florida, during World War II.
8. Victor Ah-Tye participated in tennis, softball, basketball, bowling, and golf. The latter was his "second love," and Swenson Park Golf Course, his "second home." In 1977, a monument and drinking fountain were dedicated in Victor's memory near one of his favorite spots, the sixteenth tee at Swenson Park, Stockton.
9. Bishop Wilbur W. Y. Choy, letter in tribute to Rose Ah Tye, May 7, 1975, Seattle, Washington.
10. Rose's twelve grandsons were Robert Ah-Tye, Gordon Ah Tye, Dale Ah Tye, Fred Cheung Jr., Marshall Cheung, Terry Ah-Tye, Denny Ah-Tye, Elliott Kai-Kee, Kirk Ah-Tye, Kenneth Ah Tye, Curtis Chong, and Mitchell Ah-Tye.

Chapter Fifteen

1. *Young China,* December 15, 1977. The 1866 Kong Chow deed described the piece of land in San Francisco as: "Commencing on the North line of Pine Street ninety five feet ten inches West from the North West Corner of Kearney and Pine Streets . . ."
2. Lillian Chang, interview by author, Foster City, California, July 11, 1985.
3. Manchester Fu, Manny and the Celestials—"Kong Chow Temple," *East/West,* October 27, 1968.
4. *Chinese Times,* March 28, 1969. A "mu" is a sixth of an acre of land.
5. Gordon Lau, telephone conversation with Rachelle Chong, March 1984, San Francisco, California.
6. *San Francisco Chronicle,* April 29, 1969.
7. "Origins of the Kong Chow Temple," *Asian Week,* February 3, 1983.
8. Lillian Chang, interview by author, Foster City, California, July 11, 1985.

Chapter Sixteen

1. Since January 1994, all Chinese money has been the "people's money" or Renminbi (RMB). It is denominated into the yuan. Foreign Exchange Certificates (FEC) are no longer in use.
2. Zhen-Ya (Grace) Wu and Si-Jing (Ann) Zeng, interview by author, Stockton, California, March 23, 1996.

Chapter Seventeen

1. William Miguel, interview by author, Oakland, California,

December 22, 1988.

2. LeRoy Post, interview by Jann Garvis, Oroville, California, November 28, 1985.

3. Hughes Chin, interview by author, Salinas, California, June 21, 1986.

4. Richard O'Rourke, interview by author, La Porte, California, July 19, 1985.

5. "Summer Vacation Guide: La Porte's Union Hotel Renovation," May 22, 1991.

Chapter Eighteen

1. *Daily Alta California,* January 10, 1864.

2. Mariann Kaye Wells, "Chinese Temples in California," University of California Thesis, July 20, 1962, p. 31.
   From Wells' investigation and observation, the shrines in the two Chinese cemeteries in Colma were almost exactly like the temple described in the *San Francisco Daily Alta,* January 10, 1864, article.

3. Emma Cheong is buried with her son, Chew, in the Chinese Presbyterian Mission section of the Mountain View Cemetery, Oakland. Hong Yen, Charlotte, and Ora Chang are buried in the Chapel of the Chimes, Memory W–7–9. Oliver and his wife, Lillian, are buried in the Chapel of the Chimes, Court of St. Paul W–5–26. Chee Soo and Bessie Lowe are buried in the Chapel of the Chimes, Gentle Spirit E–3–11.

4. L. Eve Armentrout Ma, "Genealogy and History: The Yu of Yi-mei and Chang-wan in Kwangtung's Xin-hui xian," pp. 124, 126.

5. Bessie and Chee Soo Lowe's daughter, Grace, married Hock S. Ong, who in 1965 became a high-court judge in Kuala Lumpur, Malaysia. In 1994, Dilly Sr. and Rose Ah Tye's granddaughter, Rachelle B. Chong, became the first Asian American to be appointed to the five-member Federal Communications Commission in Washington, D.C. The appointment was made by President Clinton. Rachelle is the daughter of Dr. Edmond and Barbara (Ah Tye) Chong.

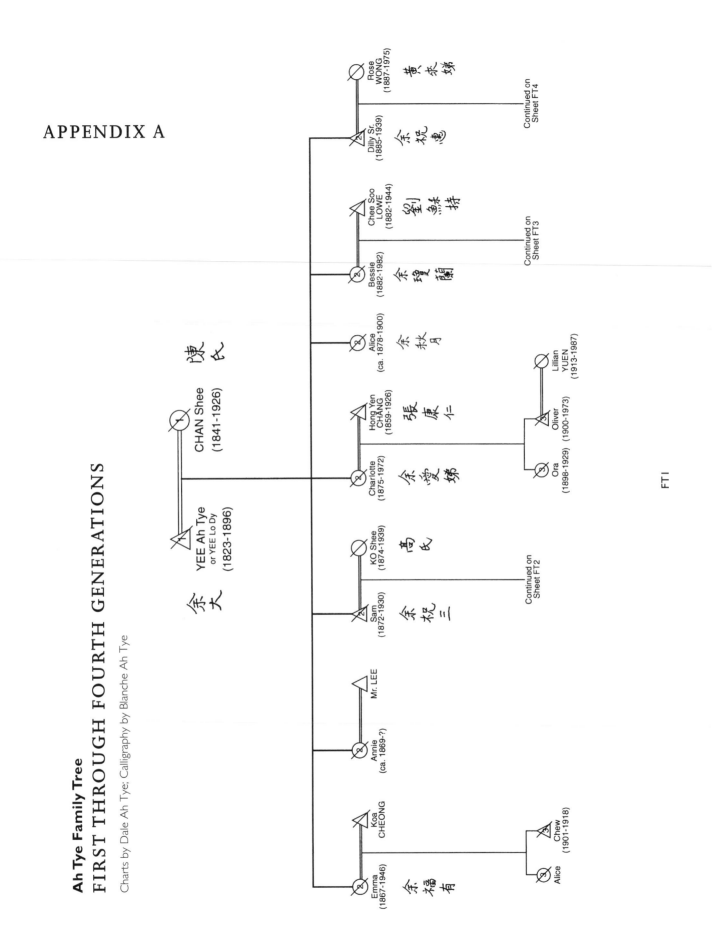

Ah Tye Family Tree
FIRST THROUGH FOURTH GENERATIONS

Charts by Dale Ah Tye; Calligraphy by Blanche Ah Tye

陳
氏

CHAN Shee
(1841-1926)

YEE Ah Tye
or YEE Lo Dy
(1823-1896)

余
大

Rose
WONG
(1887-1975)
黃
來
娣

Continued on Sheet FT4

Dilly Sr.
(1885-1939)
余
祝
德

Chee Soo
LOWE
(1882-1944)
劉
金
枝

Continued on Sheet FT3

Bessie
(1882-1982)
余
瓊
蘭

Alice
(ca. 1878-1900)
余
秋
月

Hong Yen
CHANG
(1859-1926)
張
康
仁

Charlotte
(1875-1972)
余
愛
嫦

Lillian
YUEN
(1913-1987)

Oliver
(1900-1973)

Ora
(1898-1929)

KO Shee
(1874-1939)
高
氏

Sam
(1872-1930)
余
祝
三

Continued on Sheet FT2

Mr. LEE

Annie
(ca. 1869-?)

Koa
CHEONG

Emma
(1867-1946)
余
福
有

Chew
(1901-1918)

Alice

FT1

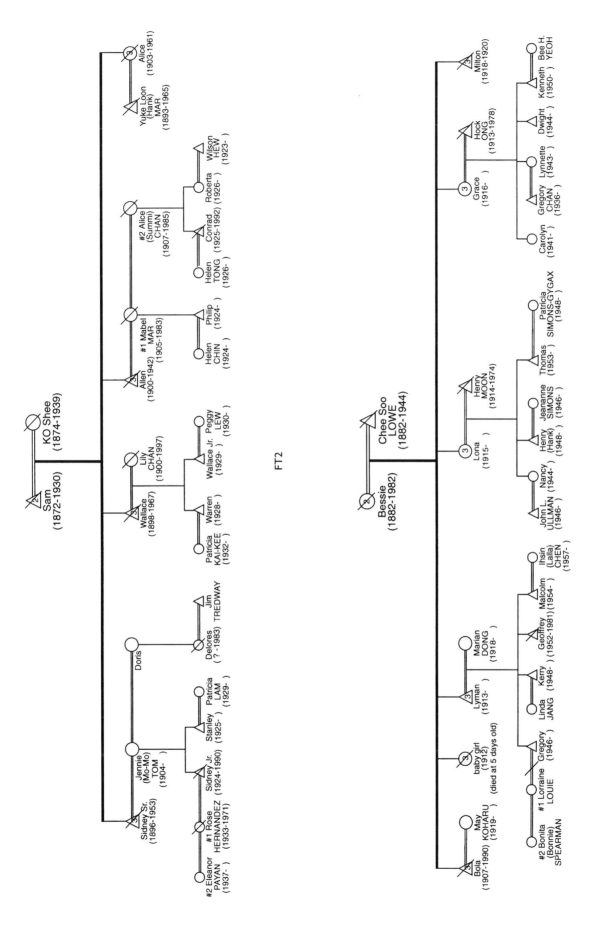

FT2

FT3

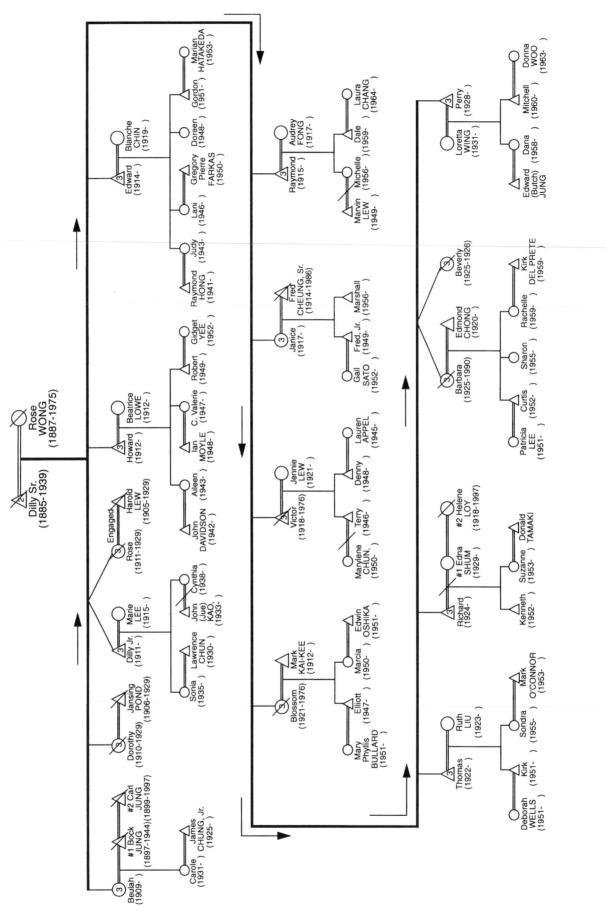

FT4

APPENDIX B: LOTTERY TICKET TRANSLATION

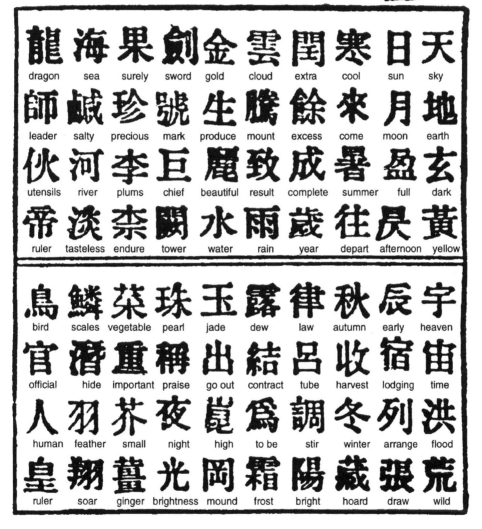

Layout by Doreen Ah Tye.

LeRoy Post was born in La Porte in 1900. He was quiet by nature, but took things in like a "sponge," becoming a living encyclopedia of La Porte's history. Since Post's death at age ninety-six, his son, John and La Porte historian Jann Garvis have carried on his legacy of historical preservation. Photograph by Doreen Ah Tye, La Porte, 1985.

ACKNOWLEDGMENTS

La Porte historian, Jann Garvis, has been indispensable in every phase of this book. She has generously shared her knowledge, documents, photographs, interviews, maps, and connections with important people.

I was fortunate to have the help of my paternal cousin, Elliott Kai-Kee, who has a Ph.D. in history. He emphasized the importance of documentation to make our family history as accurate as possible. In addition to Elliott's help in interpreting data, he edited my first draft manuscripts.

Him Mark Lai generously shared his insights, data, and expertise on Chinese American history. He gave key clues in helping to find my great-grandfather in San Francisco.

Mr. Harry L. Chin helped to translate and interpret the Chinese documents used in this book. He also made the text based on these documents more smooth and comprehensible.

The reference librarians and staffs at the Stockton-San Joaquin County Library and the Bancroft Library, University of California, Berkeley, were especially helpful in my research.

I thank my publisher, Carl Mautz, for believing in my story. Copy editor, Patricia Devereux, refined my manuscript. Rosemarie Mossinger shaped my manuscript into a more well-structured and professional work. She led me through the steps of publication with thoroughness, sensitivity, and understanding.

Richard D. Moore has designed my book with skillfulness and artistry

My husband, Gregory Pierre Farkas, was my constant support. My appreciation also goes to Edward and Blanche Ah Tye, Mary Anne Ahtye, Mo-Mo (Mrs. Sidney Sr.) Ahtye, Stanley and Patricia Ahtye, Wallace and Peggy Ahtye, Warren and Patricia Ahtye, Dale Ah Tye, Dilly and Marie Ah Tye, Doreen Ah Tye, Gordon Ah Tye, Howard Ah-Tye, Kirk Ah-Tye, Mitchell Ah-Tye, Dr. Perry and Loretta Ah-Tye, Raymond and Audrey Ah Tye, Richard Ah Tye, Terry Ah-Tye, Thomas Ah Tye, Evans G. Beltran, Charles Bloch Sr., Esther Bonta, Jerry and Lydia Brady, Linda Brennan, Dr. Teresa M. Chen, Fred Cheung Jr., Janice Cheung, David W. Chin, Hughes Chin, Curtis Chong, Dr. Edmond Chong, Rachelle Chong, Sharon Chong, Philip P. Choy, The Connecticut Historical Society, Lawrence and Sonia Chun, John and Aileen Ah-Tye Davidson, Kirk Del Prete, Elisabeth Farkas, C. Valerie Fintel, Florence (Mrs. S. L.) Fong, Sue Hess, Holly Hong, Beulah Jung, Mark Kai-Kee, Cynthia Kao, Richard Kingdon, Scott Lawson, Dr. and Mrs. Gary E. Lee, Eve Armentrout Ma, Glenn Mar, Ruthanne Lum McCunn, William Miguel, Sylvia Sun Minnick, Lona Moon, Melinda Peak, John Post, Nancy Price, Nanying Stella Wong, Zhen-Ya (Grace) Wu, and Si-Jing (Ann) Zeng.

I am grateful to those family and friends who contributed to this book but did not live to see its completion.

BIBLIOGRAPHY

Books

Barth, Gunther, *Bitter Strength: A History of the Chinese in the United States 1850–1870*, Harvard University Press, Cambridge, Massachusetts, 1964.

Borthwick, J. D., *Three Years in California*, Biobooks, Oakland, California, 1948.

Brady, Jerry, *You Bet Gold Fever*, Golden Harbor Press, San Pedro, California, 1982.

California Alumni in China, compiled by China Alumni Association of the University of California, Peking, 1916.

Chinn, Thomas W., Him Mark Lai and Philip P. Choy, editors, *A History of the Chinese in California: A Syllabus*, Chinese Historical Society of America, San Francisco, 1969.

Colville, Samuel, *City Directory of Sacramento for the Year 1854–55*, Samuel Colville, San Francisco, 1854.

Dicker, Laverne Mau, *The Chinese in San Francisco: A Pictorial History*, Dover Publications, Inc., New York, 1979.

Gong, Eng Ying and Bruce Grant, *Tong War*, Nicholas L. Brown, New York, 1930.

Gould, Helen Weaver, *La Porte Scrapbook*, Helen Weaver Gould, La Porte, California, 1972.

Gudde, Erwin, *California Place Names: The Origin and Etymology of Current Geographical Names*, University of California Press, Berkeley, California, 1969.

Hoy, William, *Kong Chow Temple*, Kong Chow Temple, San Francisco, 1939.

Kennedy, Glenn A., *St. Mark's Methodist Church, Stockton, California—1849–1968*, Stockton, California, 1968.

Labatt, Henry J., *Reports of Cases Determined in the District Courts of the State of California*, Volume 1, Whitton, Towne and Co., San Francisco, 1858.

La Fargue, Thomas E., *China's First Hundred*, The State College of Washington Press, Pullman, Washington, 1942.

Lai, Him Mark, Genny Lim and Judy Yung, *Island: Poetry and History of Chinese Immigrants on Angel Island 1910–1940*, History of Chinese Detained on Island Project, San Francisco, 1980.

Lydon, Sandy, *Chinese Gold: The Chinese in the Monterey Bay Region*, Capitola Book Company, Capitola, California, 1985.

Mark, Diane and Ginger Chih, *A Place Called Chinese America*, Kendall/Hunt Publishing Co., Dubuque, Iowa, 1982.

McClain, Charles J., *In Search of Equality: The Chinese Struggle Against Discrimination in Nineteenth-Century America*, University of California Press, Berkeley, California, 1994.

McCunn, Ruthanne Lum, *Chinese American Portraits: Personal Histories 1828–1988*, Chronicle Books, San Francisco, 1988.

Minnick, Sylvia Sun, *Samfow: The San Joaquin Chinese Legacy*, Panorama West Publishing, Fresno, California, 1988.

Nee, Victor G. and Brett De Bary Nee, *Longtime Californ': A Documentary Study of an American Chinatown*, Pantheon Books, New York, 1972.

Oakland Unified School Directory—1935–48, Oakland, California.

Polk's Oakland (California) City Directory including Alameda, Berkeley, Emeryville, and Piedmont, R. L. Polk and Company, 1928, 1930, 1931–1935, 1937–1938.

Pomeroy, C. P., *Reports of Cases Determined in the Supreme Court of the State of California*, Volume 84, Bancroft-Whitney Company, San Francisco, 1890.

Praetzellis, Mary and Adrian, *Archaeological and Historical Studies of the IJ56 Block, Sacramento, California: An Early Chinese Community*, Sonoma State University, Cultural Resources Facility, Anthropological Studies Center, Sonoma, California, June 1982.

San Francisco City Directory, 1856.

Senior Record Book of the University of California, 1906, Berkeley, California.

Sinnott, James J., "Over North," *Sierra County*, Volume 5 of *History of Sierra County*, Downieville, California, 1977.

Social Register, Washington, (D.C.) 1914, Social Register Association, New York City, 1913.

Speer, William, *The Oldest and the Newest Empire*, H. H. Bancroft and Co., San Francisco, 1870.

Yale Obituary Record—1927, Yale University, New Haven, Connecticut, 1927.

Yung, Judy, *Unbound Feet: A Social History of Chinese Women in San Francisco*, University of California Press, Berkeley and Los Angeles, 1995.

Yung, Wing, *My Life in China and America*, Henry Holt and Company, New York, 1909.

Unpublished Material

Ah Tye Family Collection.

Ah Tye, Edward, "They Call Me Lucky," speech presented at Stockton Cathay Club, June 1987.

Ah-Tye, Terry, "Victor for Victory," Kailua, Hawaii, 1985.

Cayot ledgers.

Chang Family Collection.

Chong, Rachelle B., "Kong Chow Temple Litigation," 1984.

Davis, H. P., "Other Times, Other Manners: Another Commentary on Early Revisions of the Ordinances of the City of Nevada," Searls Library, Nevada City, California.

Davis, H. P., "You Bet," Searls Library, Nevada City, California.

Jann Garvis Collection:
    Howland Flat ledger books.
    La Porte Bank copy book, 1876–1880.

Lowe Family Collection.

Slyter, Robert J. and Grace, "Historical Notes of the Early Washington, Nevada County California Mining District," Searls Library, Nevada City, California.

Personal Communications

Mary Anne Ahtye, Stockton, California, August 24, 1985.

Mo-Mo (Mrs. Sidney Sr.) Ahtye, Salinas, California, July 12, 1981; December 29, 1984; March 23, 1985 (telephone conversation); Cameron Park, California, June 19, 1989.

Sidney Ahtye Jr., Cameron Park, California, September 14, 1985.

Stanley and Patricia Ahtye, San Jose, California, February 18, 1985.

Summi (Mrs. Allen) Ahtye, San Francisco, California, October 20, 1984.

Warren and Patricia Ahtye, San Francisco, California, September 21, 1996.

Blanche Ah Tye, Stockton, California, October 5, 1984; February 8, 1985; January 20, 1986; November 20, 1986.

Dilly Ah Tye Jr., Stockton, California, January 23, 1985.

Edward Ah Tye, Stockton, California, July 13, 1983; October 5, 1984; July 4, 1985; January 20, 1986.

Howard Ah-Tye, Stockton, California, June 29, 1985.

Kirk Ah-Tye, letter to author, June 4, 1986.

Dr. Perry Ah-Tye, San Diego, California, May 26, 1986.

Raymond and Audrey Ah Tye, Sacramento, California, May 29, 1985.

Richard Ah Tye, Stockton, California, November 25, 1984.

Rose Ah Tye, Sr., Stockton, California, summer 1971.

Thomas Ah Tye, Simi Valley, California, May 24, 1986.

Charles Bloch, Sr., Stockton, California, March 5, 1994.

Jerry Brady, Nevada City, California, October 28, 1984.

Thomas W. Brady, San Bruno, California, April 29, 1987.

Charlotte, Oliver, and Lillian Chang, Berkeley, California, July 24, 1971.

Lillian Chang, Foster City, California, July 11, 1985.

Janice Cheung, Simi Valley, California, May 24, 1986.

Harry L. Chin, Stockton, California, January 18, 1978; January 30, 1986; Lodi, California, April 7–10, 1997.

Hughes S. Chin, Stockton, California, March 2, 1985; June 21, 1985; March 6, 1993; Salinas, California, June 21, 1986; letters to author, September 17, 1996; December 22, 1997.

Dr. Edmond and Barbara Chong, Stockton, California, August 18, 1985.

Florence (Mrs. S. L.) Fong, Stockton, California, March 13, 1985.

Jann Garvis, Stockton, California, November 17, 1985; March 22, 1987; La Porte, California, July 21, 1987; Berkeley, California, January 24, 1996.

Sue Hess, letter to author, May 24, 1996.

Beulah Jung, Stockton, California, October 6, 1981; February 15 and 19, 1985; September 9, 1986; letter to author, June 1, 1986.

Carl Jung, Stockton, California, September 9, 1986.

Mark Kai-Kee, letter to author, March 9, 1996.

Richard Kingdon, La Porte, California, July 19, 1985.

Him Mark Lai, San Francisco, California, December 4, 1985; letter to author, December 23, 1996; telephone conversation, December 27, 1996.

Bola Lowe, Kaneohe, Hawaii, March 25, 1985.

William Miguel, Oakland, California, December 22, 1988.

Lona Moon, San Mateo, California, November 20, 1984.

Claire Cayot O'Rourke, Quincy, California, July 23, 1987.

Richard O'Rourke, La Porte, California, July 19, 1985.

John and LeRoy Post, letters to author, January 1986; July 6, 1987.

LeRoy Post, La Porte, California, July 18 and 19, 1985; November 28, 1985; June 24, 1986.

Mary Schwegler, telephone conversation, December 15, 1988.

James Sinnott, Downieville, California, June 23, 1986.

Zhen-Ya (Grace) Wu, Stockton, California, March 23, 1996.

Si-Jing (Ann) Zeng, Stockton, California, March 23, 1996.

Interviews by Jann Garvis:

Bud Adams, Clipper Mills, California, August 1982.

Donna Day, La Porte, California, July 19, 1985.

LeRoy Post, Oroville, California, November 28, 1985; La Porte, California, January 1986.

Interview by Jerry Brady:

LeRoy Post, Yuba City, California, April 19, 1984.

Telephone conversation by Rachelle B. Chong:

Gordon Lau, San Francisco, California, March 1984.

Articles and Papers

Ah-Tye, Howard, "The Kong Chow Temple of San Francisco," *Chinese World,* October 7, 1967.

"The Ah Tye Family—Growing up in Stockton," *East/West,* September 27, 1978.

"A Chinese American in World War II," *Asian Week,* May 6, 1982.

"Chinese Americans in World War II," *Asian Week,* June 3, 1982.

"Origins of the Kong Chow Temple," *Asian Week,* February 3, 1983.

Chin, Harry L., "The Chinese Mid-Autumn Festival," Stockton Unified School District.

Chong, Rachelle B., "Present Achievements Honor Past Efforts," *The Recorder,* San Francisco, December 20, 1991.

Choy, Philip P., "The Architecture of San Francisco Chinatown," *Chinese America: History and Perspectives 1990,* Chinese Historical Society of America, Brisbane, California, 1990.

Fong, Walter N., "The Chinese Six Companies," *Overland Monthly,* Volume 23 [second series], 1894.

"From the Orient Direct," *The Atlantic Monthly,* Volume 24, 1869.

Fu, Manchester (nom de plume of Ken Wong), Manny and the Celestials—"Kong Chow Temple," *East/West,* October 27, 1968.

"Gold Districts of California," *California Division of Mines and Geology, 1970,* Bulletin 193.

Hendel, Charles W., "Report on the Plumas Consolidated Gravel Mining Company," *Gold, Historical and Economic Aspects,* Part I, California, 1974, advisory editor, Kenneth Carpenter.

Journals of the California Legislature, Assembly Journal 1853, Fourth Session, "Report of the Committee on Mines and Mining Interests," Document 28.

Kip, Right Reverend Bishop, "Idol-Worship in San Francisco, *Colonial Church Chronicle,* October 1856, Chinese in

California pamphlet boxes, The Bancroft.

Lai, Him Mark, "Historical Development of the Chinese Consolidated Benevolent Association/Huiguan System," *Chinese America: History and Perspectives 1987*, Chinese Historical Society of America, San Francisco, 1987.

Ma, L. Eve Armentrout, "Genealogy and History: The Yu of Yimei and Chang-wan in Kwangtung's Xin-hui xian," *Asian Folklore Studies*, Volumes 43–1, Nagoya, Japan, 1984.

McCunn, Ruthanne, Philip Choy and Judy Yung, Letter in Society for Historical Archaeology newsletter, March 4, 1986.

"Summer Vacation Guide: La Porte's Union Hotel Renovation," May 22, 1991.

Wells, Mariann Kaye, "Chinese Temples in California," University of California thesis, July 20, 1962, reprinted by R & E Research Associates, San Francisco, 1971.

Wong, Nanying Stella, "Kong Chow, USA," *Ting: The Caldron—Chinese Art and Identity in San Francisco*, Glide Urban Center Publications, San Francisco, 1970.

Newspapers and Periodicals

Asian Week, 1982, 1983
Chinese Times, 1969
Chinese World, 1967
Daily Alta California, 1850–1856, 1864–1865, 1885
East/West, 1968, 1978, 1982
Hartford Daily Courant, 1887
La Porte Union, 1896
Marysville Daily Appeal, 1897
Mountain Messenger, 1863–1897, 1905, 1920
Oroville Register, 1896
Plumas National, 1873–1879, 1886, 1896, 1930
Police and Peace Officers' Journal, 1926
Sacramento Bee, 1861, 1929
Sacramento Union, 1854–1857, 1929
Salinas Index Journal, 1930
San Francisco Call, 1896, 1906
San Francisco Chronicle, 1896, 1926, 1969
San Francisco Daily Herald, 1851, 1853, 1856
San Francisco Evening Post, 1900
San Francisco Examiner, 1890
San Francisco Morning Call Supplement, 1885, 1890
Shasta Courier, 1854
Stockton Record, 1929
Washington Post, 1913
Young China, 1977

Libraries, Archives, and Cemeteries

Bancroft Library, Berkeley, California:
    Auerbach Collection
    Chinese in California pamphlet box
    John Manion Collection
Butte County Recorder, Oroville, California
California State Law Library, Sacramento, California
California State Library, Sacramento, California:
    Great Register of Voters
    Charles William Hendel Collection
    Photographs
    United States Census Records
Chapel of the Chimes, Oakland, California
Chinese Presbyterian Church, Oakland, California

The Connecticut Historical Society, Hartford, Connecticut
Marysville County Clerk, Marysville, California
Mountain View Cemetery, Oakland, California
National Archives of the United States, San Bruno, California
Nevada County Courthouse, Nevada City, California
Park View Cemetery, French Camp, California
Phillips Academy, Andover, Massachusetts
Plumas County City Hall, Quincy, California:
    Births
    Deeds
    Miscellaneous Records
    Placer Claims
Plumas County Museum, Quincy, California
San Francisco City Hall, San Francisco, California:
    Deeds
    Superior Court Records
San Francisco Public Library, Main Library, Larkin & McAllister Streets
San Joaquin County Recorder's Office, Stockton, California
Searls Library, Nevada City, California
Sierra County Courthouse, Downieville, California:
    Assessments
    Deeds
    Superior Court Minutes
State of California, Department of Health Services, Office of the State Registrar of Vital Statistics, Sacramento, California
Stockton-San Joaquin County Library
Washington State University Library, Pullman, Washington:
    Thomas La Fargue Collection
Woodlawn Memorial Park, Colma, California
Yuba County Library, Marysville, California

INDEX